Boston Theater Marathon XI
2009 ANTHOLOGY

SMITH AND KRAUS PUBLISHERS
Short Plays and 10-Minute Plays Collections

Christopher Durang Vol. I: 27 Short Plays

Frank D. Gilroy Vol. II: 15 One-Act Plays

Israel Horovitz Vol. I: 16 Short Plays

Romulus Linney 17 Short Plays

Terrence McNally Vol. I: 15 Short Plays

Lanford Wilson: 21 Short Plays

Act One Festival 1995: The Complete One-Act Plays

Act One Festival 1994: The Complete One-Act Plays

EST Marathon 1999: The Complete One-Act Plays

EST Marathon 1998: The Complete One-Act Plays

EST Marathon 1997: The Complete One-Act Plays

EST Marathon 1996: The Complete One-Act Plays

EST Marathon 1995: The Complete One-Act Plays

EST Marathon 1994: The Complete One-Act Plays

Twenty One-Acts from 20 Years at the Humana Festival 1975–1995

Women's Project and Productions Rowing to America & Sixteen Other Short Plays

8 TENS @ 8 Festival: 30 10-Minute Plays from the Santa Cruz Festivals I–VI

30 Ten-Minute Plays from the Actors Theatre of Louisville for 2 Actors

30 Ten-Minute Plays from the Actors Theatre of Louisville for 3 Actors

30 Ten-Minute Plays from the Actors Theatre of Louisville for 4, 5, and 6 Actors

2004: The Best 10-Minute Plays for Two Actors

2004: The Best 10-Minute Plays for Three or More Actors

2005: The Best 10-Minute Plays for Two Actors

2005: The Best 10-Minute Plays for Three or More Actors

2006: The Best 10-Minute Plays for Two Actors

2006: The Best 10-Minute Plays for Three or More Actors

2007: The Best 10-Minute Plays for Two Actors

2007: The Best 10-Minute Plays for Three or More Actors

2008: The Best 10-Minute Plays for Two Actors

2008: The Best 10-Minute Plays for Three or More Actors

2009: The Best 10-Minute Plays for Two or More Actors

2010: The Best 10-Minute Plays

Visit smithandkraus.com to see our complete list and
to order, or call toll-free (888) 282-2881.

Boston Theater Marathon XI

2009 ANTHOLOGY

Edited and with an Introduction
by Kate Snodgrass

CONTEMPORARY PLAYWRIGHT SERIES

A Smith and Kraus Book
Hanover, New Hampshire

Published by Smith and Kraus, Inc.
177 Lyme Road, Hanover, NH 03755
www.SmithandKraus.com / (888) 282-2881

First Edition: May 2010
10 9 8 7 6 5 4 3 2 1

Manufactured in the United States of America
Book production: Freedom Hill Design, Cavendish, Vermont
Cover design: Michael Duncan Smith

ISBN-13: 978-1-57525-771-6 ISBN-10: 1-57525-771-8
Library of Congress Control Number: 2010926154

Contents

FOREWORD

For eleven years now, the Boston Playwrights Theatre has been doing the impossible, which is to commandeer ten hours on a single Sunday in May in order to greatly enlarge the creative, civic, and charitable dimensions of our city. This phenomenon has become known as the Boston Theater Marathon, obviously named after another famous local endurance test. Only instead of tireless sprinters we now have tireless spectators, willing to spend all day in theater seats just to watch a sequence of short plays.

Theatre people have traditionally been known for generously sharing their talents in a good cause, possibly because talent is often all they have to contribute. Remember the celebrated Juggler of Notre Dame who, having nothing else to donate, performed his craft before a statue of the Virgin Mary, who thereupon laid her hand upon his head in blessing? (In one version, no doubt apocryphal, the statue was said to have added the words, "Don't call us; we'll call you"!)

Now, in an unprecedented outpouring of generous artistry, scores of local jugglers, whether called playwrights, actors, directors, technicians, administrators, or theater groups, now participate in fifty ten-minute plays each year, five each hour, chosen out of four hundred applications, and performed before over three hundred and fifty people. In the first few years, the BTM, under the benign and brilliant leadership of Kate Snodgrass, used to provide two performances of each play. Now that the event has moved to the larger Calderwood Pavilion, only one performance has been deemed necessary. Even more people are now able to see the plays than before; but I personally miss the bustle of moving from theater to theater, greeting spectators on your way to the stage, getting the chance to see some growth in a second performance. Still, these short pieces often serve as ideas for longer plays. To speak personally, at least four of my own full-length works grew from ten-minute seedlings first planted at the BTM.

But more important than the advantages to the artists are the blessings bestowed by the Marathon upon the Boston theater community. The BTM essentially functions as a fundraiser for an undernourished artform. All net proceeds go to the Theatre Community Benevolent Fund, a charitable organization that helps New England theater artists, technicians, and companies in times of need (providing funds for medical emergencies, fires, vandalism, loss of property, and the like). It is besides perhaps the greatest camp ground for

New England theater artists available, providing retreats for the elite and the beat, havens for mavens, and a center where one can mingle freely with the entire theater community, audience members included.

Long may this Marathon run — and run — and run.

Robert Brustein
Founding Director of the Yale and American Repertory Theatres
Distinguished Scholar in Residence, Suffolk University
Senior Research Fellow, Harvard University

INTRODUCTION

Fellow Play Lovers,

At 12 Noon on Sunday, May 17, 2009, 50 theaters in the Boston area (and one from NYC, collaborating) came together at the Calderwood Pavilion at the Boston Center for the Arts in Boston's South End to perform one ten-minute play each (that's five plays per hour). Think about it. From 12 noon until closing — 10 PM sharp — the performers played to SRO crowds, some of whom had spent the last 10 hours rooted to their seats by the exciting, funny, tragic, absurd, surprising wealth of new works for the stage. Welcome to a Boston theater community tradition — the Boston Theater Marathon! And the crowds come back for more — in May every year we trod the boards to showcase these wonderful New England playwrights, the plays culled from over 400 entries from all over New England. It doesn't get better than this.

But wait, yes it does! First, all net proceeds go to the Theatre Community Benevolent Fund, a charitable organization that helps New England theater artists, technicians, and companies in times of need (help with medical emergencies, fires, vandalism, loss of property, you name it). Plus, in the last 11 years, over 20 playwrights' full-length plays have been performed by the very theater companies introduced to these writers at the BTM. Finally, the BTM pulls brand new audiences into the theater. These plays are like crackerjacks — you can't eat just one. The BTM experience is very like that other Boston Marathon (the foot race): it's fast, it's furious, it's dramatic, it's funny, and it's over all too soon.

So . . . Read on. The plays in this wonderful anthology have the flavor of the first day we ran the BTM 11 years ago — they're exciting, witty, surprising, and infinitely entertaining. NOW it doesn't get better than this. Enjoy!

Sincerely,
Kate Snodgrass
Artistic Director

P.S. We could not perform the BTM every year without the kind support of the Humanities Foundation at Boston University. Thank you BUHF!

THE SECOND COMING

ROSANNA YAMAGIWA ALFARO

Sponsored by the Nora Theatre Company
Directed by Daniel Gidron
Half-Human/Half-Bird. . . . . Ramona Lisa Alexander
Dr. Castelo-Branco, Man, Male Peacock . . . . Owen Doyle
Woman, Female Peacock. . . . . Claire McClanahan
Fernando. . . . . Stacy Fischer

After the apocalypse a man-bird, created in the lab of a murderous scientist, is pleased that the only survivors are himself and a human child.

Rosanna Yamagiwa Alfaro's plays have been produced by Pan Asian Repertory, East West Players, the Edinburgh Fringe, the Magic Theater, New Theatre, Women on Top, La MaMa, and the Boston Theater Marathon. Her short plays have been published by Baker's Plays, Heinemann, Meriwether Publishing, Charta Books, Ltd., and Smith and Kraus.

CHARACTERS

    BIRD, 35, half human, half bird, observant and literary.

    DR. CASTELO-BRANCO, 65, scientist, terrified by his creation.

    MAN, early 30's, jobless, fed up with his family.

    WOMAN, late 20's, still capable of wonder.

    MALE PEACOCK, anxious to mate.

    FEMALE PEACOCK, anxious to eat.

    FERNANDO, 5, eager to be just like the Bird.

SETTING

    Lisbon.

TIME

    Before, during, and after the Apocalypse.

NOTE

    There are four actors. Except for the Bird and Fernando, all the other characters are played by the same actor and actress. The Bird (who can be played by a man or woman) is dressed in tux with tails.

. . .

The human cry of a bird. Lights up. The snow is falling. A large BIRD stands on the windowsill of the bedroom and looks through the glass at an unseen baby in his crib. The BIRD cocks his head, and emits a soft trill. A baby gurgles. The BIRD emits a louder trill, this time followed by a baby's crow of delight.

    In another area of the stage the MAN reads the paper as the WOMAN looks out the kitchen window. They are both in their bathrobes.

WOMAN: It's still snowing.

MAN: *(He speaks from behind his newspaper.)* So what? Practice getting dressed. Next week at this time you'll be gutting fish at the cannery.

WOMAN: Where's your sense of wonder? This is Lisbon. It's summer, and it's been snowing all night.

MAN: So?

WOMAN: You're the one who should be getting dressed. When are you going to start looking for a job?

MAN: And who would look after Fernando? You're the one who wanted a baby. Guess who'll be stuck at home looking after him.

WOMAN: *(She's about to argue, then thinks better of it.)* Isn't it weird the way all the pigeons disappeared? All ten thousand of them.

BIRD: *(He hops downstage to address the audience.)* The centripetal movement of the air, a dip in the earth's magnetic field — birds sense these things; people, in spite of all their calculations do not. *(beat)* Take my father, Dr. Gonzales Castelo-Branco. His calculations led him to believe that I somehow posed a threat to his precious species.

(DR. CASTELO-BRANCO sprinkles some powder over a plate of fish. He whistles, calling the BIRD to dinner.)

DR. CASTELO-BRANCO: Oh, there you are. Look at this. *(He puts the plate of fish at the BIRD's feet.)* Soused mackerel. Your favorite.

BIRD: *(He hops over.)* It smells funny.

DR. CASTELO-BRANCO: What do you know about smell? You have a beak, not a nose. It smells the way it always does. Well, not quite. I added an extra pinch of saffron to give it color.

BIRD: It's poisoned.

DR. CASTELO-BRANCO: Don't be silly.

BIRD: I saw you add the arsenic.

DR. CASTELO-BRANCO: Don't look at me like that. Don't come near me. *(He moves awkwardly behind a chair.)* I created you so I've every right to destroy you. *(He swings the chair at the BIRD, who attacks him.)* I'm bleeding! Mother of God, you've bitten off my ear! *(He calls out the window as the BIRD takes flight.)* Come back! Come back! They'll kill you out there.

BIRD: That was seven years ago. He ended his life a few days later, convinced that by letting me escape he had single-handedly brought about the end of the world. What an idiot! *(He dips and swoops over the city.)* Lisbon could not have been more beautiful the day I took flight from my father's laboratory. I circled over the city until I found a park favored more by birds than people — the secluded gardens of Saint George's Castle. Peacocks in the courtyard, swans and ducks in the moat — the endless variety of the species filled me with delight.

(As the BIRD speaks two PEACOCKS appear. The FEMALE is busy eating as the MALE struts and preens. He lifts and spreads his feathers, which make a whirring sound as he moves behind her. He jumps on her, bringing her to her knees as he digs his claws into her shoulders.)

But my happiness was short-lived. The birds, using their sixth sense, mistook me for a person. What my father had rejoiced in, the creation of a remarkable new being, half-bird, half-human — what this really meant was that I could circle the entire globe and find no mate. *(beat)* A long year passed. Then one spring morning a baby was born. Fernando's parents lived in the stone building just across from my niche in the castle wall.

(A baby's crow of delight. The BIRD hops on the windowsill to take a closer look. The MAN enters, waving his arms.)

MAN: Shoo! Shoo! *(The BIRD flies off. The MAN speaks to the unseen baby in the crib.)* Damn your mother! *(Cries from the baby.)* Damn that stupid woman, leaving the window wide open! That was the largest bird I've ever seen. He could have picked you up in his yellow beak, dropped you on the rocks to crack you open, then shared you with the gulls for breakfast. *(The baby's cries intensify.)* Not that that would have been so bad. You've given us nothing but trouble. Did I ever tell you? The day you arrived I got laid off my job.

WOMAN: What are you mumbling about? Come to bed and bring Fernando with you. It's Sunday.

MAN: What have I told you about bringing Fernando to the bed? We'll roll over and crush him. Besides, you know what they say about letting little children witness the . . .

WOMAN: He's only a baby.

MAN: They say the memory of it can ruin the rest of your life. But what do you care? Think only of yourself.

BIRD: *(He watches with interest just as he watched the peacocks.)* The skin is an organ. Skin on skin, organ on organ, they rubbed and squeezed. Afterwards, he brought the baby to the bed, and she nursed him.

MAN: *(He stretches.)* You start your new job tomorrow.

WOMAN: What am I going to do when my breasts fill up with milk?

MAN: That's your problem, not Fernando's. He'll be in his crib with his bottle of orange juice.

BIRD: At first Fernando cried inconsolably for his mother, but soon he was wholly dependent on a big yellow cat and me for entertainment. He loved the cat, but I knew she couldn't be trusted. So early one morning I lured her out onto the windowsill and then to the roof, where I picked her up by the scruff of the neck and dropped her into the moat. *(beat)* Yes. From that moment on I was the undisputed center of Fernando's life.

THE BABY'S VOICE: Bird! Bird! Bird!

MAN: "Bird." "Bird." Most babies say "Dada" or "Mama." What's wrong with him anyway?

WOMAN: Maybe he knows the birds are acting funny.

MAN: How silly you are.

WOMAN: No. You don't notice because you never leave the house, but everyone's talking about it. Yesterday the birds were in hiding. Today they're everywhere. They don't even bother to get out of the way when you walk down the sidewalk.

MAN: Just take a look at this. *(He shows her the newspaper.)*

WOMAN: Eugh. What is it?

MAN: A grasshopper the size of a rat. There seem to be ten million of them migrating across Poland. *(He teases her.)* Shhh! Hear that? It's them. The grasshoppers have finished with Poland and are cutting their way across Germany and France.

WOMAN: The lights are flickering.

MAN: Nonsense. Come here and sit on my lap. Now tell me, why is it that we're the only ones untouched by these disasters? That the earthquakes stop right at our borders? I haven't been to church in twenty years, but I'm turning into a true believer. God is Portuguese.

WOMAN: Did you hear the strange news from Madrid? The reporter at the zoo? He said the gorillas were swinging on the ropes like gibbons. He said the flock of pelicans started mooing like cows and trampled a baby in its stroller.

MAN: Mooing like cows. Turn on the radio. We can't afford to miss news like that.

BIRD: They were just in time to catch an eyewitness account of the last great earthquake that buckled the Iberian Peninsula and would take both their lives.

(The BIRD picks up the baby in its blanket and flies away. Sound of the earthquake. Blackout.)

WOMAN'S VOICE: Fernando! He's gone!

BIRD: Moments later there was a fine spray of black and white stone chips from the lovely mosaic sidewalks of Lisbon and then a single giant wave from the Tagus that broke over the city and pulled it into the sea. A subtle slippage of the earth's crust and not a trace of man's civilization remained. *(beat)* Except Fernando, of course. It's amazing. He's already five years old.

FERNANDO: Grass!

BIRD: The smell of new grass. Fresh air.

FERNANDO: Stars! Orion. Cassiopeia.

BIRD: Very good. You're very bright. Your parents never knew those names. They never saw so many stars. Or birds.

FERNANDO: *(He hops like a bird.)* Or insects. The dragonfly, the caddis, the e-phe-me-rid.

BIRD: Excellent. And on the ground, reptiles, distant cousins of the birds. They survived. Only in the highest orders not a trace remained. *(He tilts his head.)*

FERNANDO: *(He tilts his head.)* Except you and me. You picked me up with your claws and flew away with me.
(He runs his hand through the bird's feathers and puts his finger on the bird's hard tongue.)

BIRD: Because I love you.

FERNANDO: Show me how Dr. Cas-te-lo Brrranco tried to kill you. Tell me more stories about the cat.

BIRD: First run and get me an apple.

FERNANDO: I'll get one for me. O.K.? Not for you. For me.
(He exits.)

BIRD: I have planted no metaphysical trees, only those that bear real fruit. With one small peck I've made sure Fernando will feel no uncomfortable yearning for an unseen Eve. Like me he'll never understand what it is about a homely female bobbing away at the ground that can cause a male peacock to raise and spread its feathers like a quivering crown.
(FERNANDO returns, eating the apple.)

FERNANDO: You love me more than anything else, don't you? You'll be with me always.

BIRD: Since you've eaten the apple bring me a fig. There's one that's golden brown, just about to split its sides.

FERNANDO: It's mine! It's mine!
(He runs out.)

BIRD: My interest in Fernando is not as it once was. I'm distracted like a mother watching the antics of the first child when the second turns in her womb. I feel a stirring, the undulations that accompany the downward passage of an enormous egg. *(He squats, ruffling his feathers.)* My feathers have grown softer, more glossy and luxuriant. What strange creature, I wonder, lies curled up in its shell? I feel it pulsing in my loins, eager to be born.
(He coos, emits a short cry, then a long trill of satisfaction.)

END OF PLAY

LIFER
(World Premiere)

TOBY ARMOUR

Sponsored by Our Place Theatre Project
Directed by Dawn M. Simmons
Fred . . . . Edward M. Barker
Lorraine . . . . Gwen Mason

Lorraine is about to be evicted. She is alone, desperate, and ready to try anything. Fred, the State Marshall, just wants to get the grim job done and go home for a quiet drink. Surprise awaits them.

Toby Armour has been stagehand, dancer, choreographer, director of a dance company, as well as playwright. She has received grants from the NEA, the Jerome Foundation, and the Massachusetts Arts Council. Her plays have been done in NYC, Boston, LA, Edinburgh, and London. Her play, *Voices from Black Canyon*, won the Lewis National Playwrighting Competition.

CHARACTERS
   FRED, State Marshall, African-American, middle-aged.
   LORRAINE, Woman, white, 70s.

SETTING
   Living room of Lorraine's apartment, which is empty of Furniture.

TIME
   The Present.

. . .

At Rise FRED is talking into his mobile phone.

FRED: *(LOW)* OK, are you guys in position? . . . NO! NO! Just hold it! Wait
till I give the signal- I hope to God I don't have to!..The Chief wants you
to go in? No! Tell him I'm still talking to her. For Chrissake, everybody,
stand-by! Just let me handle it.. *(Turns off his phone. Moves to 'doorway'
and in a gentle voice —)* Ma'am? . . . Can we uh talk about this? . . . Look,
the gun doesn't solve anything . . . no one wants you to hurt yourself
— *(Takes a step, freezes, lifting his hands high.)* OK,OK! I'm not moving,
see? . . . Look, it's Christmas eve- don't you have anyone who could take
you in? Brother? Sister? . . . *(Unintelligible words from Lorraine offstage.)*
Ma'am, I'm just doing my job- believe me, I don't want to put you out in
the street! Have you got any kids? Any grown kids? Grand kids?.. *(More
unintelligible words from Lorraine offstage. Sighs.)* OK . . . How about if
there's space in a shelter-*(This time her unintelligible words sound an angry
desperate rhythm. Interrupting & overlapping her.)* Who said it was your
fault? I never said- *(Her sounds continue.)* You already told me- nine years,
never missed a month's rent . . . I can't ask your landlord, he's skipped
town!*(Patiently.)* Look, we went through all this. The property belongs to
the bank, because he didn't pay his mortgage.*(Her sounds again.)* It has
nothing to do with you . . . I mean it has nothing to do with you, but
there's nothing you can do about it. You're going to be evicted.*(Sounds.)*
No, it's not fair . . . of course, it's not fair. You think I like doing this!
For Christ's sake, please! Listen, this is my last week. I'm retiring after
New Year's . . . *(Unintelligible congratulations from Lorraine.)* Thank you,
yeah, it's a lousy job, and good riddance *(Again from Lorraine.)* A beer
to celebrate? Sorry, I don't drink on the job. *(Again from Lorraine.)* You
have one beer left in the refrigerator. *(And again.)* They took everything

else, I know, I know. I can see. Look, if you kill yourself tonight, how am I gonna live with that? Huh? You're going to spoil my last week after 30 years! I'll be spending my whole retirement thinking about it. Will you just put the gun down for my sake? Not in your face like that, Ma'am! It could go off! Hey, things may look bad, but there's always hope . . . *(Again from Lorraine.)* You're 75 years old, what 'hope'? . . . well . . . there's got to be a way out- *(Quick response.)* no! I didn't mean *that* way!*(Phone rings. He answers in low voice.)* I told you guys to wait — What do you mean *you've* got a problem? . . . So, go take care of the guy in the basement apartment. Look, if anyone's going in, it's got to be me. Nobody else, no surprises. She's shaking so hard, she could blow her head off — no, I can handle it. Go on. Go on. *(Presses phone off. To himself-)* Shit! Christmas eve, and here I am, doing this shit. And for what? After thirty years, a lousy pension — ah, let's get it over with! *(In his gentle voice,)* Ma'am, I can see your hand is shaking a little. I'm afraid you might shoot yourself by mistake. Can we just calm down here? No one's going to hurt you. See? Just give me the gun, OK? *(Stepping forward.)* and we'll straighten this all out-*(A shot from offstage.)* Jesus!!*(Staggers, clutching his arm.)* You shot me!

LORRAINE: *(Entering.)* . . . I'm sorry.

FRED: I thought you were going to kill yourself.

LORRAINE: I did too.

FRED: Then you had a better idea. Great.

LORRAINE: Well . . . you see, I thought I'd probably miss.

FRED: Sure. *(Holding his arm.)*

LORRAINE: Is it bad?

FRED: A scratch. Nothing. *(Grimaces.)* Jeesuz!

LORRAINE: *(Peering.)* There's hardly any blood.

FRED: I said it was a scratch, OK!?

LORRAINE: They cleaned out the medicine chest, or I'd get you a bandaid.

FRED: Never mind.

LORRAINE: — and the phone doesn't work.

FRED: I said 'never mind'. *(On his phone.)* Hey, send an ambulance! No, she's all right . . . No, don't come up. Finish with the guy in the basement . . . I'm fine! I'm fine! I'm telling you! Just call the goddam ambulance! OK?

LORRAINE: I'll go quietly.

FRED: Right.*(Turns off phone.)*

LORRAINE: *(Drags out a chair.)* Sit down. You look a little shaky. *(Offering him her chair.)* Good thing you left me the chair.

FRED: *(Sits.)* Why did you do this?! I wasn't going to hurt you.

LORRAINE: It seemed like the best thing.

FRED: Shooting me?

LORRAINE: I'll have to confess, won't I?

FRED: Confess? Are you kidding?! You're going to jail, lady.

LORRAINE: They keep them nice and warm, don't they?

FRED: *(Holding his arm and grimacing.)* Huh?

LORRAINE: The cells, they'll be heated, won't they?

FRED: Of course, air conditioning in summer, heat in winter. What do you think, this is some third world country?

LORRAINE: That's all right then.

FRED: You're going to lose your freedom. Did you think of that? You won't be able to go out ever.

LORRAINE: Who goes out? The neighborhood is too dangerous.

FRED: Ah, well.

LORRAINE: I bet there's three cooked meals a day, nice hot showers, television- I can watch Oprah again, and for a change . . . I'll have company. I suppose they're mostly young people.

FRED: 'Young people'?! They're convicted felons.

LORRAINE: No landlords, no bank managers? *(He shakes his head.)* Just ordinary hopeless folks like me . . . I'd like that.

FRED: There's only one catch.

LORRAINE: What?

FRED: The judge will probably feel sorry for you and let you off.

LORRAINE: Oh . . . how about I shoot you again?

FRED: No! that's all right. Look, I'll testify that this was premeditated.

LORRAINE: You'd do that..for me?

FRED: A hate crime. She was screaming racial slurs. Called me a 'goddam nig-ger'! *(She recoils.)* They'll put you away for years.

LORRAINE: Would they really!? *(Concerned.)*What about parole?

FRED: If they let you out, you just go hold up a bank somewhere. That'll get you life.

LORRAINE: A bank..why not?..What if I get away with it?!

FRED: If you get away with it, you'll be rich.

LORRAINE: *(Nods slowly as she understands.)* Is this what's called a 'win-win' situation?

FRED: You got it.

LORRAINE: Thanks for the advice.

FRED: Don't mention it. Ah, what the hell? In a week, I'm out of all this. *(Grunts in pain.)*

LORRAINE: I can't tell you how sorry I am.

FRED: Don't mention it.

LORRAINE: Will they fire you for getting shot?

FRED: Fire me? They'll give me a nice fat bonus for being wounded in the line of duty. Believe me, I can use it.

LORRAINE: That's all right then.

FRED: I wouldn't go that far.

LORRAINE: Your wife will be upset.

FRED: My wife? *(Shakes his head.)* nothing upsets her . . . not anymore..

LORRAINE: I'm sorry..is she?..

FRED: We're divorced. She took the kids, she took the house, she's got herself a new boyfriend. She's fine, don't worry about her.

LORRAINE: And you?

FRED: Me? What about me?

LORRAINE: Do you . . . have somebody?

FRED: Look, I'm fine. All I want is some peace and quiet.

LORRAINE: Oh..so, you're alone too.

FRED: *(Annoyed.)* I didn't say that, did I?

LORRAINE: I'm sorry. I didn't mean to pry.

FRED: Forget it. Where the hell is that ambulance?!

LORRAINE: I'll never forgive myself.

FRED: I told you, it's nothing. I just need to get checked out for the record.

LORRAINE: You mean, for the record so you get the bonus?

FRED: Yeah, then I can get this whole thing over with and go home.

LORRAINE: And?

FRED: What do you mean, 'and'?

LORRAINE: Is anybody waiting for you at home?

FRED: A nice drink is waiting for me.

> *(She exits.)*

Where are you going? . . . Ah, shit! what's she up to now? Jeesuz!! Where'd she put the gun?!

> *(He starts to get up. She enters, holding a can of beer.)*

LORRAINE: It's warm. They took the refrigerator too.

FRED: What is this?

LORRAINE: A drink. You're not on the job anymore, are you?

FRED: Well..

LORRAINE: Budweiser..I don't have whiskey, I'm afraid. Better have some. You don't want to go into shock.

> *(She hands him the can.)*

FRED: Listen, Lady, after thirty years in this job, nothing shocks me.

LORRAINE: Lorraine.

FRED: Huh? Oh, well, here's to you, Lorraine! Next time, may you miss. *(He *lifts can, and drinks, hands her the can.)* You better have some. You'll be spending a long night at the station.

LORRAINE: And many years in jail, I hope. *(Lifting can.)* Here's to you-

FRED: Fred.

LORRAINE: Fred.

(She drinks.)

FRED: Have a seat, Lorraine.

(Starting to get up.)

LORRAINE: No, I'm fine here. *(Perching on an arm of the chair.)* You should conserve your strength.

(Handing him the beer.)

FRED: *(Drinks.)* Tell me something. You weren't really going to commit suicide, were you? *(She doesn't answer.)* You were?

LORRAINE: *(Nods.)* . . . then I thought 'If I could live just a little longer, only . . . not here! and not alone', and then like a kind of miracle, it came to me —

FRED: A miracle? To shoot me and be safe and warm for the rest of your life?

LORRAINE: I really tried —

FRED: — to miss, I know. *(Shakes head, holds up can.)* Well, here's Merry Christmas to both of us.

(Drinks, hands beer to her.)

LORRAINE: Do they have Christmas in jail?

(Drinks, hands to him.)

FRED: Sure, decorations, everything.

LORRAINE: If there's a party, I'll invite you.

FRED: I'll come.

LORRAINE: *(Nods happily.)* Good.

(Suddenly upset, she gets up, turns away.)

FRED: What is it? What's wrong?

LORRAINE: If the find me out!? *(He looks puzzled.)* If they find out I'm happy?! . . . they can't evict you from jail, can they?

FRED: Nah, don't worry, a trouble-maker like you? They'll throw away the key. Lorraine, if ever there was a natural-born 'lifer', you're it. Enjoy!

(He drinks, passes her the beer. Lorraine salutes him with the can, drains it as — fade with ambulance siren, church bells.)

END OF PLAY

THE GREAT MAIL ROBBERY

A Ten Minute Play

JEANNE BECKWITH

Performed at the Boston Theater Marathon XI
Sponsored by Shakespeare & Co.
Directed by Kelly Galvin
Red . . . . Ryan Winkles
Jimmy . . . . Scott Renzoni

Jimmy Grace is lonely and drunk. He has stolen a mail truck to learn about writing letters. His old friend Red finds him and tries to help him find a way out of this dilemma. Jimmy seems unconcerned

Jeanne Beckwith currently teaches English and theater at Norwich University in Northfield, Vermont Her full-length plays, *Companion* and *Broken Circle* have been named by Portland Stages as the 2008 and 20010 Vermont State Winners of the Clauder Award for New England Playwrights. *Companion* will be presented by Mountain Road Productions in May of 2010 at the Enosburg Opera House. Another full length, *Love Letters Made Easy*, will be produced in 2010 by Lost Nation Theater in Montpelier, VT.

CHARACTERS

Jimmy, Late thirties. A Hairdresser. He yearns for something new in his life.

Red, A few years younger than Jimmy who used to hang out with Red's older brother in the neighborhood. He feels responsible for the old gang.

SETTING

A clearing in a woods overlooking a reservoir in Lynn, Massachusetts. The weather is warm

TIME

Late afternoon, the present.

. . .

JIMMY sits on the ground. There is a mailbag beside him. He has been sifting through its contents and many letters, flyers, etc. lie scattered around him. He is intently reading one letter, pausing to wipe his eyes. He is obviously moved. He is obviously drunk. RED enters.)

RED: For Chrissakes, Jimmy! The cops are looking for you. Annie says they've been round to the shop twice now.

JIMMY: *(Snuffling.)* Hello, Red:. You come to look out at the water too?

RED: What the fuck you been up to? They say you stole a mail truck.

JIMMY: Who says I stole a mail truck?

RED: They all say you stole a goddamned mail truck, Jimmy. Did you?

JIMMY: Why would you think I had stole a mail truck?

RED: 'Cause you're sitting here with a mailbag, Jimmy. You've got a U.S. mail-bag and a bunch of mail. You don't have to be much of a detective to figure it out.

JIMMY: I want to know who exactly is saying that I stole a mail truck?

RED: Everybody says you stole it. It's all over the city. It'll be on the six o'clock news.

JIMMY: Oh.

RED: That redhead with the wide mouth is gonna be saying, "The authorities are seeking James Grace of Lynn, Massachusetts for questioning in the recent theft of a U.S. Postal truck."

JIMMY: She's a good looking woman, that redhead.

RED: What the Christ you go and do something like this for?

JIMMY: The truck was just sitting there. It was running. Nobody was looking after the mail. I got worried.

RED: It was Johnny O'Connor's truck. He was just delivering a package to Mrs. Peterson.

JIMMY: Looked to me like he had just left it there.

RED: He says he only left it for a minute. He gets back just in time to see you driving off.

JIMMY: That's a nice thing, Mrs. Peterson getting a package. Was it from her kids?

RED: You stole a mail truck, Jimmy. You'll be in jail for twenty years.

JIMMY: I still know a couple of guys on the job. We go way back.

RED: Since they caught you growing the Marijuana out back of the shop, they ain't been so friendly, Jimmy. You got off with a warning. This is different. You stole a mail truck!

JIMMY: I was gonna bring it back.

RED: You're dead drunk, aren't cha?

JIMMY: I went down the Blue Moon after the shop closed. I might have had a few.

RED: This is serious, Jimmy. You stole a U.S. mail truck. You'll get sent to federal prison for something like that. It won't be like spending a couple of months in Salem.

JIMMY: Rosie Callaghan died. You remember Rosie Callaghan?

RED: Of course I remember Rosie Callaghan. She taught me how to drive. What's her dying got to do with you stealing a mail truck?

JIMMY: I went down the Blue Moon and I heard the news, and I felt really bad. I went to high school with her boy, Seamus. You remember Seamus? He died about ten years ago. He had the cancer, and now old Rosie's gone on too.

RED: At the risk of repeating myself, what does that have to do with you stealing a mail truck, Jimmy?

JIMMY: I just got to thinking about how Rosie used to send us both letters when we were in the army. She'd send Seamus one every week and she'd put a note in for me. I always liked those notes. They always said exactly the same thing. "How are you, Jimmy. . .Take care of yourself, Jimmy." She used my name a lot. I liked it that she used my name like that.

RED: How many did you have at the Blue Moon? More than a couple, I bet. Maybe that's a good thing. Maybe that could get you off.

JIMMY: I got to thinking how I wish I'd get a letter now and then. I got no one ever writes me a letter.

RED: Nobody writes anybody letters, Jimmy. It's old school to write letters. You need to get yourself a computer or something.

JIMMY: I was cutting Teddy Shane's baby sister's hair the other day.

RED: Tell me where the truck is, Jimmy.

JIMMY: She's going to college somewhere out in Pennsylvania.

RED: We gotta do something about the truck.

JIMMY: She's a smart girl — a really smart girl. You ever seen her with Teddy?

RED: I'm sure she is a smart girl. Where's the damn truck!?

JIMMY: Pennsylvania's a long way from here.

RED: It ain't as far as Leavenworth 'cause that's where you're headed if we don't fix this.

JIMMY: She told me she'd write to me, Red.

RED: That's nice, Jimmy.

JIMMY: She said we could be pen pals. She's got the most beautiful hair of any of the Shane girls. It curls around your finger like a baby's.

RED: Teddy Shane's sister is about half your age.

JIMMY: She says she don't know what she'll do without me there to cut her hair. She says, nobody cuts hair like I do.

RED: I am aware of that Jimmy. You are the best hairdresser in the whole Boston area. You are a real artist — maybe they'll mention that on the six o'clock news. Now tell me where the Goddamn truck is.

JIMMY: I got to thinking, I don't actually know how to write letters. It ain't like I ever wrote Rosie Callaghan back. I just had Seamus tell her 'Hello' for me. Then I saw the truck sitting there with nobody looking after it, and I thought, well why the hell not?

RED: It makes perfect sense, Jimmy — why the hell not?

JIMMY: Rosie sent us socks once. Not just for Seamus. She sent me some too. They were the nice kind, not like the army gives you. They were warm and soft. I hope Mrs. Peterson got something warm and soft in her package.

RED: I'm pretty sure it was her blood pressure medicine, Jimmy.

JIMMY: How'd you know to find me here?

RED: Where else you gonna be but the Wolf Pits? This is where we always went when things got rough. We'd come out here and watch the water, and no cops or anybody ever bothered us. How'd you get here? You walk? I kept looking out for the truck? Where'd you leave the truck?

JIMMY: I come up through the woods. The city owns those woods, you know, so it's kinda like we all own them.

RED: You carry that bag the whole way?

JIMMY: Only nobody really owns them. A trust owns those woods. The city can't ever sell them, so it's not like they own something if they can't sell it. I think it's a good thing that nobody owns them, don't you?

RED: Oh Jesus, Jimmy. This is gonna be a mess. Maybe if you hadn't stolen the mailbag and taken it away with you and ripped all the letters open — why'd you have to go and do that?

JIMMY: Thought I'd see how a letter was supposed to sound, but there was hardly anything worthwhile in it. Junk mail, they call it and junk mail it is. I got my own junk mail at home. I didn't have to steal a mail truck for that.

RED: Don't say that you stole it, Jimmy.

JIMMY: But you keep saying that I stole it, and now that I think about it, I'm pretty sure you're right.

RED: I know what I said, but you gotta say it different when you talk to the cops. We gotta start thinking about how you're gonna "phrase" things.

JIMMY: I'm not talking to the cops now, Red. I'm talking to you. You know there's just one real letter in this bag of crap, and guess what? It's from a kid in the navy to his drama teacher. His goddamn drama teacher, and he ain't even talking about Shakespeare or big ideas. The poor kid is lonely, and he's bored. He's a Goddamn actor for Chrissakes, and now he's in the navy.

RED: Time's gonna run out on us Jimmy.

JIMMY: If I knew how to write letters, I'd write to this kid.

RED: I know you would Jimmy.

JIMMY: I'd send him some socks.

RED: You could still do that. You could get a card or something to put in with them. That's what you do these days. You buy a card at the card store. You don't steal a goddamn mail truck!

JIMMY: I could send him Teddy Shane's baby sister's address. This is a kid who knows how to write letters. He could write her, and it would kinda be like my writin' her only he wouldn't be twice her age, but it would be on account of me that he was writing her.

RED: That's a good idea, Jimmy. You can write to them both from jail.

JIMMY: But she'd never know it was really me inside those letters. I'd be kinda like that guy in the movies with the big nose, only not quite the same. *(Pause.)* You know, I think I am drunk, Red.

RED: Stay with me, pal.. Just tell me where you left the truck.

JIMMY: In Margaret Ryan's garage. I go over there every other Tuesdays to cut her grandmother's hair. She can't stand it growing. Says it will be growing when she's in her grave, so she don't want it growing now. But they're in Florida this week, so I just fed the cats. I left the truck there and came up here because I thought it would be nice to read some letters and look out at the water, but there aren't any letters.

RED: Good! This is good. We can tell the cops where the truck is before they have to call in the FBI, and even if they already done that I can call Trish Malone. She works at the FBI.

JIMMY: Trish Malone works for the FBI?

RED: She works in one of the offices. She's bound to know somebody who knows somebody.

JIMMY: I thought Trish Malone was a librarian.

RED: Yeah, yeah, but now she's a librarian who works for the FBI.

JIMMY: I went to school with Trish Malone

RED: *(Beginning to help JIMMY gather up the scattered mail.)* If she helps get you out of this, you can write her a thank you letter.

JIMMY: Maybe you're right about getting all this stuff back. I gotta make sure this letter from the navy kid gets to his English teacher.

RED: You do, and that's a fact, Jimmy.

JIMMY: The kid was in an important play once. He says that right here. I don't know if Teddy Shane's baby sister would be interested in writing to an actor.

RED: *(Helping JIMMY to his feet.)* She was gonna write to freakin' hairdresser, Jimmy. Believe me, she would probably write to an actor.

JMMMY: Look out at the water, Red. The sun's going down.

RED: I see it.

JIMMY: You wanna drive down by the beach and go walkin' later?

RED: If they don't send you off to Fort Leavenworth, I will hire us a goddamn boat, Jimmy and we can sail way out on the sea and watch the sun go down from there.

JIMMY: We could take Trish Malone with us, Red.

RED: If she's in the mood after getting you out of prison, Jimmy, I expect we could ask her along.

JIMMY: I'll write you from jail, Red.

RED: I'll look forward to it, Jimmy. I'll look forward to it.

(He hoists the mailbag on his shoulder, and the two men exit.)

END OF PLAY

LOCKDOWN
(World Premiere)
A Ten Minute Play

George Brant

Sponsored by Perishable Theatre
Directed by Vanessa Gilbert
Sergeant . . . . Anthony Jarrod Goes
Bassist . . . . Dave Rabinow
Guitarist . . . . Brien Lang
Drummer . . . . Kerry Callery

A washed-up heavy-metal band is summoned to a military base and asked to reunite for an unexpected command performance.

George Brant's scripts have been produced and developed by Trinity Repertory Company, the Kennedy Center, Premiere Stages, Trustus Theatre, the Drama League, and the Disney Channel. His script *Elephant's Graveyard* was awarded the David Mark Cohen National Playwriting Award from the Kennedy Center and the Keene Prize for Literature and is published by Samuel French.

CHARACTERS

SERGEANT, early 30's, male — confident, matter-of-fact, closet heavy-metal enthusiast

BASSIST, 30's, male — the leader and singer of the band, what passes for its brains

GUITARIST, 30's, male — generally pissed off, the songwriter of the band

DRUMMER, 30's male — amiable, a little on the slow side, goes with the flow

SETTING:
A military base

TIME:
Present

.   .   .

(*A spartan office room. The Guitarist, Bassist and Drummer from the band formerly known as Lockdown sit awkwardly on stiff wooden chairs in front of a metal regulation desk. An American flag and picture of the President are present. An awkward pause, then —)*

BASSIST: So, how you guys been?

GUITARIST: Fine.

DRUMMER: Real good, Mike.

BASSIST: Did you see the VH1 thing?

GUITARIST: Bullshit.

DRUMMER: It was all right.

GUITARIST: Bullshit. VH1?

BASSIST: They got most of it right.

GUITARIST: Yeah, all except the music. Couldn't bother to play more than 10 seconds of our songs. But the bullshit personal shit? The break-up? Oh, yeah, they got that right.

BASSIST: Yeah.

DRUMMER: Yeah.

BASSIST: Anyway. It's good to see you guys again.

DRUMMER: Good to see you too, Mike.

(*No reply from the Guitarist. The door suddenly swings open and a Sergeant in full uniform enters.*)

SERGEANT: Boys! Thanks for coming down. First, let me start by saying I'm a big fan. The biggest.

BASSIST: Yeah?

SERGEANT: I'm pinching myself right now. Lockdown. The Lockdown. In my office.

DRUMMER: C'mon.

SERGEANT: Got 'em all. Every album. From Rude Awakening to Onslaught.

DRUMMER: Thanks, man.

GUITARIST: You missed one.

SERGEANT: Hm?

BASSIST: Rick —

GUITARIST: There's one before Rude Awakening.

SERGEANT: No, I'm pretty sure I —

BASSIST: Rick —

GUITARIST: Tarantula Dream.

SERGEANT: Haven't heard of it.

DRUMMER: *(to the Sergeant)* It's a bullshit album.

GUITARIST: It's not a bullshit album.

DRUMMER: It is. Wanky guitar all over, 20 minute song on each side.

SERGEANT: No, no, I'm sure it's great. I'll look for it.

BASSIST: Well, don't look too hard.

GUITARIST: It was not bullshit.

DRUMMER: It was, all right! Fuck, that was the one with Lem!

GUITARIST: Exactly.

BASSIST: *(remembering, embarrassed, but fond)* Keyboards. Shit. Wait, what was — *(singing in a heavy metal shriek)* "Why don't you get away?"

GUITARIST: Bwow bwow bwow bwow bwow wow wow

DRUMMER: Duh guh duh guh duh guh duh guh

BASSIST: *(singing)* "Why don't you get away from me!?"
    (Big finish.)

SERGEANT: *(clapping)* Hey! Hey! That's great, great! You boys are great!

GUITARIST: Thanks. It's a good album.

SERGEANT: It'll be on my desk tomorrow. I promise.

DRUMMER: Yeah, well, it's outta print.

SERGEANT: I'll find it. eBay or something.

DRUMMER: Sure.
    (The Sergeant stares at them for a moment, then —)

SERGEANT: Lockdown.
    (Uncomfortable silence.)

DRUMMER: Yeah.

SERGEANT: So, let's talk, huh?

BASSIST: Sure. So . . . are you guys looking for a tour of bases here? Support the troops? 'Cause I think we're down for that. As long as we're not talking four months or something. Or outside the Green Zone in an empty parking lot.

SERGEANT: No, no, nothing like that.

BASSIST: Good, well, we can give you a week free — with expenses here and there, meals and shit — otherwise, it's gonna run into actual cash.

SERGEANT: Sure, sure. Well, let's talk.

GUITARIST: More? *(than this?)*

SERGEANT: Yeah, more. Now you guys aren't . . . I'm not exactly tearing you away from anything, am I?

GUITARIST: Huh?

SERGEANT: Work. "Gigs." I mean, you're not in the middle of anything. Recording, touring, writing?

GUITARIST: What the fuck business is it of yours?

BASSIST: Rick, hey -

GUITARIST: No, no, we're not. We've been broke up for years. So what?

SERGEANT: Thought so, just checking.

GUITARIST: For your files? What?

SERGEANT: No, I just keep up on you. Read the magazines. Hell, I'm a member of your fan club.

DRUMMER: Yeah?

SERGEANT: 3rd level. I even made a donation to studio time a few years back.

BASSIST: Oh well, thank you, Sergeant.

SERGEANT: You got it. It was my pleasure. Got a good song out of it. "Brainstorm."

DRUMMER: Yeah.

SERGEANT: Kinda felt like it was my song. Like I had some ownership, you know?

BASSIST: Sure.

GUITARIST: Well, I wrote it.

SERGEANT: Oh, I don't feel I deserve royalties or something. Just pride that I had a part in it. A part in Lockdown. You understand?

BASSIST: Sure.

SERGEANT: So I was naturally upset to hear you'd broken up.

DRUMMER: Us too.

SERGEANT: And I got all the solo stuff, but . . . if you don't mind my saying so, those albums were louder, but that's about it. Not better, just louder.

BASSIST: That's probably fair.

SERGEANT: Something about the chemistry of a band. Something you can't put your finger on. Like the chemistry of a platoon. They all have a different reason they work.

GUITARIST: I wouldn't know.

SERGEANT: You try not to break up a platoon.

BASSIST: Sure.

SERGEANT: 'Cause just look what happens. Rick, you teach guitar now?

GUITARIST: That's right.

SERGEANT: Oh, how the mighty have fallen.

GUITARIST: Let's go.

SERGEANT: *(to the Bassist)* And you're not much better. That's your voice on the carpet commercial, right? Singing about carpet?

BASSIST: . . . yes.

SERGEANT: *(the Drummer)* And I don't even know what you're doing.

DRUMMER: Just keeping it real.

SERGEANT: Sure you are. So when this gig came up, I naturally thought of you all. A chance to get you back together. A big reunion.

BASSIST: I said we'd do a tour. I offered free.

SERGEANT: That's not necessary, we'd pay you. That's the beauty of this. You'd be an independent contractor. Helping us out.

GUITARIST: What the fuck are you talking about?

SERGEANT: Well, some of our guests have been here for some time. They've grown a bit . . . immune. We have found, however, that the use of certain musics can prove quite useful with even the most hardened visitor. Your music, "Brainstorm," in particular. Almost works on its own, without the car batteries.

DRUMMER: Without the — ?

SERGEANT: But a recording only gets us so far. You see?

(Beat.)

BASSIST: You want us to play.

SERGEANT: Yes.

BASSIST: Play while you — ?

SERGEANT: You'd be surprised. It works.

GUITARIST: Fuck you.

SERGEANT: Whatever you want backstage. Like the old days. Korbel, coke, and a bowl full of nothing but yellow M&M's.

BASSIST: Done his homework.

SERGEANT: You'd do 30 minute set, one hour break, 30 minute set, so on. Kick-ass sound system. And you can play as loud as you ever wanted.

DRUMMER: Wait, wait, so — what? I play high-hat while you're pounding some guy's head in?

SERGEANT: You're the Artist. What you play is up to you.

GUITARIST: Fuck off.

SERGEANT: You'd be jamming again.

GUITARIST: No.

SERGEANT: For a very appreciative audience.

GUITARIST: No.

SERGEANT: Serving your country. Money. Women.

GUITARIST: Fuck you.

SERGEANT: I see. Is this all of you?

(They band looks at each other, nod.)

Sure?

(They nod again.)

That's too bad. Goodbye, then.

(Sergeant opens door for them. Lockdown moves to exit.)

(sighing) The General told me you were no Stillborn.

(The band stops in their tracks.)

BASSIST: What?

DRUMMER: What do they have to do with this?

SERGEANT: Oh, I'd placed a friendly wager with General Myers. Bet him you'd get more confessions than Stillborn.

GUITARIST: Stillborn is here?

SERGEANT: Goodbye, boys.

GUITARIST: Wait. Stillborn? They're here?

SERGEANT: Sure. They've been playing for months in Block 4. Block 5 was going to be yours. Much cleaner.

GUITARIST: Hold on, hold on.

SERGEANT: Like I said, I like you all better, but —

GUITARIST: Sign us up!

BASSIST: Rick?

GUITARIST: Sign us up! No way those hair metal posers are better than us!

DRUMMER: Fuck, no!

BASSIST: *(to the Drummer)* Jerry?

DRUMMER: Rick's right, Mike. You know it.

SERGEANT: Well? Michael?

(All look at the Bassist.)

BASSIST: . . . All right. We're in.

SERGEANT: Super. You won't regret it. Rehearsal room's down the hall. Loaded with gear.

BASSIST: Thanks.

SERGEANT: You might want to wear blindfolds or dark glasses for the first few times. Stillborn found some of it a bit unsettling at the start.

GUITARIST: We'll be fine.

SERGEANT: I know you will. And boys? If you ever need an extra push up the mountain — I do play keyboards.

(The Sergeant salutes and exits.)

GUITARIST: Oh my God.

BASSIST: What?

GUITARIST: I hear something. A song. The first song I've had in years.

DRUMMER: Shit!

BASSIST: Write it down, Rick, write it down!

GUITARIST: Yeah, yeah!

(He does so, then stops —)

Guys? It's good to be back.

(Lights out.)

END OF PLAY

ABRAHAM AND SARAH

(World Premiere)
A Ten Minute Play

ALAN BRODY

Abraham And Sarah was originally produced at the Boston Theater Marathon in May, 2009 sponsored by Underground Railway Theater.

Directed by Adam Zahler

Assistant Director/Stage Manager Danielle Kellerman

Abraham . . . . Stephen Russell

Isaac . . . . Tim Traversey

Sarah . . . . Debra Wise

Abraham, alone in his tent, prepares for the sacrifice of his son, Isaac. His wife Sarah discovers his plan tries to stop him.

Alan Brody is Professor of Theater Arts at MIT. His award winning plays including "Invention for Fathers and Sons," "The Company of Angels"and "The Housewives of Mannheim" have been produced at such theaters as The Cincinnati Playhouse in the Park, The Aspen Playwrights Conference, The Live Oak Theater in Austin, Texas and The Berkshire Theater Festival. A production of his play "Greytop in Love" at The Walnut Street Theatre in Philadelphia starred Kim Hunter.

CHARACTERS
    ABRAHAM, 60-70
    SARAH, his wife, 60-70
    THE VOICE OF ISAAC, their son, 10 years old

SETTING
    ABRAHAM's tent in Beersheba

. . .

Beersheba. ABRAHAM's tent. ABRAHAM is alone, sharpening a sacrificial knife. SARA comes in.

SARAH: Not again. *(No response)* Enough with the sacrifices, Abraham . . . What is it this time? A camel?

ABRAHAM: Don't be foolish.

SARAH: You've already done the sheep, the goat, the cow and the horse. There's nothing left but the camel . . . You're trembling.

ABRAHAM: Leave me alone.

SARAH: You've already got a tribe full of followers. You don't have to keep proving yourself.

ABRAHAM: Go away.

SARAH: All these public sacrifices are getting on my nerves. Everybody standing around while you slaughter some new victim, telling them the One God demanded an offering.

ABRAHAM: That's how they come to believe and give up their idols.

SARAH: Yes, well it's a very expensive visual aid. A waste of good livestock. You made a mess of the cow. All because you wouldn't let anyone help you. And then I'm the one who has to lay out the feast. This time you didn't even warn me. How many are you expecting? Fifty? A hundred? Two hundred? How am I supposed to feed them without any warning? You've got enough followers. How big a tribe do you want?

ABRAHAM: He wants all mankind to know he is the one God.

SARAH: Look, Abraham. You've found a very good idea with this One God thing. A lot of people can see how efficient it is. No more carving idols and daily mumbo-jumbo for this god and another one and never being sure which one will get jealous. But you can't expect all mankind to go along with a good idea. People have reasons for staying with what they know — or going with someone else who might have just as good an idea.

ABRAHAM: The One God is the truth.

SARAH: You prophets are so intractable.

ABRAHAM: Save your pragmatism for the cooking pot.

SARAH: Sure. All you have to do is gather a crowd, make an inspirational speech, slice up a goat and then depend on my cooking to seal the deal.

ABRAHAM: Ungrateful. Who made you pregnant when you were long past child-bearing? Who made you a queen among women?

SARAH: Yes, well. . .

ABRAHAM: When those two strangers came to our fields and I invited them in according to the laws of hospitality, when later, the next morning, they revealed themselves as His angels and foretold you would be with child and changed your name to queen among women, you laughed your practical laugh. But nine months later it was the One God who laughed.

SARAH: *(Dryly)* Yes. It was some miracle. So what's the sacrifice this time?

ABRAHAM: It won't be public.

SARAH: Why do it, then? All this rigamarole without an audience?

ABRAHAM: The One God has commanded it.

SARAH: When was this?

ABRAHAM: Last night. While you slept, He spoke to me.

SARAH: Like when He told you He was going to destroy Sodom?

ABRAHAM: Yes.

SARAH: And you bargained with him to save it?

ABRAHAM: Yes.

SARAH: Well, you did a great job.

ABRAHAM: It was His will.

SARAH: So I'll finally say it. These visits from the One God. Did you ever think they might be you talking to yourself?

ABRAHAM: Don't blaspheme.

SARAH: It's a theory. I mean, He's just as capricious as you are, just as demanding of attention.

ABRAHAM: I hear Him. He comes to me in thunder.

SARAH: So if it's not a camel, what is it?

ABRAHAM: I can't tell you.

SARAH: Why not?

ABRAHAM: Enough!

SARAH: Good argument. What's going on?

ABRAHAM: Leave me to the work.

SARAH: No. This is something new. Usually you're tearing around getting things ready. I've never seen you like this.

ABRAHAM: He's testing me.

SARAH: Testing you . . . *(Silence)* I don't like the smell of this. A private sacrifice with a mystery victim.

ABRAHAM: It's not your concern.

SARAH: I think it is.

ABRAHAM: Be grateful you don't have to cook for the multitudes.

SARAH: What is this sacrifice?

(ISAAC calls from outside)

ISAAC: *(Offstage)* Are you ready, father?

ABRAHAM: *(Calling off)* I'm coming.

ISAAC: *(Offstage)* I've got all the wood.

ABRAHAM: *(Calling off)* Good boy. I'm coming.

ISAAC: *(Offstage)* It's heavy.

ABRAHAM: *(Calling off)* Put it down till I come.

SARAH: You're taking Isaac? Why are you taking Isaac? *(No response)* Why are you taking my boy?. . .What's the sacrifice?. . .

ABRAHAM: This is my One God's greatest test!

SARAH: You're not. . .No! No! Give me that!

(SHE goes for the knife. HE strikes HER and SHE falls.)

ABRAHAM: Women mustn't touch the sacrificial instrument.

SARAH: You've lost your mind!

ABRAHAM: *(Kneeling over HER and holding HER down)* He came to me in thunder. He said I must do this as a covenant. He said I would be the father of multitudes.

SARAH: He said! He said! How can He be the One God if He tells you to sacrifice your own son?

ABRAHAM: Never question!

SARAH: You won't take my son.

ABRAHAM: He's my son, too. I love him. Do you think I don't weep inside for what I have to do? But the One God commands it and I must obey or all my life is meaningless.

SARAH: What about my life without my son?

ABRAHAM: Perhaps He will take me to the brink and then have pity on me.

SARAH: And if He doesn't?

ABRAHAM: I will sacrifice my Isaac to the truth.

SARAH: Your truth, not *the* truth. There is no *the* truth! And what will happen after?

ABRAHAM: Every man will know my story.

SARAH: And every father with his own truth will follow your example and sacrifice his son for it. For his God, his tribe, his land. And nothing will have meaning anymore.

ABRAHAM: If the One God takes pity on me, I will bless Him all the days of my life.

SARAH: And I will curse Him! What pity?

ABRAHAM: He will spare my son at the final moment.

SARAH: Then every father will believe his God will spare him in the final moment and send his son to sacrifice for an illusion. And leave their mothers screaming in anguish — and hatred of their men.

ABRAHAM: God is the business of men.

SARAH: Madman! *(SHE breaks away from HIM and runs to the opening)* Isaac! Run! Run away!

ISAAC: *(Offstage)* Father said to wait.

SARAH: Run!

ABRAHAM: Stay where you are! I'll be right there! *(HE pulls HER back and puts the knife to HER throat)* If you move, if you try to come after us, Ill slit your throat before the boy's eyes.

SARAH: Monster!

ABRAHAM: I will prove my faith in Him.

SARAH: And bring endless destruction.

ABRAHAM: Then that will be His will.

SARAH: Yours. Not His. And I will hate you to the end of your days. And Him for eternity.

ABRAHAM: Don't move. *(HE backs away from HER toward the opening.)* Nothing will stop this. *(HE reaches the opening. Calling as HE leaves)* I'm coming, son!

(HE's gone. SARAH stands frozen, then crosses HER arms over her belly and doubles over in pain.)

SARAH: *(Wailing)* Isaac!

END OF PLAY

SEX FOR A CHANGE
(World Premiere)

ROBERT BRUSTEIN

Sponsored by American Repertory Theatre
Directed by David Wheeler
Doctor . . . . .Steven Barkhimer
Nurse . . . . .Bobbie Steinbach
Patient. . . . . Robert Bonotto

A tender blend of love between the transgendered, rendered in a comic hailstorm of scalpels and sutures.

Now Senior Research Fellow at Harvard and Distinguished Professor of Theatre at Suffolk University, Robert Brustein was the founding director of the Yale Repertory Theatre and the American Repertory Theatre and founded the ART Institute for Advanced Theatre Training. Playwright, director, scholar, and theater critic, for over sixty years, Robert Brustein has overseen 200 productions and is the author of 16 books on theater and society, his latest being a new book on Shakespeare called *The Tainted Muse*.

CHARACTERS
Doctor
Nurse
Patient

SETTING
An operating room.

TIME
Now

. . .

An operating room. Patient on an operating table, under anesthesia, with a tag on his toe. Female nurse waiting for the doctor. After a moment he enters in his scrubs, holding up his washed hands.

DOCTOR: Good afternoon, Nurse, what's on the menu today?

NURSE: Appendectomy.

DOCTOR: Really? I was told it was a sex change.

NURSE: Could be the wrong O.R.

DOCTOR: Could be the wrong patient. Check out his chart.

NURSE: He has no chart.

DOCTOR: *(Irritated)* Well, then, read his wrist bracelet.

NURSE: *(Squinting)* Caravelle. Club Med. Guadaloupe.

DOCTOR: That accounts for the flushed complexion and the bloated abdomen. But it doesn't explain why he's lying anaesthetized on an operating table. What's that on the toe tag?

NURSE: *(Reading one side)* "Drastic reduction." *(Reading the other)* "Everything must go."

DOCTOR: Just as I thought. It's a sex change. Scalpel please.

NURSE: *(Handing him the instrument)* Shouldn't we call Receiving first?

DOCTOR: Forceps. What for?

NURSE: This patient's HMO may not cover genital confirmation surgery.

DOCTOR: Thingamajiggy. *(She hands him a clamp)* What the hell is genital confirmation surgery?

(He drops a round object into a bucket)

NURSE: A sex change.

DOCTOR: Well, if it's not covered, the patient pays the hospital, who pays the surgeon, and I'm richer by a thousand shares of Microsoft.

(He drops another round object into the bucket)

NURSE: I thought Microsoft was in a dive.

DOCTOR: Google then. Here's the HMO Expense Manual. Look up Fees for Surgical Services. It's right under my broker's phone number.
(He takes a book out of the pocket of his scrubs and throws it to her, and continues operating.)

NURSE: According to this, health plans only cover sex changes for government employees in certain areas of Northern California, where the procedure is called a salpingo-oophorectomy, or a bilateral salpingo-oophorectomy if both ovaries and tubes are removed.

DOCTOR: We can't do a bilateral salpingo-oophorectomy. Our patient is — was — a male.
(One longer object is dropped in the bucket.)

NURSE: *(Checking the manual)* The males are being offered feminizing genital-plasty. But the only patients eligible for this procedure are fire fighters in the city of San Francisco.

DOCTOR: As I see it, we either fly this patient out to San Francisco, register him as a fireman, and charge the city government for a thousand shares of Microsoft — er, make that Google — or we operate here and have him transfer the fee directly into my broker's account. What's the limit on the San Francisco insurance?

NURSE: Up to $50,000 if the surgery involves penile inversion vaginaplasty.

DOCTOR: What the hell is penile inversion vaginaplasty??

NURSE: *(Reading the manual)* A procedure that turns the skin of the penis inside out and uses it for a vaginal cavity.

DOCTOR: Very creative. Let's do that one. And if the HMO rejects his application, he's in a perfect position to go and fuck himself.

NURSE: *(Hesitant)* Pardon me, Doctor, but are you absolutely certain you have the proper authorization for this procedure? The Medical Board could make waves if you undertook an expensive surgical operation without appropriate clearance. Why not give the patient an appendectomy and tell him it's a vaginaplasty?

DOCTOR: Why not give him a vaginaplasty and tell them it's an appendectomy? That way we could keep the Medical Board out of the loop entirely without disturbing their customary coma.

NURSE: I hesitate to mention this, Doctor, but you seem unusually eager to proceed with this surgery. Is vaginaplasty a speciality of yours?

DOCTOR: Nope. This will be my virgin voyage.

NURSE: Excuse me, Doctor, but professional ethics oblige me to observe that your decision might be a little problematic.

DOCTOR: How so?

NURSE: I mean, even under the best of circumstances, like when the surgeon is trained and qualified, and might even have some experience with the procedure, there's no guarantee of absolute success.

DOCTOR: And how would you define "absolute success"?

NURSE: Aside from persuading the HMO to pay the hospital bill and the doctor's fee, I would say that absolute success is defined by the patient's total satisfaction with his new circumstances.

DOCTOR: Well, then, Nurse, you see before you a shining example of absolute success.

(Turning proudly in a complete circle.)

NURSE: You?

DOCTOR: *(Nodding)* I had the procedure performed on me last year. In this very hospital.

NURSE: *(Amazed)* No kidding! Who was your surgeon?

DOCTOR: Jimmy Levinson.

NURSE: Not Jenny Levinson?

DOCTOR: No, Jimmy Levinson.

NURSE: Formerly Jimmy. He operated on herself just three weeks ago.

DOCTOR: And you know him . . .

NURSE: . . . her . . .

DOCTOR: — on a first name basis?

NURSE: He operated on me last Christmas before he became she.

DOCTOR: You are transgender, too, then?

NURSE: We prefer to say "transwoman."

DOCTOR: I thought your face was familiar. Weren't you that hunky attendant with the big biceps that used to hang out in Dispensary?

NURSE: That was me. Abe Teitelbaum in Radiology.

DOCTOR: And I was Rose Lafferty in Gynecology.

NURSE: The famous Doctor Rosie! I thought I recognized you.

DOCTOR: The obstetrical surgeon with the cobra tattoo on her shoulder.

NURSE: I loved that tattoo! I always had a kind of crush on you except you were a woman.

DOCTOR: And I always had a kind of crush on you except you were a man.

NURSE: Think of it, under other circumstances, you could have been Abie's Irish Rosie.

DOCTOR: What do you mean other circumstances? Those other circumstances are now.

NURSE: By God, you're right. These other circumstances are now.

DOCTOR: And what is your newly gendered name, Abe?

NURSE: Guinevere Teitelbaum, R.N.. And yours, Rosie?

DOCTOR: Lancelot Lafferty, M.D.

NURSE: I believe we are a match.

DOCTOR: One last question, Nurse Teitelbaum. And your answer is very important to me. Are you a virgin?

NURSE: *(Delighted with herself)* Two days after my vaginaplasty, Dr. Levinson offered me a hymenectomy as a bonus. I am as impregnable as the Khyber Pass.

DOCTOR: My virginal Nurse Guinevere!

NURSE: My virile Doctor Lancelot!

(They embrace passionately.)

PATIENT: *(Rising from the table in an anesthetic daze, speaking with a high voice)* Is the operation over? Are my tonsils out yet?

(BLACKOUT.)

END OF PLAY

GONE
(World Premiere)

ED BULLINS

BOSTON THEATER MARATHON
May 17, 2009
Sponsored by Roxbury Crossrsoads Theatre
Directed by Jackie Davis
Amber. . . . . Jade Guerra
Bartender Robbie . . . . Tom Graves
Toby . . . . Keith Mascoll

Gone by Ed Bullins is as severe as a Harlem Renaissance painting by
Jacob Lawrence.

Ed Bullins left Philadelphia prior to his writing with a vengence. In
1965, during the Watts Riots, he stood on the stage of San Francisco's Fire House Repertory Theatre, challenging his audience to concede the possibility that there existed a dangerous, famished entity
in America which fed off the life and spirits of black people. From
that first telling experience, bringing "Clara's Ole Man" to the stage,
Bullins has followed the message of enlightenment to the masses. He
has numerous awards, plays, and artistic works.

CHARACTERS

> BARTENDER ROBBIE, in his 50s, of European extraction.
> AMBER, mid-20s, African-American woman.
> TOBY, early 30s, an L.A. wannabe movie thug.

SETTING

> A bar.

TIME

> Night.

. . .

A youngish black woman enters a bar room. She heads for her favorite stool and sits. The bar room is empty except for the bartender. He goes to the woman.

BARTENDER: How's it goin', Amber? Have you heard anything?

AMBER: I'm great, Robbie . . . I've got offers.

BARTENDER: You have? In this economy?

AMBER: Look, just because the two diners where I was a waitress closed, don't mean that this whole town is goin' under.

BARTENDER: That's right, Amber. You're right. I tell my father-in-law, owner of this dive, every day that things are getting better.

AMBER: Yeah, you're right.

BARTENDER: No, I'm not . . . He knows I'm lyin'. That's just my way to save my salary . . . Joke, right? . . . I've been behind this bar for thirty years. And do you know what that walkin' mummy says? . . . *(Rough voice.)* "It's gone. Everything is gone."

AMBER: I know what everybody's saying . . .

BARTENDER: Yeah, but he spends his winters in Boca Raton . . . and us?

AMBER: *(Shrugs)* He's gone. But we still hangin'. *(She makes a gesture.)* I didn't know how hard it was to quit smoking. Now I know I can't afford it.

BARTENDER: Yeah . . . I know. My father-in-law who owns this joint burns up his cell phone every day in my ear . . . and, and . . . Hey, you ready for your regular, Amber?

AMBER: Why not, player? As long as it's a "Shirley Temple."

BARTENDER: Hey, honey, I'm glad that you still into your plan. And I'm glad that I was the one to help you do it.

(He starts fixing her drink.)

AMBER: My plan? . . . Right, Robbie. I didn't have much of a plan until then. And then it became . . . a vow, like my soon-to-be marriage.

(A man enters the bar. He looks around and sits two stools away from Amber.)

BARTENDER: How ya doin', Toby?

TOBY: Okay, man.

BARTENDER: Hey, I haven't seen you this year. Where . . .

TOBY: I went back to where I was born . . . L.A.

(BARTENDER places Amber's drink in front of her.)

BARTENDER: *(To Amber.)* Here it is, Ms. A.

TOBY: Give the lady another drink on me.

AMBER: *(Surprised.)* No, mister. I don't want another one.

BARTENDER: She's got enough now, Toby.

TOBY: What's wrong. My breath stank or something? (To Bartender.) And take care of your boss's interests, Robbie. Get me my usual.

BARTENDER: That's how you learn how to talk to people out on the Wrong Coast?

TOBY: Listen, I'm just too through with punks and bitches rejecting me. (Mimes.) No, Toby, that part was cast this morning. Besides, you're not the type . . . Too bad, Toby, if you were a bit more handsome, well . . . you know what I'm gonna say, sweetcake.

BARTENDER: Hey, man, I know the drill, even if I never visited the back lot.

(Amber gets off her stool and walks toward the Ladies Room.)

AMBER: Robbie. I don't want any more. I'm going to the little girl's room

BARTENDER: Long as you're not smokin' in there, kid.

AMBER: *(Surprised.)* Robbie . . . you know better than that.

(Pause. Toby nods his head toward Amber's exit.)

TOBY: *(To Bartender.)* You chippin' on that, Robbie? What's a shortie like that hangin' with you for? She's got an insurance policy with your name on it, or something'?

BARTENDER: *(Annoyed.)* Gone! She's got a plan. She's . . . she's . . .

TOBY: Lookin' for a sucker!

BARTENDER: Nawh, she's clean, I said. She don't even drink booze anymore or mess'around with any of that shit they got around here. *(Warning.)* Now if you don't . . .

TOBY: Gone, man. I'm just tryin' to have a little fun, chump. You know what? You stuck on her!

BARTENDER: Her boyfriend, Dingle's comin' off his second bit in Afghanistan soon. They getting' married.

TOBY: How romantic . . . With her girlfriend? . . . What's she askin' for head?

BARTENDER: *(Angry.)* Hey! What the fuck did you say?

TOBY: You heard what I said, Robbie. You big sucker. *(The bartender rushes from behind the bar empty-handed. Toby pulls a handgun and points it at the bartender's face. The bartender stops and waits.)* Robbie . . . big ole Robbie. When I was a kid, you used to smack me around and kick my ass out the door. Remember that, old man? Or has Alzheimer's caught up with you yet? . . . Hey, cat's not dancin' on your tongue? But I can tell by your eyes that you ain't scared. You never dreamed that you would have this moment . . .

BARTENDER: Let her go, Toby. You ain't . . .

TOBY: Let who go? There's nobody here to go, but us.

BARTENDER: Her man's comin' back in a week or two. He's saved enough for a down payment on a Dunkin' Donut stand . . .

TOBY: What army is he in?

BARTENDER: No army . . . Contractor.

(Pause.)

TOBY: You say his name is Dingle? . . . Hey, I know a Dingle. Live over by Mission Point.

BARTENDER: That's Big Dingle. Amber's fiancé is Little Dingle. Weighs two hundred fifty pounds even.

(From the Ladies Room, sound of a cell phone giving a short ring.)

TOBY: *(Edgy)* What's that?

BARTENDER: Little Dingle calls her every night.

TOBY: Well, you better get her out here!

(Amber enters from the Ladies Room.)

AMBER: Oh, my god! What the hell is this?

BARTENDER: Toby's just passing through . . . Ms. A . . . .

TOBY: Shut up, Robbie! . . . *(To Amber.)* Throw that cell phone over here!

AMBER: My phone?

TOBY: Throw it over here or I'm shooting your old friend in the face.

(Amber goes into he jacket pocket, brings the cell phone out and tosses it to Toby. Toby throws the cell phone on the floor and stomps on it.)

AMBER: *(Distressed.)* Oh . . . my god.

BARTENDER: So, what now, Toby?

TOBY: I'm glad you asked, old friend . . . I'm taking you back to the big refrigerator and locking you in there. That's after you show me where the cash is stashed. And I make friends with your girlie here.

AMBER: No!

BARTENDER: Amber?

TOBY: She's coming with me. I can use her on my journey.

BARTENDER: *(To Toby.)* You stinkin' . . .
(Bartender takes two steps toward Toby.)
AMBER: Wait, Toby . . . I have a better idea. Robbie's couch is in the men's room. I can go back there with you now.
(She gets close to Toby.)
BARTENDER: Amber! What the fuck is wrong with you?
AMBER: Don' you want me, Toby? I bet you've had lots of girls in your life. You've been to so many places. And done so many things. You must be like those hipster cats of the last century, diggin' life, now ain't that sweet? *(Amber gets within Toby's reach, gravs his gun barrel, pointing it toward the ceiling, while drawing a canister of pepper spray from her pocket, and spraying it toward Toby's eyes.)*
TOBY: Bitch! You're dead meat! Dead!
(Bartender Robbie dives at Toby's back and grabs his throat in an arm lock. He strangles Toby into unconsciousness. Amber cries softly, having pulled the gun from Toby's fingers.)
AMBER: *(To Bartender.)* The gun isn't real. It just looked that way.
BARTENDER: Is he dead? . . . Is he gone.
AMBER: I don't know . . . I'm scared to touch him again.
(A bullhorn is heard from outside: "You people in there. This is the police. Come out in two minutes, or face the consequences!!!")
BARTENDER: How did they know we were in trouble?
AMBER: I heard you and him shouting at one another. So I called 911. I had my pepper spray that Dingle had gave me. It's a good thing that I didn't know about the gun then and told the cops . . . They would have had the SWAT team burst in here terminating us . . . We'd all be gone by now.
BARTENDER: I've raised you to do the right thing, Amber, and you've always have done it. C'mon. They're waiting.
(Robbie and Amber help each other to their feet and go out the door.)

END OF PLAY

LAYING THE SMACK DOWN IN CAMBRIDGE
(or WRESTLING WITH INTEGRITY)

Jonathan Busch

Laying the Smack Down in Cambridge was orignally produced by the Lyric Stage Company of Boston, May 17, 2009, as part of the Boston Theater Marathon.
Directed by Brett Marks
Donald . . . . Alex Wyse
Cindy . . . . Maureen Keiller
General Dismay . . . . Tim Smith

A struggling, young poet must weigh his artistic integrity against his need for cold, hard cash when he is offered a job as a writer for professional wrestling.

Jon Busch's full-length *Pet Shop Days* received 2nd prize in the 2008 Firehouse Theatre Festival of New American Plays and was a finalist for the Reva Shiner Award. He works for an ad agency in Boston and daydreams about writing for video games, soap operas and pro wrestling.

CHARACTERS

DONALD, 23, a struggling, young writer
CINDY, an attractive, 35–40ish businesswoman
GENERAL DISMAY, 30–40, a professional wrestler

SETTING

DONALD's apartment

TIME

The present

. . .

DONALD returns from work in a huff, carrying his mail. There's a big pile of crumpled paper on the floor.

DONALD: (*Muttering to himself*) Stupid day. Stupid work. Stupid Barnes and Noble. No, Brenda, I can't work late tonight. You know I have writers' group. Well, you know what, Brenda? I know you think you're like a big shot cause you're a manager and you teach like one course in English Lit for Losers at EastWestern Technical College of Computing Software or whatever, but you can't tell me what to do. I'm outta here. . . . That's what I shoulda said. (*He sits down on his ratty, old sofa and begins sorting through his mail.*) I'll show her. Soon as I get published I'll take my nametag and throw it in her stupid face. I'm outta here, Brenda.
(*He opens a letter and reads. A VOICE comes from offstage and acts as a narrator, letting the audience hear the words that DONALD reads.*)

VOICE: Dear poet: Sorry, but your work has not been selected for our upcoming issue. Please keep writing and don't hesitate to send us more of your poems.

DONALD: (*Disappointed, then noticing a postscript*) Oh well. Ooh, what's this?

VOICE: P.S. — Donald, the above is simply a form letter. In your case we'd like to make a special request that you to refrain from sending us any more of your work.

DONALD: Ouch. Well, a poet's gotta have a thick skin . . . (*He crumples the rejection letter and adds it to the huge pile of paper on the floor. Obviously, this is a nightly ritual for him.*) They'll feel stupid one day. They'll say, "What were we thinking? How did we miss him? The great Donald Chesterton. Poet of a generation!"
(*He opens another letter and reads.*)

VOICE: Dear Donald: Your poetry, if one could reasonably call it that, is fraught with juvenile, melodramatic cliché. Here's a tip: Leave all references to the devouring of souls to B-grade horror films. Sincerely, the Editors. *(DONALD crumples the letter and tosses it onto the pile.)*

DONALD: *(muttering)* B-Grade horror films. I'd devour your stupid soul . . . *(He opens the last of the letters.)*

VOICE: Donald. We tried to be nice. Please stop sending us your shitty poems. Henceforth, all your submissions will be shredded, unread. The paper will not be recycled.

DONALD: Dammit! *(He adds this letter to the pile and buries his face in his hands. Then, there is a knock on the door.)* Oh crap. Is it time for writers' group already? Just a second!

CINDY: *(From outside the door)* Donald?

DONALD: Who is it?

CINDY: Donald Chesterton?

(DONALD doesn't recognize the voice. He leaves the papers, gets up and opens the door. CINDY MAHONEY, an attractive, professional woman stands in the doorway.)

CINDY: Are you Donald Chesterton, the poet?

DONALD: Who? Do I know you? Wait . . . what did you just call me?

CINDY: Okay, try to stay with me here. Are you Donald Chesterton, the poet?

DONALD: Um . . . well, I'm Donald Chesterton, yeah. And I write poetry. So I guess . . . yeah, I guess that's me.

CINDY: Fantastic. How would you like to live in a mansion, Don?

DONALD: What?

CINDY: A mansion. It's like a really big house. Do you like martinis?

DONALD: Sure, but —

CINDY: You wanna go to parties? Meet chicks? Get some action? How much do you make now? Ten, twelve bucks an hour?

DONALD: Hey, now, just —

CINDY: How would you like to be rich and famous, Donald Chesterton, the poet?

DONALD: Look, lady, I don't even know who you are. And poets don't get rich and famous.

CINDY: Well, lemme ask ya this, Donnie boy: How'd ya like to share your poetry with the world?

DONALD: Are you a publisher?

CINDY: The name's Cindy Mahoney and I am very interested in your work. *(CINDY extends a formal hand. DONALD takes it tentatively and they shake.)*

DONALD: Don't you usually just send a letter or something?

CINDY: I'm not talking about one poem here, Chesterton. I'm talking about your entire body of work.

DONALD: Really?

CINDY: *(reciting)* How squelch the flaming fires that reside within my barren soul? How quell the rage of the beast inside me?

DONALD: Hey, those are my lines.

CINDY: Poetry! Raw! Angry! Vulgar! We want it all.

DONALD: You want to publish a book of my poetry?

CINDY: Well, let's just say we'd like to bring you on full time. We'd start you off with a six-figure salary, full benefits, 401K . . .

DONALD: What? Wait. Wait a minute now, what are you getting at?

CINDY: Paid vacation. Gym membership.

DONALD: Okay, lady, even I know there's no poetry job that pays a regular salary — let alone six figures with benefits.

CINDY: I'm with the WWC.

DONALD: That's not any publisher I've heard of.

CINDY: It's the World Wrestling Coalition.

DONALD: The what?

CINDY: We think you'd be a great fit for us.

DONALD: You want me to write for professional wrestling?

CINDY: That's right. Your work has a certain spirit — a certain violence, a certain angst that would be the perfect voice for one of our characters.

DONALD: Unbelievable. How did you find me anyway?

CINDY: Next time you happen to be perusing some of the more well-regarded literary journals, take a look at their list of underwriters. You'll probably find WWC near the top.

DONALD: You're kidding me.

CINDY: We have a deal with a number of journals. We support them and in return, whenever they come across a poet of a "certain type", well, they pass the work along to us. We've had your work forwarded to us from *several* sources. They hate it. We love it.

DONALD: This is absurd. And . . . and insulting as a matter of fact. I'm a poet. I'm not about to write for pro wrestling. I'd be the laughing stock of the literary world.

CINDY: I'm giving you the chance to share your poetry with millions of people.

DONALD: Through the mouth of a guy wearing tights!

CINDY: Look, you've got a BA in English, you work in Barnes & Noble, and you've got hundreds of rejection letters scattered across your floor for some reason.

DONALD: What's your point?

CINDY: Let's take a look at a few of these, shall we?

DONALD: No!

(CINDY grabs a few rejection slips off the floor. DONALD tries to snatch them away from her but she eludes his grasp.)

CINDY: Why not? Let's just have a little look. *(she reads)* Donald: Your poem, *The Me Inside*, amounts to nothing more than an exercise in self-pity. And its companion piece, *Die Jocks Die*, is perhaps the most ignorant, morbid and offensive piece of writing I have ever come across in my many years as an editor. *(Reading another)* Donald, your poetry is a chronicle of nauseatingly self-righteous, self-absorbed angst. We have burned all of your recent submissions. We pray they were your only copies.

DONALD: But I thought poetry was supposed to be a way to express how you really feel!

CINDY: Exactly! These journals don't appreciate the fact that you're pouring your sweat and blood onto every one of these pages. But we do. We love your work. The righteous indignation. The white, middle-class angst. The sexual confusion.

DONALD: Sexual confusion?

CINDY: It's perfect for our audience.

DONALD: No. This is insane. I'm not writing scripts for a fake sport that targets the lowest common denominators in society. I have some integrity, okay?

CINDY: Don, I want to introduce you to someone who I hope will change your mind. *(She calls off-stage)* General Dismay!

(GENERAL DISMAY storms into DONALD's apartment. He recites DONALD's poetry in the tone of a classic pre-wrestling-match trash talk.)

GENERAL DISMAY: HOW SQUELCH THE FLAMING FIRES THAT BURN WITHIN MY WRETCHED SOUL!? HOW QUELL THE RAGING BEAST INSIDE ME!? YOU IGNORANT DRUNKARDS. YOU COPULATING THRONGS. SOON YOU WILL LAY IN TATTERS ABOUT A THRONE OF BLOOD!

DONALD: Whoa. Who the hell is this guy? How does he know my poetry?

CINDY: This is General Dismay, your character.

GENERAL DISMAY: TWO SOULS DIVERGED IN A YELLOW WOOD — AND I CRUSHED THEM BOTH!

DONALD: My character?

GENERAL DISMAY: Help me, Donald. Everything you stand against stands against us in our next match.

DONALD: What are you talking about?

GENERAL DISMAY: Pretty Boy Jacobs and Charming Chet Chandler.

CINDY: It's a tag team, Don.

GENERAL DISMAY: Those nancy boys think they've got us beat. Those ponies are riding high on the hog. They say they're too busy partying and banging chicks to even train for our match. But together we could put Pretty Boy Jacobs and Charming Chet Chandler back in their place.

DONALD: Do you really expect me to buy all this?

CINDY: What do you mean? Pretty Boy Jacobs and Charming Chet Chandler represent those jocks you find so disagreeable.

DONALD: But it's not real. It's all a show. I don't want any part of it.

CINDY: Okay. Have it your way, Don.

(CINDY gives a solemn nod to GENERAL DISMAY. He leaves the apartment.)

DONALD: Is he leaving already?

(GENERAL DISMAY returns carrying a stack of gymnastic pads. He calmly lays them out on the floor.)

DONALD: What's he doing? Hey, nobody said you could set up your stuff here.

GENERAL DISMAY: YOU ARE ENTERING A WORLD OF HURT! COME WITH ME INTO THE DEPTHS OF PAIN!

DONALD: Is he talking to me? Or still reciting my poetry.

CINDY: Hard to say.

GENERAL DISMAY: I WILL WRENCH YOUR SOUL FROM YOU DISEMBOWELED BODY AND EXPUNGE THE PUNGENT INNARDS WITHIN!

DONALD: Ploughshares called that line redundant. Should I be frightened?

(GENERAL DISMAY charges at DONALD and clotheslines him. He falls onto the mat.)

DONALD: AAAGGGHHH!! What the hell?

(GENERAL DISMAY lifts him back to his feet and pummels him with exaggerated wrestling style punches, stomping his foot with each blow for effect.)

GENERAL DISMAY: OH YEAH! FEEL THE HURT!!

DONALD: I thought this was supposed to be fake!

(GENERAL DISMAY jogs to the other side of the room. As DONALD stumbles around, GENERAL DISMAY tackles him.)

CINDY: Don't worry. He won't do any permanent damage.

GENERAL DISMAY: TIME TO DROP THE BIG ELBOW!!

(GENERAL DISMAY rises and pats his tricep twice before proceeding to drop a 'big elbow' on DONALD.)

DONALD: OOOOOMMMPPHHH!!! I give, I give.

GENERAL DISMAY: FEEL THE PAIN THAT GENERAL DISMAY BRINGS! TO YOUR RIBS! TO YOUR SPINE! AND TO YOUR SOOOOOUUUUULLLL!!!

(He finally pins DONALD. CINDY drops down and bats a three-count on the mat.)

DONALD: Oh, the pain. It's so real.

GENERAL DISMAY: *(Still laying on top of DONALD)* OH YEEEAAAHHH!!!

DONALD: Oooooooooh.

GENERAL DISMAY: *(with sudden calm)* Let me level with you, Don. Why spend your life compromising who you really are? Why measure your greatness as a poet against the standards of an insular, academic elite? Why pander to a handful of ivory tower bureaucrats, when it means so little in terms of material wealth or spiritual fulfillment? Who is to say that they have a better grasp of the aesthetic than the rest of us? Who are they to judge what qualifies as art? What matters is being true to yourself, Don. And you could be sharing your true self with millions who have the same feelings you do, but can't quite put them into words.

DONALD: *(Squeaking under the weight)* I'm in pain. Real pain.

GENERAL DISMAY: That's right, Donald. Share your pain with millions who feel it exactly as you do.

DONALD: I feel it.

(CINDY nods and GENERAL DISMAY releases DONALD. DONALD struggles to his knees.)

DONALD: Oh. That really hurt. And yet . . . it's . . . such a rush. It's . . . everything I've felt over the years. You're right. Right about everything. All the anger and the pain. All crashing down on me, slamming me to the ground. It's finally real and it's amazing.

GENERAL DISMAY: *(Extending his hand)* What do you say, Don? Be the voice of General Dismay!

DONALD: I'll do it.

(GENERAL DISMAY helps DONALD up.)

CINDY: Come on. There's a limo waiting out front.

DONALD: Nice.

GENERAL DISMAY: OH YEAH!!

(DONALD and GENERAL DISMAY clasp hands and flex.)

(Blackout.)

END OF PLAY

LAST MEAL

Julia Harman Cain

Last Meal was originally produced in the Boston Theater Marathon in Boston, MA, on May 17, 2009, by the Salem Theatre Company. Directed by Catherine M. Bertrand.

Ann. . . . . .Caroline Watson-Felt
Nik . . . . .Natalie Cowell

A veteran cook in a state prison, ANN seeks help from a young innmate, NIK — revealing the skills that she has mastered and the secrets that she keeps.

Julia's full-length plays include *Four Rooms Waking, The Labyrinth* (musical), *Trinity,* and *Honor Not My Name.* Her work has been produced at Manhattan Theatre Source, the Boston Theater Marathon, Princeton University, Charles River Creative Arts, Princeton Summer Theatre, and the Capitol Fringe Festival. Julia is a 2007 graduate of Princeton University, where she studied playwriting with Ellen McLaughlin, Lynn Nottage, and Charles Mee.

CHARACTERS
  ANN, Female. Older.
  NIK, Female. Younger.

SETTING
  A prison kitchen. Harris County, Texas.

TIME
  Winter of '95.

. . .

A table littered with cooking utensils: mixing bowl, measuring cups, peeler, spoon, and one dull knife. Ingridients for apple pie: brown sugar, butter, dough, pie crust wrapped in plastic. ANN takes apples from a bag, counting them on to the table. Smelling each one. She wears a sweater and a plastic cap over her hair. NIK enters. Also wears a baggy sweater and plastic cap. Her eyes dart everywhere. ANN smiles when she sees her.

ANN: Good. So you found your way here all right, that's good. Sit down, sit. Glad to have you, sure couldn't do this alone anymore, I'll tell you that much. You know, funny thing about the new ones. Always have that little twitch in the corner of the eye. Sometimes the right, sometime the left. But you just can't make up your mind, huh?
  (From her seat, NIK shrugs her answer. ANN keeps unpacking the apples, but does not sit. Rarely does. She thumbs through a cookbook.)
ANN: All right then. You'd think I'd know how to do apple pie, by now, right? Not too many guys go for it though. Like to tell how they ate up something with a good long name. This one's a funny little fuck though. Asked him if he wanted, I don't know, bourbon. Raisins, maybe. Anything to liven it up. But no, sir. So. What do you say you watch me for today and you'll soon have a feel for things, okay? (. . .) You like apples? I like apples. Always did.
NIK: Not bad.
ANN: Never did like the green ones much. What do you call those red ones, you know, with the little bits of green? You can buy them with wrinkly leaves still stuck to the stem? My niece loves those. She's, God, she'll be five next month. Last time I saw her, she was spitting up that baby mush all over her mama's face. But now her mama tells me she won't eat nothing

but those red apples, all covered in peanut butter. I say that girl's going to look like a fucking hippo by the summer. Not like she listens to me. Not now anyway. (. . .) So why don't you slice these up for me? *(She holds out the knife. NIK flinches.)* I don't bite. *(A brief silence. Indicating herself—)* Possession with intent to distribute. *(NIK takes the knife. She slices quickly and sharply through the apples. ANN watches her. Smiling.)* You got nice hands, you know. Long fingers, wide palms. First thing I noticed about you, you know? Lizzie, or was it Grady, said you worked at that Guido place in East Houston? Not for too long, I hope. Ate there once, maybe five, six years back and my pasta was drowning in a green and piss river. (. . .) "Authentic Italian" my ass. (. . .) No offense or anything.

NIK: It's fine.

ANN: You're real good with that thing. Your mama teach you?

NIK: Taught myself.

(A brief silence. Then NIK takes off her sweater. Adjusts her uniform. ANN pours lemon juice into a bowl and sprinkles in some cinnamon.)

ANN: The trick for apple pie. You got to let the apples soak in lemon juice and cinnamon before you stick them in the crust. Keeps them from getting brown and fucked up. *(Pushes the bowl to NIK.)* Give that a good stir, will you? *(NIK takes the bowl. ANN rolls out the dough and kneads it.)* So the guy also wants a roast chicken, which should be nice and easy. Some peas and roast corn I think. Cherry Coke. You like that?

NIK: Tastes like crap.

(ANN rolls the dough into strips.)

ANN: Well, it's what he wants. Not for us to judge. (. . .) While back, we had this scrawny-ass guy ask us for rattlesnake. Goddamn rattlesnake. Old Manny says, "No way we have that 'round here. Where he think he is, Wis-fucking-consin?" And guy says, "No brother, this rattlesnake is a goddamn Texas delicacy." And Manny says, "Not in no part of Texas I ever been to." Then guy swears all over the place he was born up in Sweetwater and they host The World's Largest Rattlesnake Round-Up every year. (. . .) 'Course Manny can't believe that shit, so he gets the Sweetwater Chamber of Commerce on the phone and the secretary says, "Damned if I know, I just moved here last week," so she passes him to to Chief Chef Corky, that's his real name too, and he says they got them The World's Largest Rattlesnake Round-Up every year. Every damn year. And would we like us some snake meat shipped from Sweetwater? (. . .) Don't do that normally, not procedure, you know? (. . .) But Manny said why not. Why not? *(ANN finishes rolling. NIK finishes stirring the cinnamon and lemon.)* Here, just start counting the apples in there. One, two, there you go. I do it so they don't think we snuck none for ourselves. Picked up that trick from the lady before me. (. . .) Rita Lee. Rita Lee Wilson Barnes. Poured motor oil on some guy when he flipped her the bird on the bus. Got two and half for assault and battery, plus resisting arrest. Bit the cop on the neck. Left one hell of a scar. (. . .) Poor fucker's got a life-long hickey.*(NIK mixes the apples into the lemon and cinnamon. Then she carefully lifts the bowl and pours everything into the pie crust.)* Now, you — There. There, just like that. *(ANN smiles. NIK does not look up.)* Rita. Rita Wilson. She'd always pour real slow. (. . .) You know, she had this idea, some crazy notion that your soul went out of you just like this, these little pieces, first one, then another and another. Slap, slap, little hunks of your heart go dropping down into someplace else, where there'd be a nice silver bowl to catch you as you came apart. *(NIK finishes pouring. Spreads out the apples with her fingers.)* She liked to think you held together. In your way. Few little pieces of you, they always stuck together. (. . .) Her brother died here, you know. Men's prison across the way. Got himself stabbed in the neck with a toothbrush out in the yard, just two weeks before he was due to get it from the state. She had to laugh when she found that one out. Got his dumb ass off-ed before Harris County could do it for him. (. . .) Did you know, you know they clean off the arm with alcohol before they do it? Got to guard against disease. Can't even get a last smoke no more. Health reasons, governor said. *(NIK takes her hands from the pie. She gets it.)* We'll set up the tray when this is done. Nice trays today. China. Little pictures of kids with blue faces. I used to add a flower until I had a guy eat that too. *(ANN indicates the strips of dough.)* You know what to do next, right?

NIK: *(standing up)*: This is fucked —

ANN: Where you going?

NIK: I won't do this —

ANN: You got to —

NIK: I said no —

ANN: *(standing up)*: You want to go, then go. Go pace in that yard until your brain goes to mush. Go read poems with a college boy trying to make himself a better citizen. Go on then. You think that keeps you good and innocent?

(A brief silence.)

NIK: Said you wanted a cook.

ANN: I do. Someone with hands like yours. (. . .) Think of it. To everybody else, they're just the poor lost fucks who couldn't afford no fancy lawyer and hundred-year appeals process. But to us, to you, they'll be apple pie and chicken and cherry coke. Enchiladas. Deep-dish pizza. Peach cobbler. Bologna and cheese on a white roll. And Bran flakes. Whole milk. That's somehing.

(NIK looks at the pie.)

NIK: Think I'd ask for steak. And chinese food.

ANN: Bananas and flat soda. Anything else and I'd puke it up. You know, I heard this fuck from Atmore went with a sandwich from the vending machine and a lady over in Louetta chose milk and water. Had to maintain her figure, she said.

(She laughs. NIK does too.)

NIK: *(breathes)*: How many? Each year.

ANN: Three, five. Least twenty since I got here.

NIK: They stay with you?

ANN: Sure. Some.

NIK: Like who?

(No answer. NIK turns to go.)

ANN: He was a kid — Late twenties, at most. Skinny thing.

NIK: Yeah?

ANN: Got the needle for shooting two teenage girls behind a department store while they were smoking. They went there every Sunday. Same spot. Same cigarettes. He planned for weeks: how he'd crouch behind a car with a Smith & Wesson. How he'd chop them up and shove their bodies in an oil drum. (. . .) How he'd take their shopping bags and give everything to his sister. (. . .) See, he did it for the clothes. (. . .) He swore that, when he talked to me, he said that it was all for the clothes. It was just him and his sister, ever since he was twelve, just them. Kid had three jobs, sometimes four, was always careful. But you can't prepare yourself for everything. The rain. Prices going up. Or some asshole on the six o'clock bus who pushes your sister into the mud, rips her jacket down the back. Something came apart inside him. Three jobs and his sister deserved a new jacket. Gold lining, designer label. She had to have it. What would his father think if he knew, if he knew his son couldn't get his sister a damn jacket —

(. . .)

NIK: What'd he want?

ANN: Fruit Loops. Some sour milk. Piece of toast. Burn it, he said. So that shit breaks in half when you drop it. I looked at him. (. . .) This is yours, I said. I'll make you whatever you want and we can pretend to be someplace else, someplace fancy and far away, with your sister, all dressed up — (. . .) But those were the last things, he said. When I ate that shitty-ass cereal, that was the last morning I woke up without shaking like hell. Last morning that my life stretched so damn far I couldn't imagine the end. Now it's all I think about. How many times will I brush my teeth and look out at the sun and how many times will I slug a guy in the teeth, will I check out the ass on the night watch lady, Jesus, it's big, how many times will I fold my hands and blink my eyes and crack my knuckles. I just can't stop counting, he said. God, I can't stop — But I didn't count those Fruit Loops. I didn't —

(ANN stops. NIK picks up the pie. She inspects it.)

NIK: 400 degrees. 55 minutes.

ANN: Yeah. That's right.

(NIK stops. Realizes something.)

NIK: So. When you getting out?

ANN: *(caught)* One and a half weeks.

NIK: I'm no good with steak.

ANN: You'll learn. *(ANN starts to go.)* His was my best one, you know? Never burned toast like that ever before. Should've seen it, should've seen his face. Think of it. The last one to touch him, touch the inside of him before they strapped him down and he couldn't breathe no more. Our apples will be inside this one, right as they walk him to the northeast hall.

(She is almost gone.)

NIK: I'll be part of it.

ANN: Yeah. Yeah, that's how it goes.

(She leaves the room. NIK moves aside a strip of crust. Makes sure that someone is watching. She picks out an apple slice and swallows it whole.)

END OF PLAY

THE LIQUIDATION OF THE COHN ESTATE

EDMOND CALDWELL

The Liquidation of the Cohn Estate was originally produced by Stoneham Theatre, Boston, Massachusetts, May 17, 2009, as part of the Boston Theater Marathon XI.
Directed by Caitlin Lowans.
Abbey . . . . .Linda Goetz
Patty . . . . Laura Graczyk

A young woman must deal with a mysteriously difficult customer at an estate sale. When the past has a price tag, is a human moment possible?

Edmond Caldwell writes fiction and drama and lives in Boston. He received his PhD in English Literature from Tufts University in 2001. His work has appeared in *DIAGRAM, Word Riot, Pear Noir!, SmokeLong Quarterly, Sein und Werden, 3:AM Magazine, Harp & Altar,* and elsewhere. He blogs at http://thechagallposition.blog spot.com/.

CHARACTERS

PATTY, Early twenties, dark hair, dressed like a student. Cheerful.

ABBEY, Late forties, attractive, in sunglasses, sun-dress. Aggressively tanned, slightly drunk. Carries a large handbag.

SETTING

An estate sale in a large house in an upscale suburban neighborhood

TIME

Late spring, the present

.   .   .

The second-floor landing of a large house. Up center is a wall with a closed door. Against the wall to the right of the door is an armoire with a number of knick-knacks on it, including a snow-globe. Against the wall to the left of the door leans a stack of pictures in frames. There is a hat-rack with hats on it. Everything has a price tag. The edge of the landing is suggested by the edge of the stage.

Patty stands at attention next to the door, her back to the wall. She holds a receipt booklet and a pen. Abbey enters and crosses in front of Patty, looks around, crosses back and looks around on the other side, moves downstage to stand at the edge, looks up and down, etc.

PATTY: Are you looking for anything in particular? There's vintage clothing in the room at that end of the hall, and in the study there are a lot of old books. Furniture and pictures are everywhere — but most of the real antique stuff is down on the first floor now.

ABBEY: Now.

PATTY: I'm sorry?

ABBEY: (*She hikes her sunglasses on top of her head and leans out over the edge of the landing, looking up.*) What's up there?

PATTY: A pool table. Games.

ABBEY: (*Turning.*) You'd think those'd be in the basement.

PATTY: And some exercise equipment.

ABBEY: People usually keep that kind of thing in the basement.

PATTY: (*Shrugging.*) That's just where they were, I guess.

ABBEY: (*Pointing at closed door.*) What about in there?

PATTY: What *about* in there?

ABBEY: Ha ha. You might be cleverer than your job description requires. No offense.

PATTY: None taken. It's not open to the public today.

ABBEY: What are we, a museum?

PATTY: (*Takes a few steps stage-left, speaks to someone offstage.*) Excuse me? Would you like to purchase that? I have to write you a slip and then you can pay for it downstairs. On your way out.

(While Patty interacts with the offstage customer — writing on her pad, tearing off the slip, etc. — Abbey turns and examines the items on top of the armoire. She selects a snow globe, shakes it and watches the flakes settle, slips it into her handbag.)

PATTY: No, no, of course, feel free to keep looking around — this is for three more hours today. You can leave a bid on any item, too . . . OK, thank you! Have a nice day!

(Patty turns back around, catching Abbey with her hand still in her bag. Abbey smiles and slowly withdraws a clear plastic sports-bottle, drinks.)

ABBEY: Who died?

PATTY: Excuse me?

ABBEY: I asked, who died?

PATTY: It was a Mrs Cohn, I think.

ABBEY: <u>A</u> Mrs Cohn, or Mrs <u>A</u>. Cohn?

PATTY: (*Laughing.*) <u>A</u> Mrs <u>A</u>. Cohn — Abigail. How did you know?

ABBEY: I didn't. She sure had a lot of stuff. Why do you want to get rid of it all?

PATTY: That's what we were hired to do. We're an agency.

ABBEY: Oh, of course — you're not a Cohn. This isn't a family affair.

PATTY: (*Nods.*) But we're a family too, a family business. My uncle's the boss. That's him down there, in the entryway. With the adding machine.

ABBEY: (*Looking down over edge of landing.*) The one I hit on the ass with the door when I came in.

PATTY: That wasn't your fault. He always plants himself by the door to keep people from sneaking stuff out.

ABBEY: There's quite a line already. I've never been to one of these before. It's like a garage sale for the well-heeled. (*Pause.*) Or a feeding frenzy. (*Turning back.*) Are they always like this?

PATTY: Yes, ma'am.

ABBEY: Ma'am! My god. Please, it's Abbey.

PATTY: Well it was very nice meeting you, Abbey. On this very busy day! If you see anything you'd like to place a bid on, there are bidding slips on the table in the entryway. You can leave them in the fishbowl on your way out.

ABBEY: Oh no — did the fish die, too?

PATTY: I'm sorry?

ABBEY: The fish. And then her little fish relatives from another bowl somewhere had to hire someone to sell off the plastic scuba diver and the porcelain castle and the treasure chest and the chunks of coral . . . What did you say your name was?

PATTY: I didn't. We're Gurlekian Estate Sales.

ABBEY: (*Holding out sports-bottle.*) Care for a drink, Gurlekian Estate Sales?

PATTY: I'm all set, thanks.

ABBEY: (*Toasting with bottle.*) Oh, not like this! Mazeltov. (*Drinks.*)

PATTY: (*Turning.*) Excuse me? Would you like to purchase that? I need to write you a slip . . .

(*She interacts with another offstage customer, writes receipt, etc.*)

ABBEY: (*Peering inside bottle.*) Although the ice has melted. (*Glances at watch.*) Time of meltage, 2:43 PM. (*Goes to edge, looks down.*) So that's your uncle. Mr. Gurlekian . . . Albanian?

PATTY: (*Finished with customer.*) Armenian.

ABBEY: Father's brother?

PATTY: My mom's.

ABBEY: You're not a Gurlekian, then. You're already a different branch. That's an interesting word for it, isn't it? Branch. Because a family is like a tree.

PATTY: If you're interested in the gardening items they're on the covered porch. Downstairs.

ABBEY: (*Demonstratively.*) Oh no! Keep me away from saws! I might saw off the branch I'm sitting on!

PATTY: (*Unmoved.*) A saw is not a gardening implement.

ABBEY: You might need one for pruning.

PATTY: That's what shears are for.

ABBEY: Sometimes they're not enough. Do you garden?

PATTY: Not really.

ABBEY: Me either. (*Drinks from bottle.*) Your people had a genocide too, though, didn't they?

PATTY: Excuse me?

ABBEY: The Turks killed a bunch of your people just like the Germans killed a bunch of mine.

PATTY: (*Uneasy.*) I'm sorry, I really have to keep my eye on things.

ABBEY: (*Steps to edge of stage and looks up.*) What did you say was up there?

PATTY: A pool table and some games. I think they had a play-room up there.

ABBEY: People usually put that kind of thing in the basement. (*Turning back.*) I think there's something fishy going on around here. What did you say was behind that door?

PATTY: I didn't. You can't go in there.

ABBEY: Maybe, at one time, screams came from that room.

PATTY: I try not to think about stuff like that.

ABBEY: Maybe that's where the ghosts are.

PATTY: Maybe you should talk to my uncle. Right down there — see? He can almost see us from where he's standing . . . (*She waves frantically.*) If he would just look up.

ABBEY: You seem quite capable of dealing with the situation. Are there any Cohns here?

PATTY: (*Points to door behind her.*) You mean in there?

ABBEY: Ha ha. See? You give as good as you get. But I mean just generally — here today.

PATTY: I don't think so.

ABBEY: Would you know one if you saw one?

PATTY: My uncle handles that part of the business. We usually don't have to encourage relatives to stay away, though, because, you know, emotionally . . . But it can all depend. Sometimes they want to watch over every little thing.

ABBEY: Whereas it's the Gurlekians who need to be watching over every little thing.

PATTY: Well, we don't do this for charity. It's a lot of work.

ABBEY: (*Aside, clearing her throat.*) Pound of flesh.

PATTY: Excuse me? We read that in one of my classes, you know, so it's not over my head, if that's what you think.

ABBEY: Not at all. So you're an English major?

PATTY: Management. I want a job after I graduate.

ABBEY: That's the spirit. I was a history major. But then I made a terrible mistake.

PATTY: You started drinking.

ABBEY: Worse.

PATTY: You got married.

ABBEY: I became a lawyer.

PATTY: (*Brightening.*) I'm still thinking about law school. What kind of law do you practice?

ABBEY: Which branch, do you mean? Wills and probate. (*She uncaps her bottle.*) You know, one of these days you're going to be a good girlfriend to have a drink with. (*She drains the last sip.*) In about twenty years, I think.

PATTY: Thank you. I think.

ABBEY: I'll be long gone. What did you say your name was?

PATTY: I didn't, but it's Patty. Or that's what everyone calls me, but it's really Patil. It means 'snowflake'.

ABBEY: Incredible. I think I need to take a nap.

PATTY: It's not that I don't want you to go, but you probably shouldn't drive.

ABBEY: I took a cab. I'll just call one again. (*Searches in handbag, brings out snow-globe.*) By the way, snowflake, I have a present for you.

PATTY: (*Taking snow-globe.*) You were going to steal this?

ABBEY: I just wanted a souvenir.

PATTY: (*Looking at tag.*) It's only seven dollars.

ABBEY: (*She flips her sunglasses back down over her eyes.*) It's the thought that counts. (*Moving away.*) I have to go.

PATTY: Hey! Abbey — Abigail? I get it now — you're a Cohn, aren't you?

ABBEY: (*Stops, turns.*) If I was, I'm sure I'd be one from the wrong branch. The wrong fishbowl.

PATTY: Here — (*Hands back the snow-globe.*) I want you to take it.
(*Abbey looks at globe thoughtfully, places it in handbag. Nods and starts to move away again.*)

PATTY: Wait!
(*She writes something down on her pad, tears off slip and hands it to Abbey.*)

PATTY: This is for you, too.

ABBEY: What is it?

PATTY: The pay slip. You have to give it to my uncle along with the money.

ABBEY: I thought you were giving it to me for free.

PATTY: It's seven dollars.

ABBEY: I thought we'd shared a moment there.

PATTY: I give as good as I get, don't I.
(*Blackout.*)

END OF PLAY

SAFELY ASSUMED

Andrea Fleck Clardy

Original Production: Boston Theater Marathon 2009
Sponsored by Boston Playwrights' Theatre
Directed by Thomas Martin
Dorothy . . . . Shelley Brown
Jamal. . . . . Alex Castillo

Meeting by chance in the probation office, an elderly white woman who likes to shoplift and a young African-American man confuse and enlighten each other.

Andrea Fleck Clardy: A Dramatists Guild member, her short plays have appeared in Boston Theater Marathon, SlamBoston, Six Women Playwrights Festival, Firehouse Center, and American Globe Theatre Festival. Her play *Hide and Seek* with music by Clark Gesner premiered at the Hangar Theatre and will be produced in Ames, Iowa, by Children's Theatre.

CHARACTERS

DOROTHY FISK, A white woman in her sixties, who wears a full skirt and bright shirt, which are unstylish, vaguely eccentric. She looks unobtrusive but odd.

JAMAL JEFFERSON, An African-American man in his early twenties, who wears oversize jeans, running shoes, and a clean, white t-shirt.

SERENA PAIGE, An African-American probation officer in her forties, dressed in slacks and a jacket.

SETTING

The waiting room of a probation office, with an interior door in the back wall and a door out of the office stage left. It is sparsely furnished with folding chairs and a low table holding magazines.

TIME

Mid-morning in the spring of 2009

. . .

Jamal slouches in the chair nearest the door. He is holding an MP3 player, with wires to his ears. Dorothy enters stage left and peers into the room tentatively.

DOROTHY: Excuse me. Is this where I'm supposed to be?
(Jamal pats his thigh rhythmically, listening to his music. When he catches Dorothy's eye, he removes one ear bud.)
JAMAL: You talkin' to me?
DOROTHY: You are the only one here. Could you tell me if this is where I am supposed to be?
JAMAL: This here is the probation office, just like it says on the door. Where is it you supposed to be at?
DOROTHY: Right here then. This is where I'm supposed to be. . . at.
(She sits across from him. He puts bud back in his ear.)
DOROTHY: Before you go back inside those things. . . Please.
JAMAL: What you want to know?
DOROTHY: I have so many questions. Are you yourself on probation?
JAMAL: Else I wouldn't be sitting here. That's for sure. I got lots of places I'd rather be at.
DOROTHY: What do they do once they have you on probation?
JAMAL: What they do is they watch your every move. Means you got to follow

all their rules about no drinking and no drugs and no leaving the city and you got to get yourself down here to sit and wait every two weeks to talk to your p.o. That's about it. Except if you screw up, they nail you.

DOROTHY: What's a p.o.?

JAMAL: Probation officer. How come you want to know? You got a kid in trouble?

DOROTHY: You mean my own children? Goodness, no. My two daughters are grown now but they were never in trouble. They've married and moved away with their families. Mary Ann lives up in Albany where she is a reference librarian. Susan is way out in Duluth. It's an hour earlier in the Midwest.

JAMAL: So what you doing here? Looking out for some friend?

DOROTHY: No. I think I am the first person I have ever known who was placed on probation.

JAMAL: Whoa. What you do wrong?

DOROTHY: Well, I didn't do anything I personally consider wrong. I'm here because of the shoplifting. I do quite a lot of shoplifting.

JAMAL: That right?

DOROTHY: It's kind of my hobby, you might say. It's something I've done all my life. In the last few years, with the children grown, it has become more important to me.

JAMAL: What you boost when you go out? You talking about food?

DOROTHY: No, not so much food, although I once took a whole black truffle. Golf ball size. You know those mushrooms that pigs snuffle out of the ground somewhere in France. They are very expensive.

JAMAL: Why would you take a thing like that, what pigs snuffled out of the ground?

DOROTHY: I tried cooking it in the toaster oven. It tasted kind of earthy. That was years ago, soon after my husband died.

JAMAL: And now? What you steal now?

DOROTHY: I don't think of it as stealing. I take things I can use, like Bufferin, lightbulbs, woolen socks.

JAMAL: Uh-huh.

DOROTHY: I could buy what I need, of course. I am very careful with money. But the shoplifting gets me out into the world and it's so much more exciting than bingo or gin rummy. Why should I go to the Senior Center when I can be having more fun in the stores?

JAMAL: How'd they catch you?

DOROTHY: I used to wait until I was alone in an aisle and never look up. Just tuck things right into my big purse. Then I realized that nobody notices a woman like me. I'm assumed to be harmless. I began to feel as if I was invisible. I could walk through the store and nobody would see me at all. That was the magical power time had given me. So I became less cautious. They caught me the first time with a security person dressed as a customer. I didn't think that was quite fair.

JAMAL: That why you on probation, for getting caught that one time?

DOROTHY: Oh, no, dear. The first time they just gave me a warning. The next time, they sent me right into a program with lots of other old people who take things. We each met with a counselor and then we had group discussions. The program lasted three weeks. We were supposed to think about why we shoplift.

JAMAL: What you think?

DOROTHY: Well, of course, I knew perfectly well but I couldn't tell them about the fun of it. I never talk about that. Except here I am talking with you. Anyhow, they caught me twice more before anyone pressed charges. This last time they put me on probation. They said next time I will have to go to jail. Imagine, at my age. Imagine going off to jail.

JAMAL: I can imagine that real easy.

DOROTHY: What was it that you did to get on probation? I've told you my story and so you should tell me yours. *(Jamal is silent.)* What was it you did?

JAMAL: Same charge as you.

DOROTHY: You shoplift? What a coincidence! Then we're in this together!

JAMAL: No, Ma'am. We're not in nothing together. See, I didn't do it. I never took nothing. Flat out nothing. No Bufferin. No clothes. No bling. No mushroom. Nothing.

DOROTHY: Then why are you sitting here waiting to see your — what is it? — your p.o.?

JAMAL: Because I been to juvenile court already once before for something else I never did. Then they say I stole stuff I did not steal and that's why I'm on probation. Because all them things you just told me work the opposite for me. You so nice and so white and so old they don't even see you walking through. You so safe they don't even charge you when they catch you at it. I walk in, the guy behind the counter snaps his head up. Always. He knows me, then he nods. He don't know me, then he never take his eyes off me.

DOROTHY: Oh my.

JAMAL: I go in them big stores, the plainclothes cop just float along the end of the aisles, watching me, waiting for trouble. Or making up trouble on a slow day. If he say he saw me lift something, then who you think they going to believe? Even with Barack Obama to be president of the country, who you think they going to believe?

DOROTHY: I suppose you would not get the benefit of the doubt.

JAMAL: You got that right. I would not.

DOROTHY: I never thought about it that particular way.

JAMAL: That's right. That's because you don't have to think about it that particular way. You don't have to think about it at all, nice white lady like you.

DOROTHY: Well, dear, now I'm not asking to be safe. I like the risk. That's why I take things.

(She thinks for a minute, watching him.)

I have an idea. I just had a wonderful idea how we could even it out between us.

JAMAL: How's that?

DOROTHY: Maybe we should work together, you and I.

JAMAL: What you even talking about?

DOROTHY: Well, I was thinking over what you just told me. If you and I were in a store at the same time, weren't you just telling me that they would all be watching you? So if there was something you wanted, one of those music machines you were listening to or whatever. Why, I could just take it for you. Just tuck it into my big purse without looking up. I know just how to do it if I stay focused. And then I would leave and you would leave and we would meet up later. I could help you.

JAMAL: You could help me. That what you said?

(He looks at Dorothy a long moment before he speaks.)

Would it make any difference if I was to tell you I ain't but sixteen years old?

DOROTHY: I would be a little surprised. But it's so hard to tell about age with some people. Isn't it? I would have thought you were a little older. I don't think age is important one way or the other.

JAMAL: That right?

DOROTHY: Yes, that is quite right. What if I told you I was sixty-two? That would not change anything, would it?

(She holds out her hand.)

My name is Dorothy Fisk.

(Jamal considers, and then extends his hand.)

JAMAL: Jamal Jefferson.

DOROTHY: It's a pleasure to meet you, Jamal. A real pleasure. Well, what do you say? Do you think we can work together?

(Jamal speaks slowly, with no trace of street diction.)

JAMAL: Suppose the real truth is that I'm not sixteen, after all, and that I never got caught for shoplifting. Never got in trouble at all. Suppose what I really do is I work for the Probation Department as an investigator. I sit out here in the waiting room all morning and all afternoon because that's my job, to chat people up and see what secrets they want to tell me.

DOROTHY: That can't be true.

JAMAL: Why not? Why can't it be true? You think you know who I am because of how I look? Well, looks like you better guess again. They can dress some rent-a-cop up like a customer. You found that out yourself when you got caught that first time. You told me the story just now. So why can't they dress a p.o. up like a home boy?

DOROTHY: They wouldn't do that. They would never do a thing like that.

JAMAL: Well, of course, they would. Just shows how little you know. They pay me to keep an eye out for anyone bragging about violations. That's exactly what they do! Here's the other thing. I keep special watch out for anyone who might contribute to the delinquency of a minor. See what I'm saying?

DOROTHY: We were having a private conversation. You have no right to eavesdrop as a detective.

JAMAL: Yeah, I do. That's my job. What you was doing just now sounded to me like proposing criminal activity to a minor, suggesting larceny to a sixteen-year-old child when you knew that child is already in trouble with the law. That's serious. That's real serious. What you did was a punishable offense. You could go to jail for what you just did.

DOROTHY: Well, I was just being nice when I offered to work with you. I'm sorry I even talked with you in the first place. This is not turning out to be any fun at all.

(Back wall door opens and Serena enters, holding a clipboard.)

SERENA: Jamal, come on back.

(Jamal rises and turns to speak directly to Dorothy.)

JAMAL: No, Ma'am. It ain't no fun at all. That's exactly right. Sounds like you beginning to understand. You can't safely assume nothing. You got to learn what to say and what to keep quiet when you come in here. You got to learn to watch your back. You was asking what probation be like. Now you finally got some idea. Glad I was able to answer your questions and help you out. You have a nice day.

(He exits through door, following Serena.)

 END OF PLAY

BE THE HUNTER

Tom Coash

Be The Hunter was produced in the 11th ANNUAL BOSTON THEATER MARATHON by Fort Point Theatre Channel on May 17, 2009.
Directed by Allen Phelps.
Bobby . . . . Dave Fink
Quint . . . . .Jason Tamborini

Bobby, a United States Marine, on home leave from Iraq, asks Quint, a hunting buddy, to help him stage an accidental shooting which would excuse him from returning to the war.

A New Haven, Connecticut playwright and director, Mr. Coash has had many productions of his plays, produced numerous one-act festivals world-wide, and worked in the literary offices of such theaters as the Manhattan Theatre Club and Actors Theatre of Louisville.

CHARACTERS

BOBBY, Male, 18-21 years old, a Marine, dressed in shorts, tennis shoes with no socks, and a colorful Hawaiian shirt. Smart and a smart-ass.

QUINT, Male, 18-21 years old, known Bobby since childhood, dressed from head to toe in hunting/camouflage gear. A good old boy.

SETTING

The woods, mid-morning

TIME

The Present

.   .   .

Bright fall day. A clearing in the woods. Bobby, dressed in jeans and Hawaiian shirt, sits on a log, rifle next to him, smoking a cigarette and drinking vodka out of a quart bottle. We hear sporadic gunshots in the distance. Quint, rifle in hand, shades, dressed from head to toe in camouflage gear, rises from behind a rock and creeps up behind Bobby and raises the gun to his head.

QUINT: You're dead raghead!

BOBBY: Hoo-aah.

QUINT: Down on the ground dickweed. Fore I waste you!

BOBBY: You're forgetting something.

QUINT: What?

BOBBY: Hearts and minds, dude.

QUINT: What?

BOBBY: You're sposed to win our hearts and minds. For freedom and democracy.

QUINT: How do I waste your ass and win your heart and mind at the same time?

BOBBY: "Operation Freedom", man. Not "Operation Waste Their Asses". *(Bobby offers Quint the flask, who waves it off.)*

QUINT: Come on, get up. I wanta shoot something. *(Swings his rifle around the clearing)* Boom! Boom! Boom!

BOBBY: Nice.

QUINT: We're sposed to be huntin', not sitting here rotatin'.

BOBBY: Like there's deer round here after that.

QUINT: Like there's deer round here at three in the afternoon. What happened to "get out at the crack o' dawn"?

BOBBY: Sounds like somebody's shooting at something.

QUINT: Shit, buncha drunks haulin' around in their Ass UVs killing cows. You wanna hunt deer, you build a stand, you wear camo, you're here at dawn, you're serious about it. This is bullshit. Three in the fuckin' PM. You used to be serious about this. Fucking Deer Hunter, man. I used to look up to you.

BOBBY: Hoo-aahh.

QUINT: Fuckin' Daniel Boone.

BOBBY: Shit.

QUINT: Fuckin' Euell Gibbons with a hard-on. Living off the land!

BOBBY: Be the hunter.

QUINT: Fuckin' A, Bro.

BOBBY: That's what our Division Commander told us. Before we went in to Falluja.

QUINT: What?

BOBBY: Be the hunter.

QUINT: No shit?

BOBBY: You should hear this asshole. Feeding us all this garbage about how we were following in the footsteps of Alexander the Great. Like the fucking Hoplites.

QUINT:*(Making machine gun sounds . . .)* Buuurrrooowww, .50 caliber, buurr-rooww! Run you fuckin' hadjis!

BOBBY: Can you believe that shit?

QUINT: "Be the hunter"! I like that. *(Pause)* So I was pretty good, hunh?

BOBBY: What?

QUINT: Snuck up on your ass cold.

BOBBY: You were dead ten times over.

QUINT: No way.*(Bobby shrugs.)* No way you saw me.

BOBBY: RAP round right up your ass.

QUINT: Good cover all the way. Your ass was grass. *(Bobby smiles.)* What? I was like Rambo. Navy Seal. Slit your throat, you never hear a thing.

BOBBY: You were behind the trees?

QUINT: I *was* a tree. A fucking oak, man. Dappled.

BOBBY: There're no trees over there.

QUINT: What?

BOBBY: It's desert. No trees.

QUINT: Oh for Christ sake.

BOBBY: You're lying there in the dirt, gutshot, intestines spewing all over your lap.

QUINT: Right.

BOBBY: Lying there screaming. Sand in your eyes. Flies on your face.

QUINT: Palm trees.

BOBBY: No.

QUINT: Coconut trees.

BOBBY: There's no trees!! They all got wasted! Burned, blasted! It's a goddamn desert! All right?!!

QUINT: All right.

BOBBY: There's no trees!

QUINT: Ok, ok.

BOBBY: I oughta know! I fucking know!

QUINT: Ok, Jesus. Chill! *(Pause.)* You're wack sometimes, man. You know that?

BOBBY: *(Bobby chugs the rest of the bottle and tosses it.)*
You ever wish you were a girl?

QUINT: A girl?

BOBBY: Women in the service get pregnant, they stay home.

QUINT: Uh oh, Branson got some barracks babe prego?

BOBBY: I'm not going back, man.

QUINT: Some sweet little barracks Ho?

BOBBY: It's too fucked up.

QUINT: What? You and some chick?

BOBBY: The war, dipstick. If I was a woman, I could conveniently forget my fucking pill, get knocked up, and nobody'd care.

QUINT: Whoa, whoa, whoa, back up some.

BOBBY: And you're gonna help me.

QUINT: I'm gonna get you pregnant?

BOBBY: You're gonna shoot me.

QUINT: Shoot you?!

BOBBY: You shoot me in the leg, I don't have to go back.

QUINT: The hell you don't have to go back.

BOBBY: An unfortunate hunting accident.

QUINT: They'd throw your ass in the slammer.

BOBBY: Happens every year. Poor fucker gets mistaken for Bambi. Blammo.

QUINT: You're saying you want to go AWOL?

BOBBY: I'm saying I don't believe in what we're doing over there and I don't wanta fucking die for it. Simple.

QUINT: Simple?

BOBBY: *(Cocks a finger at his leg.)* Bam! I'm home free. Million dollar wound.

QUINT: Shit. *(Pause.)* Mr. Gung-Ho Marine! Mr. Fuckin' Devil Dog, Green Dragon gonna whip their Arab asses.

BOBBY: You don't know what you're talking about, man.

QUINT: You're on a mission! That's what you said! That you were on a mission to spread the gospel of America and the M-16.

BOBBY: Fucking recruiter fed me that bullshit. And you know what? We were! We *were* on a mission. Now we're just standing around with our dicks in our hands waiting for someone to chop 'em off.

QUINT: So all your big talk . . .

BOBBY: Listen, we're sposed to be freeing these people, right? 'Stead we're just wrecking the goddamn place. The US Wrecking Ball Corp. The old guys say it's like Viet Nam all over. No mission. Take ground and give it back. Take Falluja, give it back, take Tikrit, give it back. Nobody wants us there. You think every car on the street's an IED packed with nails and dynamite.

QUINT: Shit.

BOBBY: We're manning a road block and this beat up fuckin' Mercedes comes screaming the wrong way up the street at us. Hitting potholes, trunk lid bouncing up and down, horn blaring. We're shooting in the air, shouting, waving it off. Suicide bomber, suicide bomber! People scattering. Up-gunner on the LAV lets go with the .50 caliber and that car just disintegrates. Contents? One old fat guy in a scungy galabeya with half a head left. Two dead women in the back. Blood everywhere. Clothes shredded, brains and body parts all over the fucking upholstery. Two little girls and their fucking dolls cut to pieces in the trunk, and then this baby on the floor of the backseat screaming his lungs out. Civilians. They see a Huey overhead and a fucking M1A1 Abrams tank coming down their street and they just panicked. Freaked. God knows what. I'm standin' there like an idiot wiping the mother's brains off this baby's face, yelling for the medevac and suddenly an RPG comes whizzing past me, bounces off the tank and blows sky high. Three of our crew down. AK-47 rounds snappin' all around us. Tracers. There's a goddamn sniper! The tank lets go with the main gun. You could actually see the blast wave going down the street. Blows this building a new fucking double-wide garage door, no more sniper. The LT's yelling something but I can't hear shit. I feel this warm, wet stuff on my chest and look down thinking, fuck I'm hit! Kid's peeing on me. Street's total screaming chaos, bodies everywhere, and his little dick's waving back and forth in the air like a little firehose squirting piss all over me.

QUINT: Jesus.

BOBBY: This is being the hunter?!

QUINT: It's war dude! It's being a soldier.

BOBBY: What war? Not my war. Not their war. We haven't even declared fucking war! We're just sitting ducks minding the pond while these oil ass-holes are pumping billions out from underneath us.

QUINT: Bullshit, you know it's more then that.

BOBBY: Is it?

QUINT: We're making America safer.

BOBBY: Thank you Mr. President.

QUINT: Making the world safer.

BOBBY: Jesus that shit sounds corny when you say it out loud.

QUINT: It's not corny!

BOBBY: Right, mission accomplished. Storm troopers for world peace. Every night kicking down doors for democracy, women and children wailing and screaming, Nobody speaks English. No furniture, no toilets, no running water, no food, no lights. "Down, down, down!" Shouting "Shut the fuck up!" Trying to cuff somebody's shonky old father in his raggedy-ass underwear. Thinking some 15 year old's gonna come screaming outta the back room with an AK-47, blow your nuts off! Hearts and minds dude, hearts and minds.

QUINT: Go to Canada then. Be a conscientious, chicken-ass, objector!

BOBBY: I'm not a conscientious objector. I just object to whatever the fuck it is we think we're doing there. *(Picks up Quint's rifle and shoves it at him.)*

QUINT: No.

BOBBY: You said you wanted to shoot something.

QUINT: Shoot your own fuckin' self!

BOBBY: Can't do it. Powder burns. They'll court martial me for a self-inflicted wound.

QUINT: I can't believe this!

BOBBY: You don't know what it's like.

QUINT: No, but I'm going to.

BOBBY: Oh yeah? How's that?

QUINT: I enlisted.

BOBBY: You what?

QUINT: Volunteered for 29 Palms.

BOBBY: Desert training.

QUINT: Yep.

BOBBY: You dumb fuck.

QUINT: Don't call me that.

BOBBY: Haven't you been listening to me?!

QUINT: Hell yeah, I've been listening to you. All this last year. Spit and polish Branson, the Marine's Marine.

BOBBY: Get out of it.

QUINT: I don't want to get out of it. I'll do my duty and I won't come home cryin' about it.

BOBBY: This is classic.

QUINT: We'll have each other's backs, man. Kick some ass. See the world.

BOBBY: You wanta get my back? Then get it now. Shoot me.

QUINT: No way.

BOBBY: Come on, be the hunter!

QUINT: Jesus, you got medals, the silver star! You're a hero. You can't just throw that shit away. They tied yellow ribbons on every tree in this town when you came back. I had to drive over to Wal-Mart in Dempsey and buy their whole fuckin' stock.

BOBBY: I'm sorry! Ok?! I'm sorry I'm not the action figure of your fucking dreams! Ok?! NOW TAKE THE GUN! TAKE IT! TAKE IT! *(He shoves the gun in Quint's hands and then marches off about 20 feet. Points to his leg.)* Right here.

QUINT: No!

BOBBY: Watch my knee. I don't wanna be Johnny comes gimping home.

QUINT: I ain't gonna do it Bobby.

BOBBY: *(Pause.)* Jennie wants you to do it.

QUINT: What's she got to do with it?

BOBBY: We're getting married.

QUINT: No. Since when?

BOBBY: She's knocked up.

QUINT: You knocked up my sister.

BOBBY: You don't want her to be a war widow, do you buddy?

QUINT: You knocked up my little sister.

BOBBY: I want to hold a baby again, Quint. Just not in the middle of a firefight. I want a family. I want a wife. I want a baby.

QUINT: You fuckin' asshole.

BOBBY: So shoot me.

QUINT: You yellow fuckin' bastard.

BOBBY: Just do it before the vodka wears off. *(Quint raises gun and aims at Bobby's head.)* The leg dickweed!*(Pause.. lowers aim..he purposely fires under Bobby's feet, Bobby jumps, fires again, Bobby jumps, laughs.)* Gotta shoot better then that in Baghdad, old buddy! *(Quint fires, Bobby crumples, grabbing his calf, blood spurts out.)* Shit, shit, shit, shit, shit!!! Uunnnhhh, Jesus!

QUINT: I used to look up to you, man.

(Black out.)

END OF PLAY

BUT FOR THE GRACE OF GOD

Laura Crook

Boston Theater Marathon, Calderwood Pavilion Boston MA
Sponsoring Theatre Company: Village Theatre Project
Directed by: Dale Place
Cassidy . . . . Kortney Adams
Helen . . . . Ellen Peterson
Adelle . . . . Jennifer Valentine

On a beautiful fall day, at a public playground, three mothers find themselves with a moment to spare. In their brief exchange the complexities of motherhood begin to surface.

Laura Crook is a playwright, director and actor. She performed at North Shore Music Theatre, Gloucester Stage, Champlain Shakespeare Festival, Huntington Theatre, and Merrimack Rep. Laura directed the critically acclaimed *Queen of Wyoming* at the 2008 Edinburgh Fringe Festival. *But For The Grace of God* is Laura's first play.

CHARACTERS

CASSIDY, Late 20's, new mom. Exhausted. A Baby Bjorn hangs off her front. Her hair is pulled back in a clip.

HELEN, Mid to late 30's mother of 3. Jeans, sweater, casual. She is smart, funny basically happy with her lot and never self-pitying.

ADELLE, Mid to late 30's mother of 2. She has a laid back artistic style. Also casual. Sometimes shy, but always kind.

SETTING

A public playground. Early fall. Brilliant sunlight. Best days of fall.

TIME

3 PM, just after school.

NOTE

The word "criminy" is pronounced "CRY-mini"

. . .

Lights up on CASSIDY who mimes pushing a sleeping baby in a playground "bucket" swing. This action continues throughout the play.

Enter HELEN

HELEN: *(Out to playground).* GO, be free, be wild, run, *(more to self)* Get out of my freaking pocket! *(Stands watching for a bit then relaxes slightly, looks at watch, sips coffee, still more to self.)* I give it half an hour.

CASSIDY: *(Breaking the ice)* Yeah that's about what I've got left. The only time she's not screamin' is when she's swinging.

HELEN: Yeah it was like that for me with my Jason. I felt freaking seasick.

ADELLE: *(Off-stage)* Go on sweetheart. I'm going to be right over by the swings with Helen. Yes you do, see her? Jason, Clara and Craig's mommy? Yeah they're here. Look over by the pirate ship. Ok honey? Yup I'll be right over there. Promise. *(Enters.)* Jesus please us, it's like having an octopus instead of a son!

HELEN: Well the screws have let us out of lock up let's make the best of it.
(Toasts them with her travel coffee mug.)

ADELLE: Hey are you working on the fundraiser this year?

HELEN: Are you kidding? After last year's "Motown Hoedown"?! It looked like a Klan meeting in Harlem. This year I pleaded marriage troubles. Are you?

ADELLE: I got away with the wrapping paper drive.

HELEN: Wow, how'd you score that bullshit job?

(A football is tossed onstage ADELLE picks it up.)

ADELLE: Craig, go long. *(She throws a nice spiral offstage.)*

CASSIDY: Nice pass.

ADELLE: Oh I'm full of surprises. I'm Adelle.

CASSIDY: Cassidy.

HELEN: That's an interesting name.

CASSIDY: My parents were Deadheads.

HELEN: Well coulda been worse . . . *(thinks back,)* like "Bertha". I'm Helen.

ADELLE: *(Gesturing to swing)* How old?

CASSIDY: Five months.

HELEN: Awww, God it was so much simpler then.

ADELLE: Yeah, the Baby Mozart, the tiny toes, the way they *smelled.*

HELEN: Oh God it was like heroin. I remember thinking I could live off just the smell of the top of Jason's head.

ADELLE: *(Looking out at her son.)* Oh I loved that age.

CASSIDY: *(Tearing up.)* What am I doing wrong?!

HELEN: *(Noticing Cassidy's fragile state.)* Your first?

CASSIDY: DUH! What was your first clue? Oh my God I'm so sorry. I don't know what's wrong with me. I don't even know you! I'm so sorry. *(She is crying.)* I'm so fucking *tired.* I'm constantly losing it. It's not fair. I'm so mad. I love my baby, but I miss my *life.* I feel like such a selfish bitch when I say that. Everyone else is all glowing and Angelina Jolie. And I haven't taken a real shower in 3 days. *I want to blow dry my hair!!*
(CASSIDY bursts into sobs. ADELLE and HELEN move in to comfort her; HELEN steers CASSIDY to the bench, ADELLE takes over the swing, never altering the rhythm. CASSIDY begins to calm down.)

HELEN: It does get easier, or more familiar, or something. Here. Have a sip.
(HELEN hands CASSIDY her coffee mug)

CASSIDY: *(Taking a swig of Helen's coffee.)* What the hell is that!?!

HELEN: Margarita, straight up, no salt. *(CASSIDY and ADELLE look at HELEN)*

HELEN: WHAT?! I'm over 21. It's after 3 o'clock. Criminy! It's my damn carrot on the end of a never ending stick. For fuck's sake I have a PhD in Mediation of Civil Unrest but some days . . . . With each baby my life got smaller and smaller until the angels on the head of a pin pondered it. I'm the incredible shrinking brainiac. My house makes Pakistan and

India look like a fucking Pixar movie. The playground, this ½ hour has become a combination of The Hague and a fistful of valium. Jesus I don't know what I'm talking about. I listen to NPR and the Disney Channel and I swear sometimes I can't tell them apart. So, yes; sometimes to quiet the need to think whole thoughts I have a cocktail closer to noon than 5, so raise your eyebrows. You're just jealous.

ADELLE: Well. Don't bogart it.

(ADELLE takes the mug)

HELEN: Sorry Cassidy. My freak out probably doesn't help. But you know something — At the end of the day when all is quiet and the clichés come out. I check on the kids while they're asleep. And I'll be damned if I don't see the babies that they will always be to me. I have my Grinch moment and the frame around my heart snaps.

(She takes back her mug, drinks.)

ADELLE: *(out to playground)* Peter!! No Licking! *(to HELEN)* Did you just say Criminy?!

HELEN: Yeah I'm trying it on. I find Jesus Fucking Christ a bit strong for the 3 year old set.

CASSIDY: What about Adelle's Jeezus Pleezus?

HELEN: Too sexual.

ADELLE: What?!

HELEN: *(Shrugs. Her cell phone rings, she looks at the I.D. and answers)* Yeessss . . . ? Hi. Which one the Master or the Visa? So transfer . . . 'yeths mathtah'. Okay love you too. *(Hangs up)* Oh jeez louise now I gotta play the balance transfer game. God forbid our APR goes up. So it's 1.9 till next spring-mmm yummy 6 months of false security.

ADELLE: The modern myth of Sisyphus.

CASSIDY: Who?

ADELLE: You know the guy who pissed off the gods and had to roll the rock up the hill only to have it roll down again for eternity.

CASSIDY: Sounds like laundry.

HELEN: How do you know this shit?

ADELLE: Oh please I've got all kinds of useless crap rattling around my brain. All the words to "The Devil Went Down To Georgia," a poem I memorized in 4th grade, real handy stuff. Just God help me if I forget my list; I get to the market and it's like I've had a stroke.

HELEN: *(Out)* Clara! Please leave your underpants on. I know you want to see the princesses but they need to stay ON at the playground. Okay?

(They pass around the "coffee".)

HELEN: Oh Shit. *(Out to playground.)* Nobody move. Mommy's got band aids in the car.

(She runs off stage.)

CASSIDY: How long have you two been friends?

ADELLE: Is that what we are? It's weird. We've been in each other's orbit for about 3 years but I couldn't tell you her maiden name or where she grew up or if her grandparents are still alive. But I do know some of the more intimate details of her children's lives, her married life and her financial struggles.

CASSIDY: So, you're what? Acquaintances? Playground pals?

ADELLE: *(thinks for a bit)* It's more like casual sex. Extremely intimate but you never know when you're going to see each other again.

HELEN: *(Enters. A tin in hand. She is putting a couple band aids in it and closing it. Looks at it. Muses.)* Huh. I used to keep my dope in here, now it's filled w/ Hello Kitty and Spiderman band aids and antibacterial wipes. That was a different life.

CASSIDY: I'm just impressed that you were able to find them so fast. My car is so full of shit I swear we could survive a week on the contents, but I'd be hard pressed to produce a band aid.

HELEN: Try a mini van!! I swear I could clothe feed and probably *educate* a small village with the flotsam swirling around in my car.

ADELLE: I got you both beat. The last time my daughter was home she was obsessed with fucking pine trees. Goddamn white pine boughs. I'd look in my rearview mirror and it was like Tolkien's Ents storming Isengard! It's her latest in autistic expression: at all times two pine boughs one for each hand. It's like some crazy Greenpeace semaphore!

(Beat.)

HELEN: Your daughter? Jesus. I didn't even know you had another kid!

CASSIDY: How did you know? Was it obvious when she was born? Could you tell by looking at her? Fuck. I'm sorry I don't mean to be rude. I'm just so new at this. I'm sorry.

ADELLE: No, no, it's okay. She was a normal baby. Normal toddler. Cried. Laughed. Played peek-a-boo. It was gradual. When she was about 2 and a half . . . Little things, forgetting words, how to scribble, one day she couldn't ride her scooter, the next she forgot how to get out of bed.

(HELEN shaken by this information looks out at her kids)

CASSIDY: What did you do?

ADELLE: I shut down. Closed off. Stopped going to "toddler time" and "mommy and me's". Started going to specialists and therapists.

(Beat.)

HELEN: *(breaks out into hysterical laughter)* Oh . . . oh . . . oh . . . . My god . . . I'm
sorry. I can't help it . . . *(More laughter, the other women just stare at her.)*
It's just . . . .it's just . . . ."Autistic Expression" . . . . . . *(ADELLE begins
to giggle, HELEN still laughing, mirroring ADELLE's gesture.)* . . . .Green-
peace Semaphor!!!
*(HELEN is now incapacitated with laughter. ADELLE begins to laugh
as hysterically as HELEN. CASSIDY has no choice but to join in.)*
CASSIDY: Shh hahaha shhhhhh I can't push the swing and laugh at the same
time.
HELEN: Oh my god my stomach.
*(They take a moment to calm themselves and pass around the dregs of
HELEN's margarita. Look out at playground.)*
HELEN: Hey! Where are my kids? Oh crap, they're playing with the car. I gotta
go. See you soon. It was nice to meet you Cassidy. Good luck.
ADELLE: Helen, let me walk with you it'll be an easier extraction if we show a
united front. Bye Cassidy.
HELEN: *(Exits shouting offstage) Boys!* Stop trying to decapitate your sister.
ADELLE: *(Follows calling toward playground.)* Come on Peter time to go.
(CASSIDY remains. Still pushing swing.)

END OF PLAY

A NEW DAY

Lydia Diamond

Sponsored by Boston University New Plays Initiative
Directed by Ellie Heyman
Jordan . . . . Jordan Clark
Sarah . . . . Alejandra Escalante
Alex . . . . Alex Wyse
Forrest . . . . Chris Bannow
Jenne . . . . Jenne Claiborne

On the dawn of President Obama's swearing in, a group of college friends have gathered around the television.

Diamond's plays include: *Voyeurs de Venus, The Bluest Eye, The Gift Horse,* and *Harriet Jacobs*. Theaters include: Arena Stage, Huntington, Goodman, Steppenwolf, Long Wharf, Hartford Stage, McCarter, MPAACT, Chicago Dramatists, Congo Square, and Company One. Diamond is an '06/07 Huntington Playwright Fellow, a TCG Board Member, and is on faculty at Boston University.

CHARACTERS (all college students)
JORDAN, Asian American Female
SARAH, White Female
ALEX, White Male
FORREST, White Male
JENNE, African American Female

SETTING
A college apartment

TIME
Morning, January 20, 2009

NOTE
Races are specific and determined by the race of the actor for whom the
role was written.

. . .

*Jordan and Alex sit on couch, in front of television which is silently on.
It's morning, Jordan paints her nails, Alex eats the edges off of one pop
tart after another. Sarah sits in a chair typing furiously at her computer.
They've all been up all night. Empties, coke bottles, pizza boxes, and
snack food litter the Living Room. Sarah has her own stack of Red Bull
cans.*

SARAH: Why don't you guys go to bed?
ALEX: Why don't you?
SARAH: It's eleven thirty . . .
JORDAN: So?
SARAH: Well, my play's due at 3:00.
JORDAN: How's it going?
SARAH: I don't know. They keep talking, but seriously I don't know to what
end.
ALEX: I took that class, don't worry about it. She'll just say, "what do you think
you should have done . . . " It's like therapy.
JORDAN: *(showing Alex her nails)* What do you think?
ALEX: About your nail polish? Seriously?
JORDAN: I'm showing you two different colors. Look, this is Midnight Mad-
ness, and this is Dark til' you Drop.

ALEX: They're the same color.

JORDAN: I don't think so.

SARAH: Just give her an answer.

ALEX: Midnight Madness.

JORDAN: Thank you.

ALEX: Should you have polish all around the edges like that are you?

JORDAN: I'm doing my best . . .

ALEX: If I give you twelve dollars would you just go get them done?

JORDAN: It's not the money . . .

SARAH: Jordan had an unpleasant experience last time she was at the salon.

JORDAN: I'm not sure if I'd call Fashion Nails a "salon" . . . .

> (*The door opens. Jenne and Forrest enter, carrying a box of Dunkin Donuts.*)

JENNE: You're still watching?

SARAH: Hour 32 of all Obamavision all the time . . .

ALEX: It's history.

JORDAN: Anyway right now they're talking about the airplane and the geese.

ALEX: They should kill all the geese . . .

JENNE: They died. When they hit the engine they died.

ALEX: No . . . I mean, all the geese. That's a problem, if geese are flying into airplanes, I say, what do we need the species for.

SARAH: Listen to this . . . O.K. Greg says: Hey. And Monica says: Hey. Why didn't you call me? . . . I did. No, you didn't . . .

ALEX: Wait, who's talking?

FORREST: Here, I'll read with you.

SARAH: *(pointing to her computer screen)* start here . . .

SARAH: Hey.

FORREST: Hey.

SARAH: Why didn't you call me?

FORREST: I did.

SARAH: No you didn't.

FORREST: I did.

SARAH: No you didn't.

FORREST: I did.

SARAH: No you didn't.

FORREST: Well I meant to . . .

SARAH: Well you didn't.

FORREST: I didn't?

SARAH: You didn't.

JENNE: Seriously?

SARAH: I'm going for, like real time, realistic dialogue.

ALEX: Well . . . "what do you think you should have done?"

SARAH: I'm on like page 15, and I have at least twenty-five more to go. This sucks.

FORREST: Is there coffee?

ALEX: Could you make a pot sweetie?

SARAH: Sweetie?

FORREST: You're just jealous.

(Forrest exits to kitchen. Jenne sits down on couch between Alex and Jordan. Looking at her fingers.)

JENNE: Hey! That's Midnight Madness right? Nice. You should do your toes in Dark til' you Drop. They compliment eachother. *(beat)* You guys are seriously skipping class to watch the inauguration?

ALEX: It's history. Why would I go to a core A level poli-sci class, when I could stay home and watch this. People will talk about where they were when he got sworn in forever . . .

SARAH: Unless he gets shot . . . *(They all look at her, shocked.)* What? He's not Jesus. It would be horrible. But you haven't really considered the likelihood . . . .

JENNE: Just, don't say it out loud please.

SARAH: I'm sorry.

JENNE: Aren't you bored? Every time I turn to CNN they're like, "it's cold" now, we'll go to Marjorie standing outside near the monument, Marjorie? "It's cold here, let's go to Phil. Phil?" "Marjorie? Ted? It's cold."

JORDAN: Well that, and what will Michelle wear.

JENNE: See, now that **is** interesting.

ALEX: You're the smartest shallow person I've ever met.

JENNE: That's not shallow . . . I'm an artist. Personal adornment is a socio-political artistic statement. You're so full of shit Mr.-Carefully-studied-carelessly-casual. Everything Michelle wears, will go into the history books. The Jackie cardigan? The Jackie black shift dress . . . think, from now it'll be the Michelle kitten heel, or the Michelle brooch or something. It's like if Martha Stewart was black . . .

ALEX: I just lost you.

JENNE: Just, like, things you never thought a black woman would be famous for. But I'm taking my black ass to class, that's all I'm saying. When you're the only one in a lecture hall, the teacher notices if you're not there.

ALEX: Perhaps Obama will change all that, it's a new day.

SARAH: I just hope Michelle does better than that red and black thing she wore during the convention.

JENNE: I told you guys my older sister dated him didn't I.

ALL: Yes.

JORDAN: Yes, you've told us.

JENNE: I could have been spending like, Christmases at the White house.

(Forrest enters with coffee mugs. He hands one to Alex.)

FORREST: Is she still talking about her sister and Obama . . . Are you still talking about that?

JENNE: It's pretty amazing. That's like less than six degrees. Like, I'm closer to Obama than Kevin Bacon is.

SARAH: What happened?

JENNE: What?

SARAH: Why did they break up?

FORREST: Her sister is weird.

JENNE: She didn't like that he smoked . . . and he was really skinny, and those ears looked really big then.

JORDAN: Does he have a big, you know . . .

JENNE: Jordan!

FORREST: I'd kind of like to know.

JENNE: We never talked about it . . .

SARAH: Then she didn't sleep with him.

JENNE: We didn't talk about it.

ALEX: Please, if I'd had sex with the president elect, I'd tell everyone . . .

JORDAN: Well, that probably would have made McCain your president elect.

ALEX: Hey, it's a new day.

JENNE: I'm sure it's big.

JORDAN: You didn't ask her if they'd had sex.

JENNE: We're a very modest family. I'm sure she did though. They dated for like two months. But also why wouldn't it be large?

JORDAN: Because he's black?

JENNE: Yeah.

ALEX: Isn't that a stereotype?

JENNE: Yeah.

ALEX: I'm not comfortable with that . . .

JENNE: O.K. Oh, you think like, if I'm saying that black men have larger penises, that means yours is small?

ALEX: Well, I am Jewish so . . . .

JENNE: I do believe that our new president may have the largest penis of all the presidents in history.

FORREST: Lincoln was very tall.

SARAH: That's true . . . and was almost as black as Clinton.

ALEX: Sarah . . . write your play.

SARAH: Maybe I'll tell her that I was so moved by the inaugural events, I found myself creatively stunted.

ALEX: She'd say you should have used it.

SARAH: I'm going to take a shower.

JORDAN: Well hurry, I think they'll start soon . . .

SARAH: But first like, the homophobic minister has to pray, and then someone has to say a poem and shit like that right . . . .

ALEX: Yeah, it's gonna be a while. And you do need a shower.

(Sarah exits.)

JENNE: I'm worried about her.

JORDAN: Isn't she going to lose her scholarship if she gets another 'C'?

JENNE: I think the pressure probably makes it worse. And her dad just got laid off. *(Jenne looks at Jordan's nail job.)* This is bad. If you're gonna use dark colors you really have to get it in the lines.

JORDAN: Every time I go to the nail place, I'm waiting for my turn right, and someone walks up to me and says, are you available . . . Like, I'm standing there, holding my polish, in my coat, and all people can see is I'm Asian and in the nail place so I must work there?

JENNE: Girl, that's just Boston . . .

JORDAN: Yeah, but then I have to do this whole thing where I have to decide not to be offended, and feel guilty that I feel offended, because why should I be ashamed of being mistaken for a hard working Filipino nail technician . . . . And I'd almost stand the degradation for a nice short square tip in a dark color.

JENNE: I'll hook you up . . . *(exiting towards bathroom . . .)* You got polish remover?

JORDAN: It's in the bathroom.

JENNE *(o.s.)*: Sarah . . . . Can I come in, just to get the nail polish?

ALEX: *(to FORREST)* Have you eaten?

FORREST: I'll have a boston cream.

(Alex start for the donuts, Jordan is closest to the box.)

JORDAN: Here. *(handing Alex the box)*

ALEX: *(referring to t.v.)*Oh . . . I think it's starting.. . . . .*(he turns it up a little)*. It really is exciting.

FORREST: I know . . . I'm sorry to be jaded . . . but it bothers me. Who do *we* have, you know? He's smart, he's handsome, his family is like fricken perfect . . . . But then there's this lame ass minister doing the convocation..

ALEX: The invocation, and like 99 percent of ministers don't support gay marriage . . . .

(Jenne has returned and is doing Jordan's nails.)

FORREST: It's just like, we're all supposed to be overjoyed, like it'll all be alright tomorrow . . . how can he fix it all? And he could care less about us . . . seriously . . . our gorgeous hyper-hetero president doesn't believe in Gay marriage. That's crazy, and it feels like I'm the only one who can't get over it . . . .

ALEX: I just think it's more complicated than that . . . and I do care. But honey, it would be like if I were the first out president, and on the first day of my presidency I tried to put through legislation for reparations.

JENNE: Cool.

ALEX: So, we got the country to stop thinking of us as a freak show . . . we've shifted all these additudes, they all stepped out of their comfort zones and voted me in . . . thought clearly I was the only choice . . . So they hung there with me and my partner . . .

FORREST: Me.

ALEX: O.K. So there we are the president and the first man, and our little dog, and we're like, now we're going to re-enfranchise all the disenfranchised, overnight . . . it would be impossible . . . . .

JENNE: All I know is he's fine . . . .

JORDAN: Ssshhh . . . . It's coming on . . . .

(They turn on the T.V. We hear the procession music . . . . Sarah enters in a bathrobe, her hair wet. She stands behind the sofa, her hand on Forrests's shoulder . . . . Forrest holding Alex's hand. Jennet and Jordan fully absorbed in the events on the T.V., manicure halted. All is quiet, a very, very long silence as the friends watch the television while the lights fade, light from the television playing across their faces, stage goes to black as we hear the beginning of the swearing in . . . .)

END PLAY

SUGAR GLIDER

WILLIAM DONNELLY

Sugar Glider received its co-world premiere as part of the 2009 Boston Theater Marathon and 2009 Source Festival, Washington, D.C.

Boston Theater Marathon — May 17, 2009
Producing Theatre: Battleground State
Director: William Donnelly
Irene . . . . Shelley Bonomi
Brian . . . . .Kevin LaVelle
Special Thanks: Heather McNamara

Source Festival, Washington D.C. — June 24, 2009
Director: Jennifer John
Irene . . . . .Jessica Wanamaker
Brian . . . . Chris Mancusi

Late one night, Irene's outwardly successful brother Brian shares a story about a beloved pet, which leads to a strange and troubling revelation.

William Donnelly served as Industrial Theatre's resident playwright from 1997 to 2008. In 2005, he was awarded a Playwriting/New Theatre Works grant from the Massachusetts Cultural Council. He has twice been named a Clauder Competition Finalist, and *Magnetic North* was awarded the grand prize in 2006.

CHARACTERS
    Irene, Mid to late 30s
    Brian, Her brother, slightly older

SETTING
    Irene's kitchen.

. . .

IRENE is dressed in sleepwear. BRIAN is dressed in a suit and tie.

IRENE: *(To audience.)* My brother has done pretty well for himself.
BRIAN: *(To audience.)* How's it going?
IRENE: Minor league ballplayer —
BRIAN: Double A.
IRENE: Altoona Curve.
BRIAN: They're in the Pirates' system.
IRENE: Started for a season and a half.
BRIAN: Then I blew out my knee. Just bad enough.
IRENE: Found his way into a sales job.
BRIAN: Insurance. Solid company.
IRENE: Within five years, he won rep of the year.
BRIAN: Twice, actually.
IRENE: I was going to say twice.
BRIAN: Just keeping you honest.
IRENE: Big place in Bedford, little place in Dennis, medium-sized time share in Vermont.
BRIAN: For kicks.
IRENE: Lovely wife.
BRIAN: Kim. Grew up in Westchester.
IRENE: Lovely children.
BRIAN: Ashley and Olsen.
IRENE: Couldn't talk him out of that one.
BRIAN: I still don't see what's wrong with it.
IRENE: Lawnmower, snowblower.
BRIAN: Essential.
IRENE: Dog, cat, hamster.
BRIAN: They all sleep on the same mat. Swear to God.
IRENE: Pretty decent set up, right?
BRIAN: I'd say.

IRENE: So why is he in my kitchen, three A.M. on a Wednesday, sweating vodka, talking to me about sugar gliders?

(They sit.)

BRIAN: They're marsupials. We saw them on our trip to Australia. Just little things. Seven or eight inches. They've got these flaps like flying squirrels. If they're just hanging out, you wouldn't really notice, you'd maybe think they recently lost some weight or something. But when they open their arms, it's almost like wings, like Batman. They can do fifty yards, tree to tree, then they rear up like they're slamming on the brakes. It's badass.

IRENE: So that's the "glider" part.

BRIAN: Right.

IRENE: What's the "sugar" part?

BRIAN: Diet? I don't really know. The kids became obsessed. Olsen especially. He got online, did all kinds of research. I only came to it late, after he'd already found a dealer. Someone who farmed them.

IRENE: I've never even heard of them.

BRIAN: Me either but what does that mean? The kids were all, "Dad, dad, they're so easy, so cute . . ."

IRENE: "We'll totally take care of him."

BRIAN: "You won't even know he's there."

IRENE: Like us and the iguana.

BRIAN: Exactly.

IRENE: Miserable, shit-assed iguana.

BRIAN: What was his name?

IRENE: Gilberto?

BRIAN: Yeah. Did mom kill him?

IRENE: No. *(Pause.)* Maybe.

BRIAN: Mom killed the fish.

IRENE: That was unintentional.

BRIAN: Half unintentional.

IRENE: How could she have known that the rocks helped them breathe?

BRIAN: You never know with mom. She wasn't broken-hearted when they went, that's all I'm saying.

IRENE: Were you?

BRIAN: I got nothing against fish.

IRENE: Back to your sugar glider.

BRIAN: They painted me into a corner so we ordered it and it showed up and it was ornery and weird and it snapped at everybody when they tried to feed it. By day three the kids were done. And Kim took herself out of the mix before we even placed the order because she went on record after the dog saying a dog was the final upgrade she'd participate in. So here's this sad little sugar glider kicking around, nobody wants him —

IRENE: What did they name him?

BRIAN: Domino.

IRENE: Like the sugar.

BRIAN: That went right past me. Anyway, they hate him so the thing falls to me. Not my preference, but I feel bad.

IRENE: That's not you.

BRIAN: I know!

IRENE: That's not even you At Christmas.

BRIAN: But there was something about this thing. In the eyes, maybe. He's got these eyes you can't give up on. So I started taking care of him and don't you know he turns it around. Warms right up. Eats from my hand. Sits in my pocket, even. Becomes very gentle. Almost dainty. A spelling bee champion . . . *that* kind of disposition. Six months into this thing and I am in love. Over the moon.

IRENE: That's sweet.

BRIAN: It's disgusting. I've got his picture on my desk. I'm taking him to work. Taking him on client meetings. Right there in my pocket. He is literally and without exaggeration my best friend. *(Pause.)* So one day the kids are playing . . . they're in and out . . . backyard, kitchen, kitchen, yard . . . of course, they leave the back door open . . . out he goes. Right into the woods.

IRENE: He's not in a cage?

BRIAN: Are you listening to the story? He's a fucking superstar. We were considering night school, he doesn't live in a *cage*.

IRENE: I'm just asking.

BRIAN: No. No cage. So I get home late afternoon, they tell me, I go right out, don't come home until after supper.

IRENE: After dark?

BRIAN: Three in the morning.

IRENE: You consider three in the morning "after supper"?

BRIAN: I consider everything until breakfast "after supper". So the next night, after work, I go out again. Night after that. Night after *that*. He's nocturnal, so I figure if there's any shot —

IRENE: Bri —

BRIAN: Don't say it. Don't talk to me about owls and hawks and everything else that's running through my mind every second of the day. I don't need you to say that.

IRENE: I'm sorry.

BRIAN: On the fifth night, I go way out. And you know those woods . . . that's state forest, it goes way back. I went seven to seven. All night. Walking. Listening. Leaves under foot. Things moving in the dark. I can hear my pulse. Trees. You know when the wind's up, it sounds like the ocean. You ever hear that? Trees creaking like ships on the water? *(Pause.)* Anyway, I'm out there and I run into a coyote. I'd heard they were out there, and every once in a while I'd be walking the dog and he'd find the deer bones with the teeth marks on them, but I've never actually seen one. So we're checking each other out. I expected him to run or charge, but he just stood there. He was working on a deer. Just a young one, it looked like. He let me get right up close. He offered me some. Some of the heart. And I was kinda in the moment so took it. It was still warm. Like an engine that just shut down. Like the lawnmower. It tasted like iron. Just a little bit. Like a vitamin. I had blood on my chin. The coyote licked it off. And then he bailed. I haven't seen him since. And I'm out there every night. I've seen other coyotes, but not him. They've all got the same look. Same as people in a refugee camp — the ones who have been forged and tempered.

(Silence.)

IRENE: You didn't really eat a deer.

BRIAN: Just part of the heart.

IRENE: Does Kim know about this?

BRIAN: Kim thinks I'm working late, I don't know what Kim thinks. Kim has her own thing. Look. I love Kim. I love Kim and Ashley and Olsen. I love them all very much. But Domino loved *me*.

IRENE: Bri . . .

BRIAN: I'm scaring you.

IRENE: Kinda.

BRIAN: Come out with me.

IRENE: What?

BRIAN: Come out to the woods.

IRENE: No.

BRIAN: Not even for a night?

IRENE: How much have you had?

BRIAN: How much what?

IRENE: Come on . . . I can smell it on you.

BRIAN: That's alcohol.

IRENE: I know.

BRIAN: No. Rubbing alcohol. For the fever. And the abrasions.

IRENE: What abrasions?

BRIAN: From the forest. I've been going out barefoot. Sometimes naked.

IRENE: Okay, now you're *really* scaring me.

BRIAN: There's nothing scary here. I've never felt this right. Not in my job, my marriage, not when I was playing ball . . . *(Pause.)* Don't be scared. Just understand. You don't even have to understand all of it. Just a little. Please.

(Silence.)

IRENE: I understand.

BRIAN: Thank you.

(He embraces her.)

IRENE: God, you're burning up.

BRIAN: I know. It won't break.

(BRIAN takes off his suit jacket. He sits and removes his socks and shoes. He has abrasions on his feet. After a moment, he smiles at IRENE, stands, and moves towards her. He embraces her then exits, leaving his jacket and shoes.)

IRENE: *(To audience.)* I should've called the police, but I called Kim. In the time it took to explain — to fail in my explanation — he was gone. There are times I'll see a man walking: matted beard, roughly the same build, but leaner in the face, harder. I can't help but wonder. *(Pause.)* You don't know sometimes when you're losing someone, when they've already been lost. It's difficult to know.

END PLAY

INHERITING CLEO
(Co World Premier)

STEPHEN FARIA

BOSTON THEATER MARATHON XI
May 16–17 2009
Stanford Calderwood Pavilion
At the Boston Center for the Arts

Sponsored by The Actors Studio of Newburyport
Directed by Marc Clopton
Cleo .... Jenny Dale Richards
Dave .... Eliot Johnston
Aunt Meg .... Sherry Bonder
Cousin Jimmy........................... Tim Diering
Other Relative......................... Pam Battin Sacks

While fleeing from angry relatives in a funeral parlor, Dave enters the viewing room of a dead man he doesn't know. He meets Cleo, and the awkwardness of the situation brings the two together.

Stephen Faria is a Play Write and Composer/lyricist. Steve has had three full length plays produced; "Sense", a comedy in 2004, "Things that Matter" a musical in 2006, and "Quicksand", a Drama in 2009. Steve has had short plays selected for, "The Source Festival" in DC, "The Boston Theater Marathon", and "The New Works Festival" of Newburyport.

CHARACTERS

    CLEO, About twenty five, attractive, dressed in black.

    DAVE, About twenty five, a little disheveled, wearing an ill fitting suit, but good looking.

    AUNT MEG (off stage voice only), Middle aged, loud and pushy.

    COUSIN JIMMY (off stage voice only)

    FAMILY MEMBER (off stage voice only)

SETTING

    The back all of a funeral parlor viewing room. There is a line of chairs. Cleo is sitting in one of the chairs looking out at the audience where the body is laid out.

TIME

    An early evening of the present year

. . .

(In a funeral parlor, a young woman sits alone at what is the back of the viewing room. A young man in an ill fitting suit sits next to her. They sit in silence for a few seconds. She wipes a tear, and then speaks in a low voice to the young man.)

CLEO: He was a good man, wasn't he . . .

DAVE: *(Looking strait ahead.)* Mmm . . .

CLEO: Always making people laugh . . .

DAVE: Mmm . . .

CLEO: I know it's hard, we're all going to miss him.

DAVE: Mmm . . .

CLEO: I'm sorry, I'll stop talking . . . *(She puts her hand on his knee.)*I can see you're upset.

DAVE: *(He looks at her for the first time.)* No I'm not. I mean don't stop . . . *(Cleo pulls her hand away)* . . . talking.

CLEO: *(She looks at him a little suspiciously.)* I'm sorry, we've never met have we. I'm Cleo.

DAVE: Dave . . .

CLEO: How did you know Buddy?

DAVE: Buddy?

CLEO: Buddy, the deceased . . . *(She points to the front of the room.)*

DAVE: Oh, Buddy. *(He looks at her for a long moment)* I'm sorry, this isn't my room.

CLEO: What?

DAVE: This isn't my room. I didn't know . . . *(He points toward audience)* Buddy.

CLEO: *(She looks at him like he's a weirdo)* Well what are you doing here?

DAVE: I'm from the other room, on the other side.

CLEO: You're from the other side . . .

DAVE: I was in that room, now I'm in here.

CLEO: So the other room is your room.

DAVE: Yes.

CLEO: You're not the actual guy in the other room, you know, like the guy the room is for are you?

DAVE: No. Come on.

CLEO: Thank god, because you're acting a little strange, and that's a particularly bad suit. Just making sure I'm in a reality situation here.

DAVE: Yes, of course this is reality. Jeez, I don't look that bad do I?

CLEO: Yes actually, and you're kind of creeping me out. Why are you in somebody's room you didn't even know? Why aren't you in your own room?

DAVE: If it makes you feel any better, I didn't really know the guy over there either.

CLEO: Why would that make me feel better? Stop talking to me.
(She turns her body away from him. They are silent for a moment.)

DAVE: Look, he was a relative, I just didn't know him, that's all. I met him once, but I was only five. I really don't remember it very well.

CLEO: That doesn't explain why you're in the wrong room, and I don't know why you're telling me all this. I don't even know you.

DAVE: Well, you were really nice to me when you thought I was upset about Buddy, and I thought maybe you wouldn't mind if I talked to you or something.

CLEO: Or something? Are you coming on to me in a funeral parlor?

DAVE: I wouldn't say I was coming on to you. I mean, it crossed my mind we might get a cup of coffee some time.

CLEO: You just asked me out with a dead body in the room.

DAVE: I wasn't asking you out. I just said I thought we might get a coffee some time.

CLEO: That's asking out.

DAVE: It is?

CLEO: Yes.

DAVE: Oh . . . well . . . do you want to?

CLEO: *(Cleo goes a little spastic, waving at the air trying to erase the entire situation)* No. What are you, one of those weirdoes that comes to funeral parlors to pick up women?

DAVE: What weirdoes? Nobody does that.

CLEO: Of course they do. I saw it online.

DAVE: It must be true then. *(Dave laughs a little.)*

CLEO: What's so funny?

DAVE: I came in here to try and make myself feel bad or at least feel something appropriate for the occasion, and instead, I meet you and end up laughing.

CLEO: Why did you have to come in here to feel bad? You have a much better chance of feeling bad in the other room. At least you met him once.

DAVE: But nobody in there really feels bad about the deceased.

CLEO: The line on that side goes into the street, and everyone is crying.

DAVE: They're only crying because he didn't leave them anything. The guy was loaded. They're upset because they all had plans for the money they would be getting, and now they have to change their plans. Nobody's over there for the guy laid out in the box. They're all there to console each other for another loss entirely. That's why I came in here. I looked through the door and saw you sitting here and it seemed like this was how it should be at one of these things, so I came in and sat down next to you.

CLEO: So, what did he do with all his money, did he leave it to charity?

DAVE: No, he left it to me.

CLEO: Get out.

DAVE: Fifty seven million . . . you're sitting next to a millionaire . . .

CLEO: And you wore that suit? No, stop trying to pick me up, you do not have fifty seven million dollars.

DAVE: OK, you're right, inheritance tax is brutal. Did you know they take fifty percent? I only end up with twenty eight five.

CLEO: Why are you doing this?

DAVE: Doing what? I'm not lying, here I'll show you. *(Dave turns and calls into the next room)* Auntie Meg . . . Auntie Meg . . . Hi how are you?

AUNT MEG: *(From off, angry, through tears.)* Screw you Dave. I hope you choke on that money, you little bastard.

CLEO: Twenty eight five?

DAVE: Do you believe it?

CLEO: What did you do when you were five, when you met him? You seem to have made a big impression.

DAVE: I really don't remember that much. I do remember I dumped a potted plant in his sister's lap.

CLEO : Nice.

DAVE: Come to think of it, it was my Auntie Meg. *(He waves to the other room and then reacts as if he was given the finger.)* They're all mad at me over there. Like it's my fault Uncle Will left me all that money.

CLEO: His name was "Will?" You're kidding.

DAVE: Funny huh? They wouldn't be so mad if they knew I was going to share it with all of them.

CLEO: You're going to share it with them? Well why don't you tell them?

DAVE: I want to let Uncle Will have his fun. He obviously gave me the money because I was the last person in the family that was entitled to it. He didn't even know me, he was just trying to piss them all off. It was kind of his dying wish. Who am I to deny him that? Then again, I don't appreciate being singled out as the least important person in my entire family. Granted, the fifty seven million softens the blow a bit. But hey, I have feelings you know. Money isn't everything.

CLEO: Are you really going to give back all that money? It's one thing to give money away after you're gone, there's not much you can do with it then, but when you're alive, there's lots you can do with it, and those people in there seem so mean and hostile. I'm sorry, I know that's your family I'm talking about, but from a totally objective point of view, I wouldn't give them a dime.

DAVE: So you don't think I should assuage the angry hoard?

CLEO : You are so weird. Who says things like "assuage the angry hoard?"

DAVE: What's wrong with assuaging the angry hoard?

CLEO: It's not common language, that's all.

DAVE: Everybody's always on me about that. What's wrong with a little uncommon? Is that your goal, to do things just like everybody else? Well sue me. If I have to give a bunch of shitty people their way I'd rather call it assuaging the angry hoard. It makes me feel better. So if you have to criticize my behavior, why not call it . . . I don't know . . . putting voice to your confusion over my idiosyncrasies. Try it maybe it'll make *you* feel better.

CLEO: I'm not just like everyone else. There's nothing common about me. I may not be as out there as you, but I've done lots of crazy and spontaneous things in my life.

DAVE: Oh really, crazy and spontaneous . . . like accepting a date from a stranger in a funeral parlor?

CLEO: It's not a situation that comes up every day.

DAVE: It came up today.

CLEO: Maybe I just don't like you.

DAVE: You're spending an awful long time having a conversation with someone you don't like.

CLEO: Look who's talking. How much time have you spent talking to the angry hoard?

DAVE: Ouch, I thought you were going to say something nice.

CLEO: Ok . . . I find you . . . interesting. I might even like you a little, but I wonder — do you ever think about how much you have to give up to be a part of . . . *(She points toward the other room.)*

DAVE: . . . The angry hoard?

CLEO: Well . . . yes.

DAVE: You're worried about me. I knew you were nice, I could tell. I know you don't want me to ask but . . . would you come into the other room with me?

CLEO: . . . Over there, with Uncle Will and the angry hoard?

DAVE: Yes. I'm asking you to accompany me into the other room.

CLEO: *(Sweetly teasing.)* Oh Dave, our first date. That's so sweet. *(She changes back to serious voice.)* We're in a funeral parlor. You're asking me out in front of a dead man that you don't know, to go with you into another room with a bunch of angry people and a dead man that neither of us knew. That's going to be our first date?

DAVE: *(Dave thinks a long time, but can't think of a way to disagree.)* Yes.

AUNT MEG: *(from off)* David, who's that with you, some gold digger trying to get her hands on Will's money?

DAVE: *(To Cleo, then to Aunt Meg.)* Don't listen to her Cleo. It's all right Auntie, will you cut it out? I'm going to share the money with you, Ok?

AUNT MEG: Oh, that's rich, that's easy to say, you're going to share the money with me. You think that's going to shut me up?

DAVE: I'm sharing it with everybody, it's a done deal. Go ask the lawyer.

JIMMY: *(Starting one at a time then overlapping.)* He's sharing it with all of us?

A COUSIN: Who's sharing what with whom?

AUNTIE MEG: Dave said he's sharing the money with us.

A COUSIN: He's sharing the money with us?

JIMMY, COUSIN, &MEG: *(These lines are said by all three relatives, over lapping and at slightly different times, sounding spontaneous and excited.)* Dave's sharing the money with us! He's sharing the money with us!

JIMMY: We're all getting the money! Three cheers for Dave! Hip, hip *(All respond with "Hoorays".)* Hooray, hip, hip hooray, hip, hip, hooray . . . *(All singing.)* . . . For he's a jolly good fellow, for he's a jolly good fellow, for he's a jolly good fe-e-lohhhh . . . .

A COUSIN: Hey, wait a minute, who's us?

JIMMY: Well . . . us is us, all of us.

MEG: Certainly not all of us . . .

A COUSIN: Well not cousin Jimmy anyway.

JIMMY: Hey why not me, I sang louder than anybody.

MEG: Singing doesn't get you a piece of the pie Jimmy.

A COUSIN: God damn it I deserve more than cousin Jimmy and Dave put together.

JIMMY: Well I deserve more than you.

A COUSIN: Over my dead body!

AUNT MEG: ENOUGH! This is all your fault Dave. I hope you choke on your share — choke, choke, choke.

DAVE: (To Cleo)I'm sorry, never mind.*(Dave gets up slowly to leave. Cleo takes his hand and stops him.)*

CLEO: How about you just stay in here with me and Buddy for a while.

DAVE: Are you asking me out with a dead body in the room?

CLEO: Not exactly . . . I'm asking you in. I'd rather we have our first date here in Buddy's room. You don't have to go back in there. You can stay here with me. Buddy left something behind too you know, something that's meant to be shared. *(As she speaks Dave begins to feel real sense of loss and sadness.)* He wasn't rich, he didn't have a load of money, but he was a true friend. He had a way of pulling people together, making people happy. I don't know what you call it, I can't put my finger on it, but he left a little of it to everybody he knew. You're welcome to some if you want. Stay with me for a while, you'll see.

DAVE: He was a good man wasn't he?

CLEO: Yes he was . . . a very good man.

DAVE: I'm sorry I missed him.

CLEO: You haven't missed him. You got here just in time.

(Cleo takes Dave's hand. They sit looking forward at Buddy as the lights fade to black.)

END PLAY

PERSPECTIVE
(World Premiere)

PETER M. FLOYD

Perspective was originally produced at the Boston Theater Marathon by FortyMagnolias Productions.

Directed by Anne Gottlieb
The Man............................Robert Pemberton
The Woman ....Maureen Keiller
The Other Man.......................Steven Barkhimer

Perspective tells the story of a couple who find that their disparate memories about their pasts reveal that they've been living in two different worlds — literally.

Peter M. Floyd, of Brighton, Massachusetts, has been writing plays since 2004. His plays have appeared in the Boston Theater Marathon, the Dragonfly Festival, SLAMBoston, the New England Fringe Festival, and other venues. He is a member of Playwrights' Platform, and a co-founder of the Exquisite Corps Theatre Company.

CHARACTERS
  THE MAN, male, 25–40
  THE WOMAN, female, 25–40
  THE OTHER MAN, male, 25–40

SETTING
  A bedroom, present day

. . .

Lights come up on the bedroom in the apartment of the MAN and WOMAN. Their bed faces the audience; on each side is a small table. Several dressers and bookshelves line the walls. It is about 11:00 on a Sunday morning. THE MAN and THE WOMAN are stretched out in the bed. THE WOMAN is in a nightgown, while THE MAN wears shorts and a t-shirt. She is reading the Arts section of the Sunday Times, while he does the crossword puzzle in the Times Magazine. Various other pieces of the Times lay scattered about the bed. Several moments pass, and then THE WOMAN puts down her paper and looks at THE MAN.

WOMAN: This is nice.
MAN: *(still immersed in his puzzle)* What is?
WOMAN: This. Just lying around on a Sunday morning and not doing anything. It feels wonderfully lazy.
MAN: *I'm* doing something.
WOMAN: Doing the crossword is not really a hugely productive activity.
MAN: It stimulates the brain. Who starred in *Charade?*
WOMAN: Audrey Hepburn.
MAN: Doesn't fit. Five letters.
WOMAN: Grant. Cary Grant.
MAN: Thanks.
WOMAN: It's just been a long time since we've done this. Just have a quiet Sunday morning at home in bed.
MAN: We do this all the time.
WOMAN: We don't! We never do. We always have to go off somewhere, like your parents' or something.
MAN: No, really, I think we spend more Sundays in than not.
WOMAN: I don't think so.
MAN: You know, it's like in *Manhattan*, when Woody Allen and Diane Keaton both get asked how often they have sex. Woody says, "Hardly ever, maybe

three times a week," and Keaton says, "Constantly, like three times a week." To me, it seems like we lie in on Sundays all the time, to you it doesn't. It's just a matter of perspective.

WOMAN: *Annie Hall.*

MAN: What?

WOMAN: That scene you're talking about, it's from *Annie Hall,* not *Manhattan.*

MAN: Well, there you go. You remember it from *Annie Hall,* and I remember it from *Manhattan.* Perspective again.

WOMAN: But — No, that's not right. It's either in one movie or the other. That's not perspective, it's a fact. One of us has to be wrong.

MAN: Okay.

WOMAN: And it's you.

MAN: If you want to think so.

WOMAN: God! I hate it when you get like this!

MAN: Like what?

WOMAN: Where you sound like you're being all reasonable, but you're talking bullshit.

MAN: Well, I'm just saying what seems reasonable to me. I understand that may not be what's reasonable to you.

WOMAN: And then you get all patronizing. *(pause)* Kim was right.

MAN: About what?

WOMAN: After the two of us started dating, and I introduced you to all my friends, Kim pulled me aside and said, "I think he's a little patronizing."

MAN: Huh.

WOMAN: Of course, I defended you, and said that you weren't really, it was just the way you talked. But she was really on to something.

MAN: You hadn't met Kim yet.

WOMAN: What?

MAN: You hadn't met Kim when we started dating. We didn't meet her until, what, six months later, when she started dating Mark.

WOMAN: Uh, no . . . We met Mark through Kim. I mean, *I* met Mark through Kim, before I met you.

MAN: That's not how I remember it.

WOMAN: Well, you remember it wrong.

MAN: Actually, I remember it very clearly. We were meeting for dinner at the Four Seasons. Mark said, "Here, meet Kim," and you reached over to shake her hand and knocked over your glass of Zinfandel.

WOMAN: What?

MAN: And Kim laughed and said, "It's nice to meet you, too," and you got all embarrassed.

WOMAN: First of all, I never drink Zinfandel, as you know.

MAN: You drink it all the time.

WOMAN: I don't! I had Zinfandel once in my life, when I was maybe twenty, and I said to myself, "Not my kind of wine." I didn't like the . . . fruitiness.

MAN: Okay, maybe it wasn't Zinfandel . . .

WOMAN: And I didn't knock over any glass of any wine when I met Kim! I met Kim at a ceramics class in Brookline, and that was two — count 'em, two — years before I ever laid eyes on you.

MAN: I don't think so.

WOMAN: And she introduced me to Mark at a party at Irene's.

MAN: No, I know that's not true. We met Mark when we were going on that whale watch.

WOMAN: Whale watch?

MAN: Yes, we were out on the Harbor waiting for the whales to show up, and we started talking to him, and . . .

WOMAN: I have never been on a whale watch in my life. Are you kidding me? I get seasick when I sit on one of those floaty things in a swimming pool. You'd never get me out on a boat in the Harbor, looking for whales . . .

MAN: And yet there you were, and me, and Mark . . .

WOMAN: Look, maybe you were out there with some other girl, and meeting some other guy, but it wasn't me and it wasn't Mark . . .

MAN: No, no, it was definitely you. I can visualize you distinctly, 'cause you were wearing the same Sarah McLachlan t-shirt you were wearing that night we met . . .

WOMAN: What?

MAN: It was you all right.

WOMAN: Where do I start? A, I never had a Sarah McLachlan t-shirt in my life, because B, I don't like Sarah McLachlan, and C, the night we met I was wearing that scarlet sleeveless dress of mine, 'cause I'd never be so gauche as to wear a t-shirt to fucking Symphony Hall.

MAN: Symphony Hall? What are you talking about?

WOMAN: I'm talking about the night we met.

MAN: We didn't meet at Symphony Hall.

WOMAN: Of course we did. Bernie and Jan wanted to get us together, remember? So they thought we would all go to the BSO together. I remember it very clearly. At dinner before hand, Bernie talked about how it was going to be a concert of Conceptualist music, and you said, "I've never heard of

Conceptualist, what kind of music does he write?", which was so ador-
ably pathetic that I kind of fell for you right then.

MAN: Uh, Honey?

WOMAN: What?

MAN: Who are Bernie and Jan?

WOMAN: . . . You're fucking with me, aren't you?

MAN: No.

WOMAN: Tell me that you're fucking with me.

MAN: I'm not fucking with you.

WOMAN: I said, tell me that you *are* fucking with me. Can't you listen?

MAN: If I were fucking with you, I'd tell you. I'm not fucking with you.

WOMAN: "Who are Bernie and Jan?"

MAN: That's what I asked.

WOMAN: Bernie's your brother.

MAN: What?

WOMAN: Bernie's your brother, and Jan is his wife. Stop it, you're fucking with
    me!

MAN: Um, no. I don't have a brother. I have two sisters, Polly and Daisy . . .

WOMAN: No!

MAN: . . . and you're an only child.

WOMAN: I've got three brothers and three sisters!
    (Pause.)

MAN: Okay, something's going on here.

WOMAN: Yes.

MAN: Something is seriously going on here.

WOMAN: You sure it's not a matter of perspective?

MAN: Yes, I'm sure.

WOMAN: Maybe one of us has gone insane.

MAN: Maybe we *both* have.

WOMAN: *(Thinks about it.)* No, that would be too much of a coincidence.

MAN: True.

WOMAN: Look. It's like what I said about *Manhattan.* One of us must be right,
    and one of us must be wrong. We can tell by watching the movie.

MAN: Or we could just call Mark and Kim. We both admit we know them.

WOMAN: All right. *(She picks up her cell phone from the stand beside her.)* What
    should I ask?

MAN: How we met them.

WOMAN: Okay. *(She starts to dial a number on the phone.)*

MAN: Wait.

WOMAN: What?

MAN: What will we do when we find out?

WOMAN: Well, I guess whoever's wrong will have to go for extensive psychological treatment. Possibly involving shock therapy.

MAN: Okay, that sounds reasonable.

WOMAN: Here we go. *(She finishes dialing.)* It's ringing.

MAN: Well, yes, it would.

WOMAN: Hey, Kim? Kimbino-gal! How's it going? Uh-huh. Well, don't give up, it usually takes two or three times, at least when I try it. Hey, listen, I've got kind of a stupid question for you. Me and my man here are arguing about how we met. I mean, how and when each of us met each of you. You and Mark, I mean . . . So, we were just going to check your recollection on how we might have . . .

MAN: Zinfandel. Come on, Zinfandel . . .

WOMAN: *(to THE MAN)* Shhh! *(back on the phone)* Yeah, I know that sounds pretty ridiculous, but he has this notion that we met Mark on a whale watch, of all things, and that we met you afterwards. Hmm. Yeah, I know. Yes, he can be like that.

MAN: Like what?

WOMAN: But I know he's wrong, because obviously I remember when you and I met . . .

MAN: I can be like what?

WOMAN: *(to THE MAN)* Stuff it! *(back to the phone)* Yeah, right. That's right, the ceramics class. *(She turns to THE MAN and pumps her fist in victory.)* Yes, of course. Oh, I know, I know, it's just that he kept telling me we met Mark first and then . . .

MAN: Give me that. *(He seizes the phone from THE WOMAN.)*

WOMAN: Hey! I was talking!

MAN: Kim, it's me. Can you put Mark on the phone? 'Cause I want to talk to him, that's why. Hey, we've already got your story, I wanna get Mark's. Yeah, I'll hold. *(To THE WOMAN)* She's really in a pissy mood this morning.

WOMAN: Give it up. I've won.

MAN: Not necessarily. *(to phone)* Hey, Marcus! Hey, it's me. Listen, I was having a discussion with the little woman here *(THE WOMAN belts him with a pillow, which he ignores)*, and we had a bit of a disagreement about how we met you. I wanted to get your memory about . . . Yeah, that's right, the whale watch. Yep, I sure do. And when we met Kim . . . ? Yes, she spilled the wine! Yeah, Zinfandel! Of course I remember. How could I forget? Listen, why don't you . . . What? What's that? I can't hear . . . Oh. *(to THE WOMAN)* I think Kim's starting to argue with him. *(back into phone)* Okay, Mark, thanks. Talk to you later. You rock, dude! *(He ends the call and puts down the phone.)* Well, he agrees on the whale watch, and the spilled wine. That settles that.

WOMAN: No, it doesn't. Kim agreed with me that we met at ceramics class.

MAN: Hmm . . . So, our sources disagree.

WOMAN: It's like our disagreement has fractured the Universe. Half of it is what I remember, and half of it is what you remember.

MAN: If that's true, just how different are your world and my world?

WOMAN: Well, let's see . . . According to you, who's president?

MAN: Barack Obama. *(Or whoever is currently president.)*

WOMAN: Whose picture is on the five-dollar bill?

MAN: Lincoln.

WOMAN: What's the best flavor of ice cream ever?

MAN: Brigham's Wicked Chocolate.

WOMAN: You see? Our worlds are in accord. Mostly.

MAN: Right. It seems like the only differences are ones that involve us personally.

WOMAN: Maybe if we just accept that our memories aren't quite in synch, we can live with it.

MAN: We might have different pasts, but our present is the same.

WOMAN: Yes! Exactly. The present belongs to us. And the future, too.

MAN: *(Hesitantly)* All right. *(More forcefully.)* All right. *(Pause)* So we're okay, then? I can finish my crossword now?

WOMAN: Of course.

(The two smile at each other and, spontaneously, lean forward to kiss. Just before they do so, THE OTHER MAN enters.)

OTHER MAN: Hey, are you two gonna lay around in bed all day? Come on, come on, we've got work to do. I've got the paint all mixed for the kitchen walls and the new wallpaper prepped for the living room. So, get up, it's gonna be a long day! God, I can't believe how lazy you two are. I swear, if the sex wasn't so great I'd leave you two in a heartbeat.

(THE OTHER MAN exits. Pause.)

WOMAN: He's not one of mine. Is he one of yours?

MAN: No, not at all.

WOMAN: . . . Uh-oh.

(Lights down.)

END PLAY

RECOGNITION

Patrick Gabridge

BTM PRODUCTION, May 2009:
Sponsored by Wellesley Summer Theatre
Directed by Nora Hussey
Tanya Moncrief. . . . . .Ashley Gramolini
Allison Beckoff . . . . Sarah Barton

A chance meeting between an adoptive mother and the birth mother of her child on the subway leads to difficult questions and painful choices.

Patrick Gabridge has written numerous plays, including *Constant State of Panic, Pieces of Whitey, Blinders,* and *Reading the Mind of God.* He started Boston's Rhombus Playwrights' group, Chameleon Stage in Denver, Market InSight . . . for Playwrights, and the on-line Playwrights' Submission Binge. He is a member of the Dramatists Guild.

CHARACTERS
(Two women)
TANYA MONCRIEF, 23, A graduate student.
ALLISON BECKHOFF, 30s–40s.
DRIVER, Voice of a train conductor (over loudspeaker)

SETTING
Boston: In a car on the Green Line of the T (Boston's subway).

TIME
Now

. . .

A subway car on Boston's green line (the T). This can be represented with chairs.

A young woman, TANYA, in her 20s, dressed for a conference, but not expensively so, sits on a seat on the T. A name tag from her conference still hangs around her next. In her lap is a briefcase or bag and a stack of papers that she's looking through. She often looks up, to see what stop she's at. There might be other people on the train (if there are extra actors available), but the car is mostly empty. Tanya's seat is in an empty row of seats near the middle entrance of the car. ALLISON enters, in her 30s–40s, a canvas bag in hand, and sits in a single seat, facing Tanya, on the other side of the entrance doors, 2 rows back. Allison sees Tanya. A look of recognition. Tries not to stare, but keeps coming back to her. Notices Tanya's name tag. Tries harder to read it, without seeming too obvious, but she's very interested. Allison shifts forward to the next seat. Tanya doesn't notice her yet. Allison keeps trying to get a better look at the name tag. Certainly she's read it by now, but she keeps looking. Tanya looks up and their eyes meet. Allison smiles at her and Tanya, after the slightest delay, returns the smile.

ALLISON: Here for the APA conference?
TANYA: Um. Yeah.
ALLISON: I have a friend presenting there. Doris Schuman.
TANYA: Oh, right. She's supposed to be great. I think she's presenting tomorrow.
ALLISON: You're . . . young for a psychologist.

TANYA: Internship. Grad students don't usually get to go. I was lucky.

ALLISON: Good for you. Did you have to travel far?

TANYA: Um. Yeah. From Madison. Wisconsin.

ALLISON: Madison. Wow. Wow. U.W. That's where we lived before Boston. My husband finished his degree there.

TANYA: He's here now?

ALLISON: At B.U. Teaching.

TANYA: Good for him.

(Silence. Allison can't take her eyes off Tanya. Tanya is starting to notice.).

ALLISON: The conference is at Hynes Convention Center, right?

TANYA: I have to pay for my own lodging, so I was trying to stay cheap. Someone recommended a B&B in Newton. I didn't know it'd be so far out.

ALLISON: Yes, it goes way out there. (beat) How old are you? I'm sorry. I'm so nosy. Ignore me. Just . . . You . . . Look. You seem so young, even for a graduate student.

TANYA: I'm 23.

ALLISON: Right. Right.

(The train stops. Tanya looks up at the map above the doors. Any extra passengers should exit now.)

ALLISON: Which stop?

TANYA: Newton Centre.

(The train resumes motion.)

ALLISON: Oh. Wow. Next stop. Almost there. You'll be . . . Are you enjoying Boston?

TANYA: Yeah. It's great. Nice change. The people have been friendlier than I expected.

ALLISON: It has a reputation, I know. But there are so many of us transplants. I think it's mellowed. You married?

TANYA: Me? No. Just trying to take care of myself right now. That's all I can handle.

ALLISON: But things are working out?

TANYA: Um. Yeah. Sure. I guess so.

ALLISON: I'm glad.

TANYA: Well, this is almost my stop. It was nice, ah, meeting you.

(Tanya stands and moves to the door. Allison stands, too, very nervous.)

ALLISON: Tanya Moncrief from Madison.

TANYA: What? Oh, the name tag. Yeah.

ALLISON: I know who you are, Tanya.

TANYA: Excuse me. This is . . . I'm getting off here.

ALLISON: You placed a little girl up for adoption five years ago.

TANYA: You have the wrong person.

ALLISON: I know it's you.

TANYA: No. I'm a graduate student. I'm . . . I'm not . . . You have the wrong person. I don't know you.

ALLISON: Why didn't you come to the meeting at IHOP? We waited and waited.

TANYA: You're confused.

ALLISON: I know it's you.

TANYA: I have to go.

(The train stops. The doors open. Tanya moves to leave and Allison reaches out for her.)

TANYA: Don't touch me.

ALLISON: I'm —

TANYA: I have to go.

ALLISON: Her name is Emily. She looks just like you. I have photos.

(Tanya is paralyzed, stuck in the doorway.)

DRIVER: *(over speakers)* Stand clear the closing doors, please. Clear the doors, please. Off or on, Lady.

(Tanya comes back into the car. The train resumes motion. Tanya takes a seat and Allison sits right behind her).

TANYA: I've missed my stop.

ALLISON: Sorry.

TANYA: You're not supposed to know my name.

ALLISON: The hospital screwed up. We got the original records from the birth, and they forgot to cross out your name. Even the name wouldn't have . . . But when I saw your face, I knew. And Madison. So many times I wondered what you'd look like, what she'd . . . I've searched the internet. I knew you were out there, somewhere. And then I saw you. It's like looking at her, what she'll look like. Grown. I never knew what she'd . . . And then to see you.

TANYA: What do you want from me?

ALLISON: I . . . To say thank you. For our daughter. Emily is smart. Stubborn. Beautiful. Thank you.

TANYA: I didn't do it for you.

ALLISON: Right. I didn't mean —

TANYA: If I wanted to know you, I would have come to the meetings. I shouldn't have said yes, but you kept . . . If I wanted to know you, I would have answered the letters. The agency sent them to me. Until I asked them to stop.

ALLISON: The letters are still there. If you ever want them. It's up to you. I'm sorry. Maybe I shouldn't have said anything.

TANYA: Maybe.

ALLISON: But then you would vanish, and . . . what would I tell her, later, when she's older? "I saw your birthmother once, on the T, but I didn't say anything."

TANYA: Don't tell her anything.

ALLISON: She's going to want to know.

TANYA: She can't. That's not . . . It's supposed to be my choice. I'm supposed to have a say.

ALLISON: I know.

TANYA: But you don't care? Why can't you . . . Respect what I chose and, just let it . . .

ALLISON: I do. I do. I do.

TANYA: How? How is this . . . What, what I did, is just. You can't just. See, I have a life, my own life, and it's not spectacular, but it's what I have. I've finished school. I'm. But. There's a . . . See, for you, it was all just one thing, one big sweep of this, then this, then this. A continuum. Not for me. Before and after. That was before, and this, now, this is after. Do you, see?

ALLISON: I do. But when I saw your face, I —

TANYA: I'm lost. Where are we? Where are we?

ALLISON: You can turn around. Just get off, at the next stop. Cross over and go back.

TANYA: This wasn't supposed to happen. Now what? Now what? I have to wonder, all the time, when are you going to pop out, and Surprise!

ALLISON: No. I wouldn't. Don't worry. I wouldn't.

TANYA: I don't believe you.

ALLISON: I'll pretend we've never met. Okay? I take it all back. We rewind. You stay there. I'll move. I'm sorry.

(Allison shifts over across the car. Tanya stares blankly at her papers. Allison tries not to look at her. She takes her purse out of the canvas bag. Silence and train noises. Allison takes a photo out of her wallet, looks at it, looks at Tanya. Allison moves back to the seat behind Tanya.)

TANYA: I don't know you. Remember?

(Allison holds out the photo. Tanya almost takes it, but can't or won't move her hand to grasp it. Allison puts the photo in Tanya's fingers and then moves back across the aisle. Tanya finally looks at the photo for a long moment.)

TANYA: She's okay?

(Allison moves back over to the seat behind Tanya.)

ALLISON: She's . . . everything we wanted. She's not perfect. She's not an angel. Emily is human, with everything that comes along with it.

TANYA: We're all —

ALLISON: She knows she's adopted, but she doesn't know exactly what that means. Not yet. Maybe I don't even know. You're both human, for better and for worse. She'll understand.

TANYA: After. After. All this is after. You have to understand that. Please.

ALLISON: Okay.

TANYA: Here.

(Tries to give back the photo.)

ALLISON: You keep it.

TANYA: I . . .

ALLISON: Keep it for now. If you can't keep it, you can toss it later. But I can't take it back from you. When I think about you, I'll want to think you have a photo of her. Something.

TANYA: I don't . . .

(She doesn't give back the photo.)

ALLISON: My stop is next.

TANYA: Okay.

(beat)

ALLISON: Could I . . . Before I go . . . My phone. It takes pictures. Could I . . .

TANYA: I don't think —

ALLISON: Not now. I wouldn't show her now. But someday, when she's older, almost grown. Feeling lost. If she could just . . . just see, what you were like. How much you two . . .

TANYA: I don't . . .

ALLISON: She might not even want to. But if she ever does . . .

TANYA: Okay.

(Allison takes the phone out of her purse and slides across the aisle. Holds up her phone. Tanya looks right at the camera. Allison takes the picture, and stands, as the train begins to stop.)

ALLISON: I have to go.

TANYA: Right.

ALLISON: If you want, you could . . . It's not far.

TANYA: I. You shouldn't even.

ALLISON: I'm sorry. I . . . But I wouldn't forgive myself if I didn't offer.

TANYA: I wish I could. I wish I was someone who could. But I'm not. I can't.

(Allison moves into the doorway of the train, waits to see if Tanya will

change her mind. She doesn't. Allison exits, with a look back at Tanya.
Tanya sits alone in the car. Goes through papers. Stops. Brings out the
photo.)
(Lights to Black.).

END OF PLAY

THE SWEEP

Gary Garrison

The Sweep had its world premier at the 11th Annual Boston Theater Marathon, sponsored by Zeitgeist Stage Company. It was directed by David J. Miller with the following cast:

Johnson. . . . . .Rick Park
Frank . . . . .Michael Steven Costello

Frank summons his best friend Johnson to a hospital waiting room with an unusual post-mortem request: to be in charge of "the sweep" — removing, after his death, signs of a side of his life he's kept hidden. But what is Frank hiding from his best friend?

Garrison's plays include *The Sweep, Verticals and Horizontals, Storm on Storm, It Belongs on Stage (and Not in My Bed), Crater, Old Soles, Cherry Reds, Gawk, Oh Messiah Me, We Make A Wall, The Big Fat Naked Truth* and *When A Diva Dreams*. This work has been featured at the City Theatre of Miami, Boston Theater Marathon, Primary Stages, The Directors Company, Manhattan Theatre Source, StageWorks Hudson, Open Door Theatre, Pulse Ensemble Theatre, Expanded Arts and New York Rep.

CHARACTERS

FRANK, 45, handsome and masculine, but not overly so. Tossled hair, unshaven face. Anyone who meets him notices his smile.

JOHNSON, 42, a large man, in all directions. Frank's closest friend for twenty years.

SETTING

A waiting room in a hospital. Standard waiting room furniture: chairs, a couple of end tables, magazines, newspapers strewn about.

TIME

A cold day in December, early evening.

. . .

Lights pop up on.

FRANK, in a hospital gown, reading glasses, jeans under the gown, no shoes but one white sock, one red sock, perches on a chair, quietly and quickly ticking off and thinking through each item on a written list. The list is written on the bottom of a well-worn loafer.

JOHNSON practically bolts or bursts into the waiting room; he's run through miles of hospital hallways.

JOHNSON: (*Trying to catch his breath.*) Are you kidding me? Are you fuckin' kidding me?

FRANK:(*Checking his watch.*) You made it! With time to spare in the visiting hours. That's my boy! How's it going, Johnson?

JOHNSON: (*Overlapping.*) Next time you call me and say "meet me in the waiting room at the hospital," you might want to start with — oh, I don't know — the name of the hospital. Yeah, that'd be good. Because this city has four. Or how about a wing of a certain hospital, because this particular hospital has eight. Eight wings, Frank. Eight fuckin' wings, Frank. The only wing I didn't run up and down twice looking for your silly ass was the maternity wing because unless I'm mistaken, you're not pregnant.

FRANK: Well, there's no way I could get pregnant. But, on the other hand, I could easily GET someone pregnant. In which case . . .

JOHNSON: Shut up, Frank. Because if I had thought of that, I would have run up and down another wing of this hospital.

FRANK: Hey, wait a minute. Where are your glasses, Johnson?

JOHNSON: Left them at home; was racing to get here — like a madman, like an idiot — and forgot them.

FRANK: Johnson, you know you can't see shit without your glasses.

JOHNSON: Right. Right. Well, there's that problem. And then there's the problem of you can't really drive a car without gas, which I found out the hard way because I didn't have my glasses on to read the fuel gauge. And then there's the problem of signing the chrome countertop twice because I couldn't see the lines on the credit card receipt so I just kept signing the chrome countertop and entertaining the long line of people behind me. But enough about me. How are you, Frank? And what brings us here together on this cold, grey day in December, which I'm not dressed for.

FRANK: (*Laughing.*) Oh, my God. You are such a fuckin' queen.

JOHNSON: Wha — Whoa! Whoooooooa. Everything I just said, everything from my appearance here forward, has nothing to do with me being a queen but everything to do with you being a selfish, narcissistic, often vague, often obtuse, often . . . You know what? Forget that. Let's talk about what we're not talking about.

FRANK: Like what?

JOHNSON: (*Flatly.*) Hmmm. Hmmmmmmmm. What could it be? (*Leaning in.*) The hospital, you asshole. Why are you here? And why am I here?

(Frank studies Johnson for a short while, then:)

FRANK: I love you, man. I really love you, Johnson. And I'm just sorry that I couldn't . . . be, you know . . .

JOHNSON: Wait. Are you giving me the "I'm straight, you're gay, so I can't love you the way you want me to love you" talk? Because we had that talk, like, twenty years ago over bad nachos and imported Danish beer. So I'm cool with it, bro.

FRANK: Are you? Are you really?

JOHNSON: Yes, Franklin. And if I wasn't, I've had the last twenty years to get used to it, for Christ's sake. What's the matter with you? (*A beat, then.*) Oh, shit. You didn't get laid last night, did you? That's why you're all vulnerable and shit. What happened?

(Frank studies him a moment. How much should he say?)

FRANK: Okay, last night I'm getting ready for my date with Joanne. I get the fire going in the fireplace, but it's a little smoky in the room, so I crack the front door and stuff a rag in it. Then I go to the bedroom to make the bed and had to clear a path from the bedroom door to the bed. And, swear to God, there was, like, ten loads of laundry down there. Anyway, I'm making the bed and I'm thinking about how I'm really looking forward to seeing Joanne . . . and that's the last thing I remember. Next thing I know, I'm here. In the cardiac care unit. With, like, wires and shit hooked up to me and that annoying beep, beep, beep monitor thing that tells you that you're alive but not for how long.

JOHNSON: (*Now really concerned.*) What happened, Frank? Did you have a heart attack?

FRANK: I had an "episode." That's what they call it when they don't know what the hell it is: you've had a heart episode.

JOHNSON: (*Touching his arm.*) Frank, buddy, what's goin on?

FRANK: I don't know. They don't know. So they're all about the tests. Tests, tests and more tests. I'm supposed to be in my room right now for another test. But I had to see you first — alone — and I'm sharing this room with an Egyptian guy that's chanting loudly, with a lot of high notes. So I needed some privacy. Anyway, here's the deal. Now, I think we can agree I don't have your propensity for drama, right?

JOHNSON: Yes, bitch, fucker, go ahead.

FRANK: BUT, my "episode" got me to thinking, what would have happened if I just dropped dead? I mean, I was making the bed and then, boom, I was here. So I'm a little freaked out, and I'm thinking, what if I had just died? The will's in order, yeah, and the papers that say cremate me and scatter me to the wind are signed and sealed. But who's going to go into my apartment and dig through my shit and pack it up? And do what with it?

JOHNSON: Okay. I'm beginning to understand.

FRANK: Well, not really. You think you do, but know you don't. I mean, yes, I do want you be a person that does a part of that, but not all of that.

JOHNSON: Okay, totally lost now.

FRANK: Right. See, I figure if I croak, my ex — may she die a slow, torturous death in the fiery, molten pits of Hell — and my ultra-conservative mother and father, and my fucked up, conservative elementary school teacher sister will want to comb through my shit and take stuff. And I'm okay with that. (*Looking at him intently.*) But there is some stuff no one in your family should see, if you get my drift. (*Waiting for a reaction.*) No one who remembers you as a cute little blonde boy with dimples that always wore denim shorts and striped t-shirts and red high tops should see what you don't want them to see because it would, like, alter their memory of you in a way that maybe you don't want. Or maybe your ex-wife will see something in your apartment that will give her shit to talk about you for decades with her bitter, jaded, nasty, bitchy, diet-addicted, man-eating girlfriends.

JOHNSON: Okay . . . okay . . . now I got it: you want me to take the porno out of your apartment?

FRANK: (*Almost hugging him.*) I knew you'd understand! See, because you're my best buddy, and because we've been friends forever, and because you're gay and you live and let live, I just think you're, like, the perfect person to do the sweep.

JOHNSON: The what?

FRANK: The sweep. You know, swoop in, sweep the apartment clean of . . . of the dirt and swoop out.

JOHNSON: "Swoop in — sweep — swoop out?" You've really thought this through. Hmmm. Alright, but just tell me there's nothing weird, or nasty or I'll discover something that will keep me gagging for weeks. (*A beat, then:*) Just tell me, Frank. (*A beat.*) Franklin? Franklin, do you have — let me just ask — do you have, like, kiddie porn or some shit like that?

FRANK: Oh, my God! No! For God's sake, Johnson. Kiddie porn, no! That is just horrible and immoral and wrong . . . (*Slipping it in.*) . . . But there is a couple of d.v.d.s that maybe you shouldn't look at and just toss them out. You know, just throw them out without looking. I'll put them in box. You won't even have to . . .

JOHNSON: You think after this talk I won't look in that box? It could be encased in cement and I'd blast it out. Give me some titles. Come on. Out with it. What am I looking for?

FRANK: Okay. Okay. Uhm, well there's . . . uhm, there's Chicks With Dicks, Part One, Chicks With Dicks, Part Two, Chicks with Dicks, Part . . .

JOHNSON: I got it, I got it. Jesus! . . . Any others?

FRANK: Nope.

JOHNSON: (*Accusing.*) THAT'S ALL YOU HAVE? All the porno you have is Chicks With Dicks? (*A beat, then calmly.*) I'm going to try and take the judgment out of my voice. Please. Go ahead. Anything else in "the sweep?"

FRANK: Well, I've made a list. (*Displays the bottom of his shoe.*) I know it's a little unusual, but it's all I could find in my hospital room. And I stole the pen from the nurse's station. (*Reading his shoe.*) Okay, so besides the porn, there's a box of toys under the bed. I'd just take the whole box, if I were you, and toss it away.

JOHNSON: Without looking inside.

FRANK: Exactly.

JOHNSON: What kind of toys?

FRANK: What kind? Well, uhm, sex toys.

JOHNSON: Yeah. Got that. But after the Chicks with Dicks confession, my imagination is running a little crazy. So are we talking whip and chains?

FRANK: Oh, my God, no! Jesus, Johnson, what kind of freak do you think I am? No, there are no whips and chains. God. There a couple of butt-plugs and dildos, vibrators, wrist restraints, a ball gag, nipple clamps, rubber sheet — you know, those kind of things.

JOHNSON: (*Wryly.*) Oh. Oh, right. Those kind of things. Thank God, because I was beginning to think . . .

FRANK: No, no, none of that weird stuff.

JOHNSON: Right. Okay, you know, I think I'm ready for you to finish. Is there anything more you need to shock me with? Anything that I won't be able to get out of my mind for the decade ahead?

FRANK: That's all the sex stuff.

JOHNSON: Thank God. Wow. Well, there you have it. Sex in a box. Consider it gone, should you buy the farm. Is there anything else you want to share? *(Frank stands for the first time; moves away from Johnson.)*

FRANK: Yeah. One more thing. On my computer, in a file named "Dudley" — because I was watching a Dudley Do-Right cartoon when I made the file —

JOHNSON: Really?

FRANK: Sure. Always liked him. And Little Nell.

JOHNSON: The little things you learn, huh?

FRANK: Anyway, if you open that file, you're going to see a letter . . . a letter that no one should ever, ever read but you, and I mean it. And that letter . . . that letter tells you that I love you . . . And that letter tells you that for years, I was IN love with you, but worked really hard to not feel that. And that I know you spent years yourself quietly wishing, wondering, hoping, maybe even praying that I would love you they way I know you loved me. But I couldn't do it, Johnson; I just couldn't for a hundred fucked up reasons. So I worked really hard to honor how I was raised, and to never have to present that to my parents or my sister, and to not be the object of fuckin' heartless chat around my office, and to not live my life afraid that someone would discover a side of my life I wanted to keep hidden. I worked incredibly hard not to love you. And believe me, that's not easy because you're so fuckin' loveable. But I didn't want that life with you. I was . . . am a coward. *(He steps backwards, closer to Johnson.)* Before I turn around, I'm going to give you a moment to wipe your eyes in case you're crying and shit, because I can't . . . I can't see that. And the reason I never gave you the letter is because the letter was just for me, to remind me to love you the best way I knew how.

(Johnson wipes the tears from his eyes.)

JOHNSON: You can turn around now. (*He doesn't.*)

FRANK: (*A beat.*) Do me a favor? Could you just . . . go? Just, you know, walk out the door and we'll talk later?

(Johnson walks to the door, opens it.)

JOHNSON: (*Struggling to say something; finally:*) Don't die on me anytime soon, okay? I need a little time to forget all that you said, and all that you haven't . . . then you can go.

FRANK: It's a deal.

(Johnson shuts the door, still inside the room. Frank, thinking he's alone, collapses inward, sobbing.)

JOHNSON: What a shame.

(Lights slowly fade.)

END OF PLAY

GWEN & EVELYN
(World Premiere)

Paul H. Goodwin

Gwen & Evelyn was originally produced as part of the Boston Theater Marathon XI at the Stanford Calderwood Pavilion at the Boston Center for the Arts, Boston, MA, May 17, 2009.

Sponsored by Blackburn Performing Arts
Directed by M. Lynda Robinson
Gwen . . . . Karen Eris
Evelyn. . . . . Sally Nutt
Man . . . . Nick Neyeloff

When two women share a man who becomes disabled, they must decide what responsibility has to do with love.

Paul was the head writer of *Central Square* (a soap opera that aired on national award-winning Cambridge Community Television). His plays, *Maria's Day; Ann, Is That You?* and *Chances* have been performed throughout New England by The Arlington Players, TCAN Players, The Studio Repertory and the Newburyport Firehouse Center for the Arts.

CHARACTERS
GWEN: Thirties.
EVELYN: Thirties.
MAN: Forties.

SETTING

A beautiful sunny garden, mid autumn. Leaves have started to gather around the two stone benches.

.   .   .

GWEN pushes a MAN in a wheelchair downstage. He stares ahead, eyes unfocused, leaning slightly to one side. She places the wheelchair beside a bench, locks the wheels and sits on the bench. Gwen, sitting, stares ahead looking at the flowers, the surroundings, anything but the man, who continues to stare straight ahead. Her eyes eventually stray to his hands, which she lifts, studies them (devoid of jewelry) and places them in his lap. Without eye contact, she looks around again. Eventually, a look of recognition crosses her face (she sees someone off-stage). Gwen rises, kisses the man on the forehead and walks toward the unknown person. She stops in front of another bench and waits as EVELYN enters.

GWEN: Hello.
EVELYN: Hi.
GWEN: Did you have any trouble?
EVELYN: No, I knew where I was going.
GWEN: So, you've been here before?
EVELYN: No, I'm just good with directions.
GWEN: I thought you might not come.
EVELYN: It did cross my mind, but only for a moment.
GWEN: I wouldn't blame you.
EVELYN: I want to be here.
GWEN: Really?
EVELYN: Really.
GWEN: Maybe we should sit?
EVELYN: Okay. How is he?
GWEN: Fine. Good actually. They provide excellent care here.
EVELYN: How long before he's released?
GWEN: I'm not sure. It's still too early to tell.
EVELYN: I suppose.

GWEN: But he's young . . . healthy . . . for the most part. I don't know. Not really. They tell me a lot of things that I don't really comprehend. I guess I still don't believe it.

EVELYN: That's understandable.

GWEN: Please don't do that.

EVELYN: Do what?

GWEN: Be so compassionate.

EVELYN: I'm sorry.

GWEN: You did it again.

EVELYN: I'm . . . I do, do that.

GWEN: He always liked that about you.

EVELYN: He said that?

GWEN: No, but he would. His mother is the same way.

EVELYN: Kind?

GWEN: Saccharin.

EVELYN: I didn't think so.

GWEN: I forgot you had met her.

EVELYN: Your fifth anniversary.

GWEN: It's the only time she ever visited.

EVELYN: California is far away.

GWEN: That wasn't the reason. She never approved.

EVELYN: Why, did she say that?

GWEN: She didn't have to. I could tell.

EVELYN: I didn't see it.

GWEN: You weren't the target. Besides, you were preoccupied.

EVELYN: I wasn't.

GWEN: You were.

EVELYN: Because I was with Charlie?

GWEN: Whatever happened to him?

EVELYN: He's married, two kids.

GWEN: Is he happy?

EVELYN: I think so. He calls every once in a while.

GWEN: I never understood that.

EVELYN: Being friends with an ex?

GWEN: Yes.

EVELYN: It's not that difficult.

GWEN: But it is hard?

EVELYN: Sometimes. Weren't you ever friends with an ex?

GWEN: Good God, no.

EVELYN: Why not?

GWEN: When it's over, it's over. What's the point?

EVELYN: Maybe you haven't finished learning all the lessons you were supposed to.

GWEN: I don't believe in that new age crap.

EVELYN: I don't believe you're that solitary.

GWEN: You probably think I only care about myself. Everybody else does and if I go through with this, they definitely will.

EVELYN: I've never thought of you that way.

GWEN: That's because you're getting what you want. My mother thinks every time anything gets too much for me, I bail, but it's not true.

EVELYN: I'm sure it isn't.

GWEN: Maybe it is, but this isn't easy for me.

EVELYN: I know. He told me it was over between you, but that doesn't mean there aren't feelings.

GWEN: Yes.

EVELYN: So, he would have left anyway?

GWEN: Yes, he would have walked away from me. Pardon the pun. Funny thing, he might never again. (*beat*) I can't believe this is the first time we've really talked since I got your letter.

EVELYN: I wanted to call, but I didn't know how much you wanted me to.

GWEN: I knew on some level. Don't wives always know, I just didn't know it was you.

EVELYN: How did you figure it out?

GWEN: When you didn't call right away, I started putting it together. When he was taken from the Randolph was a big clue. Why did you just leave him there?

EVELYN: When I left he was fine.

GWEN: You almost had a wedding reception there.

EVELYN: With Charlie.

GWEN: That's right.

EVELYN: I've always loved that hotel.

GWEN: You love a lot of things.

EVELYN: I like it that way.

GWEN: It won't be easy for you, you know.

EVELYN: I realize that.

GWEN: Do you? I think you have a very romantic ideal of what this entails.

EVELYN: I don't.

GWEN: Just stop it, will you?! All these short, pat answers. Everything you say is exactly right, so understanding, so sincere, so true . . . so full of shit!

EVELYN: Is that what you think I'm doing?

GWEN: I think you have a guilty conscience and you're trying to make yourself feel better.

EVELYN: That's not why I came up with this plan. I just feel it's the best solution. It was going to happen anyway, whether he was well or the way he is now.

GWEN: I don't believe you.

EVELYN: You don't have to. So, what are your plans?

GWEN: I'm going back home.

EVELYN: To Colorado?

GWEN: Yes, maybe back to school too.

EVELYN: I wish you luck.

GWEN: Just keep it. You'll need it more than I will.

EVELYN: Can I do anything for you?

GWEN: Please.

EVELYN: Want anything?

GWEN: I took his ring. He won't need it. (*beat*) I guess I should go. I suppose I should be grateful to you.

EVELYN: For what?

GWEN: For setting me free from a dying marriage and saving me from playing nursemaid for the rest of my life to someone I don't love.

EVELYN: He won't be like that forever.

(*Gwen rises, turns back to look at the man. Evelyn goes to hug her, but Gwen backs away.*)

GWEN: I better leave.

(*She turns and leaves. Evelyn looks to the man and appears momentarily panic-stricken but immediately replaces it with a smile. She goes to the man and sits beside him, looks longingly into his blank eyes, picks up his hands and kisses them. She kneels, unlocks the wheels clumsily, then rises and pushes the wheelchair back upstage.*)

END OF PLAY

SUR LA MAISON

Michael J. Grady

Although *Sur La Maison* received earlier readings at Goddard College's *Take Ten Festival* and Image Theatre's *Naughty Readings*, its first full production took place at the 11th Annual Boston Theater Marathon on May 17· 2009. Sponsored by Elemental Theatre Collective. Directed by David Rabinow.

John . . . . Alexander Platt
Maurice. . . . . Kevin Delaney
Charli . . . . Kelly Nichols

Genre: Comedy

At a fancy restaurant Charli tells John she is leaving him, for the waiter. Charli wants to be friends but John has grieving to do. But can he hurry up?

Michael J. Grady is a playwright, performer and educator currently working at the Accademia dell'arte in Arezzo, Italy, where he lectures in comedy writing, clown-types, and playwriting. His plays include: Open House (2009 Best 10-minute Plays for 2 or More Actors) and Eralset or Scrabble in Babel (Heideman Award finalist.)

CHARACTERS:

    JOHN, a man, late 20's.

    CHARLI, a woman, same.

    MAURICE, a man of the world, mid to late 30's.

SETTING

    Chez Maurice — a restaurant.

TIME

    Evening (somewhere between 5 and 8 minutes after arriving at the restaurant.)

. . .

CHARLI sits alone at a table staring out into space, starry-eyed with a smile on her face. Over her table is a big sign that says "Chez Maurice."

JOHN: The restrooms are amazing here; you have to try them. They have towels, real towels to dry your hands, the walls are real, simulated marble and they have the sports page behind glass at the urinals. I mean it's like heaven.

CHARLI (*Dreamy*): Yes.

JOHN: They have everything.

CHARLI: And so do I.

JOHN: Did you miss me?

CHARLI: I want to break up.

JOHN: Did I take that long?

CHARLI: I'm sorry. I met someone else.

JOHN: When?

CHARLI: Just now.

JOHN: While I was in the . . .

CHARLI: (*With sudden realization*) John, this is so awkward. I don't know what to say. What do you want me to say?

JOHN: "Just kidding."

CHARLI: I didn't plan on it.

JOHN: Well, neither did I.

CHARLI: I know.

JOHN: Who is it?

CHARLI: Does it matter?

JOHN: Of course it does?

CHARLI: Why?

JOHN: What's his name?

(*Pause.*)

CHARLI: Maurice.

JOHN: Maurice?

CHARLI: Yes.

(*John looks up at the sign which says "Chez Maurice."*)

JOHN (*Laughs*): Oh. "Maurice." Good one.

CHARLI: It's true.

JOHN: (*Playfully*) Lucky I didn't take you to a Jack in the Box.

CHARLI: John?

JOHN: (*Laughing out loud.*) You really had me a moment there.

(*JOHN continues laughing. MAURICE approaches, filling up their water glasses.*)

CHARLI: Maurice!

JOHN: Maurice?

MAURICE: Oui, Maurice. 'ow es everah thang? (La Vie en Rose starts to play. Pause)

CHARLI: Perfect.

(*MAURICE and CHARLI look at each other. Long Pause.*)

CHARLI: Oh, this is John.

MAURICE: Enny frehnd of Charli ehzeh frehnd ov me. (*To Charli*) You may 'ave whatever you desire.

CHARLI: mmmm. Sounds delicious.

MAURICE: Ha ho ho. (*to both of them*) What you ordehr, eht will be sur la maison . . "on . . .ze 'ouse." May I recommend ze swardfiish?

CHARLI: Ze swardfiish?

MAURICE: Et well melt in yora mouse.

CHARLI: Ooh, melt in my mouse? Oh, Maurice.

MAURICE: Mon amour. (*They kiss aggressively*) ah, wehll let me check on your entrée.

(*MAURICE and CHARLI smile at one another.*)

MAURICE: Shoes me.

(*MAURICE leaves. La Vie en Rose ends abruptly*).

CHARLI: (*Dreamy*) Wow!

JOHN: Wow.

CHARLI: Mmmm. He has that . . .

JOHN: Je ne sais quoi?

CHARLI: Oui. (*Reviving*) Oh, gosh, I'm sorry. This must be hard on you.

JOHN: You think?

CHARLI: This is so awkward.

JOHN: I know.

CHARLI: Um . . he gets off in an hour and I want to go home and make myself look nice before we go out.

JOHN: Aren't you going to have your swordfish?

CHARLI: Oh, John, he was speaking metaphorically. The French love to speak in metaphors. They're poetic.

JOHN: I'd like to speak to you metaphorically, right now.

CHARLI: I'm sure. I'm sorry. Well, anyway, I really should get going.

JOHN: All right then, well I guess this it. Goodbye Charli.

CHARLI: John? That sounds so final. (*Pause.*) I can't leave you feeling so bad.

JOHN: It's ok. Just go, Charli.

CHARLI: Well, you see, ah, I kind of need a ride.

JOHN: I see. Well, take the keys.

CHARLI: You'll feel better in no time.

JOHN: Sure . . . I know.

(*Long pause.*)

CHARLI: Are we still going to be friends, John?

JOHN: Sure.

CHARLI: Are you going to be ok?

JOHN: I just have to get through it. It's a process.

CHARLI: What process?

JOHN: I really don't feel like talking about it.

CHARLI: Can't you just accept it and be happy for me?

JOHN: I can't just shake it off, Charli.

CHARLI: You have your process to go through.

JOHN: Yes.

CHARLI: What process?

JOHN: The Grieving Process.

CHARLI: Are you grieving?

JOHN: No.

(*John forces a smile, takes a deep breath and then weeps audibly.*)

CHARLI: John? John? John? (*Hands JOHN a napkin and he blows his nose.*) It's ok. It's ok. Do you want to tell me about it?

JOHN (*Recovering*): Telling you about it doesn't help. I just have to go through it, take it one piece at a time. It has many. . .phases.

CHARLI: Phases?

JOHN: Yes. I have to take them one at a time.

CHARLI: What's the first phase?

JOHN: Denial.

CHARLI: What's that?

JOHN: Before coming to a realization of the painful truth, a griever often denies what has happened.

CHARLI: So, you are trying to come to a realization that it's over.

JOHN: Yes. .

CHARLI: I see.

JOHN: If indeed it is over.

CHARLI: It is over.

JOHN: That's what you think.

CHARLI: So this is denial?

JOHN: No.

CHARLI: You just said you were in denial.

JOHN: No I didn't.

CHARLI: Are you denying your denial?

(Pause.)

JOHN: No?

CHARLI: John, I don't think I have ever been in love with you, but I am absolutely in love with Maurice.

JOHN: You just met Maurice.

CHARLI: Sometimes you just know.

JOHN: So what you are saying is . . . you want to see other guys.

CHARLI: I don't want to see other guys.

JOHN: Ah ha!

CHARLI: Just Maurice.

JOHN: Ahhh.

CHARLI: So what's next?

JOHN: I'm still in denial.

CHARLI: Still?

JOHN: Undeniably.

CHARLI: You can't be.

JOHN: Why?

CHARLI: You're accepting the fact that you are in denial. If you accept that you are in denial than how can you be in denial?

JOHN: Well then, maybe I'm not in denial.

CHARLI: Exactly. What's next?

JOHN: I always hated that about you. You always do that, whenever we argue I hate it when you do that.

CHARLI: What?

JOHN: Using (searches hard for a word, gesticulates and grunts, finally) reason.

CHARLI: When will you go to the next phase?

JOHN: When I am done with this phase.

CHARLI: Can't you just skip to the next phase?

JOHN: No!

CHARLI: What's the next phase?

JOHN: Anger.

CHARLI: Anger?

JOHN: Are you fucking deaf?!

CHARLI: What do you have to be angry for?

JOHN: You fucking cunt! I leave the table for five minutes.

CHARLI: Eight minutes.

JOHN: It's good to know you had time to look at your watch. Eight minutes and you're ready to outsource your vagina to the Pyrenees! You selfish, spoiled, capricious, dick-teasing, whore!

CHARLI: Feel better?

JOHN: A little.

CHARLI: What's next?

JOHN: Bargaining.

CHARLI: What's that like?

JOHN: (*Falling to his knees.*) Charli, please! If you come back to me I will never go to the bathroom again, I promise. I don't know how, but I'll find a way. Please, please, please, Charli!

(*La Vie en Rose begins again. MAURICE enters.*)

MAURICE: Iz everizang okeh?

CHARLI: Oh that accent, it drives me crazy. (They kiss)

MAURICE: Oh, dahling . . I meez'd yuzo.

CHARLI: Since we've met I've done nothing but think about you.

MAURICE: I've behn sinking of da last time we made love.

CHARLI: Me too.

JOHN (*Aside*): In five minutes?

MAURICE: Eight minutes.

JOHN: Wow.

MAURICE: Oh, mon amour.

CHARLI (*moaning*): Amour. (*looong kiss.*)

JOHN: I am so depressed.

CHARLI: Don't be depressed.

MAURICE: Zer ahh plenty of feesh in za see. But zehr arh none lahk you.

CHARLI: Ooooh.

MAURICE: I um prepeering ze swardfissh for yer, mon amour.

CHARLI: mmmm. I can't wait to taste it.

MAURICE: I yam going cross ze strait to ze market myself to mek shure et is extra frehsh.

CHARLI: Oh baby, take it to the market. (*MAURICE and CHARLI kiss.*) My my. . . oh, John, can't you speed it up?

JOHN: No.

CHARLI: How long does it take?

JOHN: A long time.

CHARLI: Why?

JOHN: Uh, well. (*To MAURICE*) Can we have a moment?

MAURICE: Ov curhhhz. (*To CHARLI*) zee yoo zoon. Au revoir.

CHARLI: Au revoir. (*MAURICE walks out the door. The music seems to follow him out.*) Now, why is it taking so long?

(JOHN plunks the ring box on the table. CHARLI is touched and a little embarrassed for JOHN. A friendship moment.)

CHARLI: That is the most pathetic thing I have ever seen.

JOHN: I know.

CHARLI: It's gallant.

JOHN: Thanks. Does that mean you're going to take me back?

CHARLI: No. Where were we?

JOHN: Depression.

CHARLI: Oh yes. So what comes next?

JOHN: Next? (*Pause. He inhales to think, pauses and lets out a calm exhale.*) Acceptance.

CHARLI: Really?

JOHN (*Rising*): Sure. Let me give you a ride home.

CHARLI: Thanks, John.

(MAURICE enters carrying a swordfish. The music follows him in.)

CHARLI: Honey. Everything's ok, now. I'll be back in 10 minutes.

MAURICE: I want to break up. (*The music stops.*)

CHARLI: What?

MAURICE: I meht someone.

CHARLI: Already?

MAURICE: Oui.

CHARLI: When?

MAURICE: At ze fish markeht. She touched my swardfiish and I knew she was se only one.

CHARLI: She touched your swordfish.

MAURICE: I yam spiking in se metahfor.

CHARLI: This isn't happening.

JOHN: (*Aside*) Denial.

CHARLI: What?

JOHN: Don't worry, Charli . . . you'll feel better in no time.

END OF PLAY

ANNIE DESMOND GETS A TATTOO

(World Premiere)

Kirsten Greenidge

Boston Theater Marathon, Sunday, May 17, 2009
Sponsored by Company One
Directed by Victoria Marsh
Annie . . . . .Nyla Wissa
Talisha. . . . . .Ashley Castillo
Margie . . . . .Lenise Ferrier
Antwoine . . . . Michael Cognata

On her sixteenth birthday Annie is faced with two questions: should she get a tattoo and should she get pregnant? The answers are not as easy as you'd think.

Kirsten Greenidge's plays combine elements of magical realism with a pronounced use of language while exploring how race, class, and culture intersect in our current America. She is current member of New Dramatists as well as Rhombus and was a recent NEA/TCG grant recipient.

CHARACTERS
> Annie, 16
> Talisha, 16
> Margie, 16
> Antwoine, 23

SETTING
> A small city in the Northeast.

. . .

A tattoo parlor. ANNIE lies on a tattoo table, shirt up, midriff bare. TALISHA, nails like talons, lacquered, sparkling, bejeweled and bedazzled. MARGIE stands.

TALISHA: It's gonna be mad cool, yo.

ANNIE: I dunno.

MARGIE (*Pulling down a corner of her jeans*): He did mine and it's mad cool.

ANNIE: Is that straight?

TALISHA: Of course it's straight.

MARGIE: He practices on oranges.

ANNIE: Maybe I should wait.

TALISHA: What you wanna wait for?

ANNIE: Oranges isn't skin.

TALISHA: You don't need to wait you need to lie down and choose your colors.

> *(A ring tone sounds and ANNIE groans in annoyance.)*

TALISHA: Yo that's a wacked out ring shit.

> *(ANNIE looks at the caller ID and groans again.)*

MARGIE: What, it's your moms?

ANNIE (*Into the phone*): I'm busy.

TALISHA: That can't be her moms.

MARGIE: If that was *my* moms I *better* stay out all night cause next time she see me she hit me upside the back my head right. ANNIE:

THIS TATTOO GUY GETS TO USE ALL THE COLORS OR JUST A COUPLE?

TALISHA: 'Course he gets to use'm all. What you think this is?

MARGIE: Was it your moms?

ANNIE: What's up with this cat yo? What's he gonna take all night?

TALISHA: Nah, it was Malik.

MARGIE: Ooooo, *Malik.*

ANNIE: Give me water.

(MARGIE takes a bottle of Alize out and hands it to ANNIE, who takes a seasoned swig.)

TALISHA: What you getting, anyway?

MARGIE: Malik's mad cool.

ANNIE: Ladybug.

TALISHA: Ladybug?

MARGIE: Cute.

TALISHA: That's kinda stupid.

ANNIE: I like ladybugs.

MARGIE: What, you not diggin' on Malik?

ANNIE: Water.

TALISHA: It's like a little girl.

MARGIE: He got one of them slider phones.

TALISHA *(derisive)*: Ladybug.

MARGIE: Real nice.

TALISHA: What was that song?

ANNIE: This kid better come give me my tattoo a-sap or I'm about to jet, yo.

MARGIE: You seen that slider phone?

TALISHA: You know that song.

ANNIE: He so good how come he letting me get this shit for free? If he's so good he should wanna get paid, right?

TALISHA: Lady bug, lady bug, rings and rosie.

MARGIE: What are these words coming out your mouth?

TALISHA: Ladybug, ladybug rings around the roses, that's it.

ANNIE *(to MARGIE)*: What is she smoking?

TALISHA: That's it, that's it, right? Ladybug, ladybug, rings around the poses.

MARGIE: Oh yeah, she's high.

TALISHA: You know, that nurseries rhyme.

ANNIE: Talisha —

TALISHA: Yo, it's "T" now.

ANNIE: Talisha, there ain't no such thing as a nurseries rhyme.

TALISHA: You know what I mean.

ANNIE: Where is this kid?

TALISHA: Sing it with me.

MARGIE: High.

ANNIE: Water.

(ANNIE swigs.)

TALISHA: Ladybug ladybug, you know . . . ladybug, ladybug?

(ANNIE swigs.)

TALISHA: Sing it with me.

(ANNIE swigs.)

MARGIE: I'm not singing with you.

TALISHA: Ladybug, ladybug. *(Waits.)* Ladybug, ladybug . . . *(MARGIE looks at TALISHA.)* Come *on.*

MARGIE: Ms. Jones down the hall watched me I didn't go to no nurseries school.

TALISHA: Come *on. Ladybug, ladybug* . . .

MARGIE *(to ANNIE)*: You seen that slider phone?

(TALISHA groans.)

ANNIE: Your house is on fire your children will burn.

TALISHA: That ain't it.

ANNIE: I should wait.

MARGIE: So like, you and Malik?

TALISHA: That ain't *it.*

MARGIE: Jerome just got a flip phone no one else wanted to buy it was 19.99 and it sucks.

ANNIE: Those are the words.

TALISHA: Fuck you Margie those are not.

MARGIE: Me and Jerome we do it but slider phones are mad cool.

ANNIE: Your house is on fire your children will burn.

TALISHA: This kid better hurry up you're pissing me off.

MARGIE: We still do it all the time right cause I want one of those joggers.

TALISHA: Me too right. In pink right.

MARGIE: Pink yeah. The army kind.

TALISHA: If you would hurry up with Malik we can have our baby showers together. I want one of those tall cakes. If it's the three of us we could get three layers right? Three layers and three pink joggers and our baby girls will go to nurseries school together and learn all the right words to these dopey songs.

MARGIE: I think you should get a rose.

ANNIE: I don't like cake.

TALISHA: What you mean you don't like cake? You sayin' you never eat cake.

MARGIE: Maybe you should get a rose?

TALISHA: You don't eat cake.

ANNIE: Where is this kid?

MARGIE: It's forever. You should get something classic.

TALISHA: Everybody eats cake. You ain't so unique and special you don't eat cake like the rest of us.

MARGIE: You get a red rose it will match Malik's phone.

ANNIE: Well I don't like it, I just eat it cause everyone else does.

MARGIE: Don't you think that's cute? If your rose matched Malik's phone?

ANNIE: A ladybug is red.

TALISHA: A ladybug is *stupid.*

MARGIE: I've already taken three tests, you gotta get your move on, girl.

TALISHA: If you want the same shower, yeah, you better hurry your ass up.

MARGIE: Sierra and Cassie already gotten to see theirs on a screen.

TALISHA: Yeah, but they did it all wrong. I seen them at McDonald's before school and you not supposed to eat breakfast if you want a girl. They did it all wrong and now they both stuck with boys. That's what the screen say for both a them. Boys. I ain't goin' through all this trouble just to have boys you can't dress cute right. Those pee sticks is mad expensive I don't want to waste em all up.

MARGIE (*To ANNIE*): How many tests you take?

ANNIE: If this fool was for real we wouldn't have to come here in the dark and crap.

TALISHA: His cousin lets him practice in here at night.

MARGIE (*To ANNIE*): How many tests you take?

ANNIE: This is forever, yo, he better've done more than just practice on some friggin fruit yo.

TALISHA: I love mine.

ANNIE: It's crooked.

MARGIE: Annie. How many tests?

TALISHA: She ain't take no tests.

MARGIE: What, isn't Malik good at it?

ANNIE: Water.

(*MARGIE goes to hold out the bottle. ANNIE puts her hand out. MARGIE yanks the bottle back, teasing.*)

MARGIE: Malik any good or not?

TALISHA: She don't know.

ANNIE: Give me that.

MARGIE: Malik any good or not?

TALISHA: She goin' back on her word.

MARGIE: Jeez, Annie, you chickening out?

TALISHA: She don't wanna share a shower with us.

MARGIE: We gonna have girls and walk em together and stuff.

ANNIE: It's my birthday give me that.

(*MARGIE teases ANNIE with the bottle, then gives it to her. ANNIE swigs hard.*)

MARGIE: You got to. A tiny little baby go'na love you all for you. We each gonna have one and they all gonna wear pink.

TALISHA: She thinks she gonna go to school and shit.

MARGIE (*To TALISHA*): We go to school and it sucks.

TALISHA: Not dinky high school. College. Scholarship. I seen how Ms. Fitzgerald calls on you, is all sweet to you. (*To MARGIE:*) Every one likes cake but Miss Ladybug here. She think she too good for us.

MARGIE: You don't think the slider's a nice phone?

TALISHA: Slider's for chumps. She into those I ones.

MARGIE: Who you know can pay six hundred dollars for a phone?

TALISHA: She goin' back on it. Look at her.

ANNIE: This fool better hurry his self up.

TALISHA: I seen Ms. Fitzgerald, Annie, I seen her.

ANNIE: This my birthday or what?

MARGIE: Who you know go to college, Annie?

TALISHA: Every body like cake.

MARGIE: Who you know really gets out of here?

TALISHA: Every body like pink.

MARGIE: You goin' back, Annie?

(ANNIE'S phone rings. ANTWOINE enters.)

ANTWOINE: Sweet sixteen right?

(ANNIE lifts up her shirt again, lies back, and ANTWOINE sits, is about to go to work. The phone rings. ANNIE looks ahead. MARGIE looks at ANNIE. TALISHA looks at her nails.)

MARGIE (*To ANNIE*): No one around here has one of those I ones.

(MARGIE and ANNIE look at each other as the phone rings. ANTWOINE leans in, starts the tattoo needle and begins tattooing ANNIE.)

MARGIE: 'Cause I think we should all get matching bottles right.

TALISHA: I'll get you a test, yeah?

(ANNIE braces her body against the tattoo table. The phone rings. MARGIE looks at ANNIE. TALISHA looks at ANNIE. ANNIE looks to both of them. Ring. Ring. Finally ANNIE answers.)

ANNIE (*Into the phone*): Fine if you want. Just don't be late right?

(ANTWOINE leans in, works.)

ANNIE: I eat cake.

TALISHA: Right yo. Just like everyone else see.

ANNIE: Right. Yeah.

(The sound of the tattoo needle whirs as ANTWOINE leans into his work and ANNIE grips the table. The sound of the tattoo whir blends into the sound of fire, which rises, rises.)

END OF PLAY

WHAT STRONG FENCES MAKE

(World Premiere)

Israel Horovitz

Boston Theater Marathon Draft — Revised May, 2009.

Sponsored by Barefoot Theatre Company &
Gloucester Stage Company
Directed by Robert Walsh & Israel Horovitz
Uri Abromovitch. . . . . Sean Meehan
Itzhak Shiffman. . . . . Francisco Solorzano

Israel Horovitz's 70+ produced plays include *Line*, *The Indian Wants The Bronx*, *The Widow's Blind Date*, *Park Your Car In Harvard Yard*. Awards include OBIEs, Drama Desk Award, European Academy Award, decoration by France as Commandeur de l'Ordre des Arts et des Lettres. Horovitz founded Gloucester Stage and NY Playwrights Lab.

A few months ago, when British dramatist Caryl Churchill's controversial *Seven Jewish Children* was first offered to theaters, world-wide, via the internet, I was contacted by Ari Roth, Artistic Director of Theater J in Washington, DC. Mr. Roth was about to produce *Seven Jewish Children*, and asked me to read the Churchill play and write what he called "a response piece". On reading Ms. Churchill's play, my initial reaction was to not respond . . . certainly not to create a "competing" play to be shown in the same evening as the Churchill play . . . And so I stayed silent. But, on reflection, a few weeks after Churchill's play had come and gone from Theater J, I felt another voice needed to be heard. Over the past three weeks, I have written (and re-written) a new short play entitled *What Strong Fences Make*.

My play is, I think, simple and clear, and certainly needs no explanation from its author. But, I hasten to add that it's a simple and clear stage-play that attempts to make a statement about a real-life situation that is anything but simple and clear. But, *What Strong Fences Make* is, most definitely, a different point of view from Caryl Churchill's point of view, and certainly no less valid.

Theater J has agreed to make my play available to theaters, worldwide, via its website (go to www.theaterj.org, then click on "Middle East Festival"). Any theater wishing to translate and produce this play may do so, royalty free. But, I ask that a collection be taken among audience members and a donation be made to One Family Fund (www.onefamilyfund.org), a charity offering aid to children wounded in attacks on Israel. (One Family Fund aids Israeli-Jews, Israeli-Arabs, Israeli-Druze, Israeli-Bedouins, and children of diplomats living in Israel.)

I am well aware that I am an American, living thousands of miles away from the profound moral dilemma that Israelis must face each and every day of their lives. But, I am very much a Jew, and, as a writer who spends nearly as much time in Paris and London, as I do in NYC, I am angered by the rise in anti-Semitism, and by the confusion so often made these days between what is a Jewish action and what is an Israeli action . . . meaning, simply, it is possible to criticize Israel without being anti-Semitic, as it is possible to criticize Palestine without being anti-Arab. Thus, those who criticize Jews in the name of criticizing Israel, as Ms. Churchill seems to have done in her play, step over an unacceptable boundary and must be taken to task.

Israel Horovitz

CHARACTERS
> URI ABROMOVITCH, Israeli, late 20s, large, strong, handsome, scruffy beard
>
> ITZHAK SHIFFMAN, Israeli, late 20s, small, skinny, sweet-faced, thick beard

SETTING
> Military checkpoint, just outside entrance to Ramallah, West Bank, dawn

TIME
> Dawn, the present

. . .

In darkness, WE HEAR — A single violin, haunting. And then . . .
URI: Hold it! Stop! Don't come any closer!141
> *(LIGHTS FADE UP on URI, Israeli "milu'imnik" (military reservist). HE is nervous, frightened, holds M-16 trained on something in shadows.)*

URI: Come forward, slowly . . . Let me see your hands . . . Slowly!
> *(ITZHAK walks out of the shadows, his hands semi-raised, palms forward, as if to show URI he isn't armed. HE has Arab home-boy look, wears jeans, baggy t-shirt, loose fitting jacket, "kafeyah" (red and white checked scarf).)*

ITZHAK: This okay? . . .
URI: Fine. Stop there, please.
ITZHAK: What's the problem?
URI: Entrance is closed til 6 am. It's not 6, yet.
ITZHAK: *(Looks at watch.)* It's 5:52.
URI: This gate's frozen. Nobody crosses til 6.
ITZHAK: Really?
URI: Really. 6.
ITZHAK: You're precise.
URI: It's my job. I'm obliged. Papers?
> *(ITZHAK hands ID to URI.)*

ITZHAK: Okay?
URI: Why are you going in there?
ITZHAK: It's my job. I'm obliged.
URI: *(Studying Itzhak's ID.)* Shiffman? Itzhak?

ITZHAK: Yuh.

URI: I thought you were . . . Are you related to . . . ?

ITZHAK: Yuh. I am. That's me.

URI: Wow! I didn't recognize you! You look different. The beard. You got skinny. *(Pause. And then . . .)* I know what happened. I . . . I'm really sorry. *(No reply.)* Must have been so tough.

ITZHAK: It was what it was.

URI: I know your cousin Tali.

ITZHAK: How do you know Tali?

URI: From New York.

ITZHAK: I was going to say.

URI: I lived in New York, when I was little..

ITZHAK: She's back living there.

URI: She moved back?

ITZHAK: Last month. After the funeral.

URI: Understandable. *(Beat.)* I'm really sorry. *(Beat.)* There's nothing anybody can say, is there?

ITZHAK: Not a lot. Unless you have the balls to say "I'm glad it was you, not me."

URI: I . . . *(Beat. And then . . .)* I'm not glad it was you. I am glad it wasn't me. I wish it was nobody.

ITZHAK: That's soft.

URI: Yuh, well . . . Yuh. *(And then . . .)* It's amazing I didn't recognize you. You really look different.

ITZHAK: I lost quite a bit of weight.

URI: Really different. *(And then . . .)* Did you go to Geulim School?

ITZHAK: I did . . . til 5th grade.

URI: Were you in Aliza's homeroom, 4th grade?

ITZHAK: I sat three seats behind you.

URI: Holy shit! That's hilarious! I never put that together. Itzhak Shiffman. Little Itzi, right?

ITZHAK: *(Smiles.)* I haven't been Little Itzi for a while.

URI: You lived in Talpiyot, right?

ITZHAK: Til 5th grade. Then, we moved to Ramot.

URI: I remember that. That's amazing! Itzi. I lived upstairs over Ziggy Levin . . . .Miriam Levin . . .

ITZHAK: . . . Ziggy.

URI: . . . Ziggy. *(And then . . .)* I'm Uri Abromavitch.

ITZHAK: I know who you are.

URI: You and Ziggy were, like, a really serious couple in high school, right? You and Ziggy used to . . . *(Doesn't finish thought. And then . . .)* I have a friend who was one of the first ones to the bus. I . . . *(Doesn't finish thought.)* There was nothing anybody . . . *(Doesn't finish thought.)* I don't know what the fuck to say, man. Itzi, I . . . I'm sorry. I can't fuckin' imagine . . . *(Beat.)* I don't think I knew your wife.

ITZHAK: She was nice.

URI: I knew it was you when the kids were born. I mean, it was on TV and all. Ziggy reminded me who you were. *(Beat.)* I guess you kept up with her.

ITZHAK: I do.

URI: I saw their picture, maybe 6 months ago, on their birthday, just before . . . Were they identical?

ITZHAK: The boys were. The girl was . . .

URI: Right. Of course. There was a girl. I'm still single, so . . . *(Beat.)* My God, I can't imagine . . .

ITZHAK: Neither can I.

URI: I thought you were working at the university.

ITZHAK: I am. I teach.

URI: Oh, I thought . . . Right. I read that. What do you teach?

ITZHAK: Poetry.

URI: Right. I read that, too. Or maybe Ziggy told me. You've gotta' be one of the youngest professors.

ITZHAK: I am. The youngest.

URI: I think I knew that. I'm teaching. High school French. Nothing compared to what you're doing. *(And then, suddenly . . .)* Why are you trying to go in there, Itzhak? It's crazy fuckin dangerous in there. You're not allowed. You know this. *(No reply.)* Answer me. I'm serious. Why are you going in, Itzi? Especially, just here. I'm, like, watching my back, bigtime. It's the worst it's been since the intifada started. Two Reservists — ordinary "milu'imnikim" like me — got shot at this check-point in the last four weeks. Did you know Tomer Ronen?

ITZHAK: It must be 6.

URI: What? . . . 6 what?

ITZHAK: 6 o'clock. It must be 6 o'clock by now.

URI: You're not answering me. I need an answer, Itzhak. Why are you looking to go in there?

ITZHAK: I've got a job to do. I'm obliged.

URI: I've got to search you.

ITZHAK: No need. It's exactly what you think it is.

URI: Are you shitting me?

ITZHAK: Tell me what you would do? Tell me what you would do? Tell me what the fuck you would do? *(And then . . .)* I cannot live with it. I cannot live with it. I cannot fucking live with it.

URI: I . . . Are you wired? Answer me! ANSWER ME! *(No reply. URI is horrified.)* No, Itzhak. Not that. Nobody's ever done that.

ITZHAK: It was their first day of kindergarten. I teach an early graduate-level class on Tuesdays and it was my first class, so . . . *(Doesn't finish thought.)* My mother slept over so she could help my wife. I felt vaguely annoyed by the commotion in the house. All the attention was on the . . . *(Doesn't finish thought.)* I was up late writing my first lecture — on Wordsworth. Innocence and Experience. I . . . *(Doesn't finish thought.)* I tried to talk to my wife and my mother about my lecture, but, you know, they weren't interested. Dressing and feeding three kids . . . *(Beat.)* I felt vaguely annoyed. *(Beat.)* Actually, I felt totally fucking trapped. *(Beat.)* Who the hell ever expected to be 28 with three kids, pulling at me . . . ? I mean, I still have friends who are single, like you — dating, shit like that, and, here I am, 28, three kids, and I . . . *(Doesn't finish thought.)* I put them on the bus and I kiss them, but, not really, you know, meaning it. Then, I take my bus. . . . I feel relieved walking away from them . . . younger. I . . . *(Doesn't finish thought.)* On the bus, I'm chatting up this grad student. She is really hot . . . I tell her who I am and she goes "Wow! You're famous!", and I'm thinking "Okay. This is good! . . . and she goes "You've got the triplets! There was a picture of you and them in the paper!" And, right then, that same instant, we start hearing this alarm and these sirens, and she goes, in this whisper, "Something bad's happening." I think that maybe I . . . *(Doesn't finish thought.)* I recognize you, Uri. You've still got the same face, it's just, like, pumped up with air, but it's definitely you. I . . . *(Doesn't finish thought.)* I knew Ziggy was going out with you, once in a while. She was still going out with me once in a while, too, Uri. You must've known that, huh?

URI: I guess I did, yuh. Ziggy let that slip.

ITZHAK: I've got a job to do in there, Uri. I chose this entrance, 'cause I knew you'd be here. It's after 6. I'm going in. Just let it happen.

URI: I can't do that, Itzhak! You can't do that! No one's ever done that, man.

ITZHAK: "No one's ever done that"?! Are you blind or crazy?

URI: Them, not us. None of us has ever done that.

ITZHAK: Then let the games begin. I'm going in, Uri. Just let it happen. No one's going to blame you. No one's ever going to know. Just let it happen.

URI: I can't. You've gotta' get help, Itzhak. There are support groups . . . You can't do that!

ITZHAK: There's a bus terminal, three blocks inside. The 1st bus leaves the terminal at 6:15. It's going to be filled with their filthy little animals. I'm going to stop their filthy little animals from growing into what they grow into. I'm going to do that, Uri. I'm going to send them a message they never fucking dreamed they were gonna get. Me. I'm going to do that. So, either let me go in, or step the fuck out of my way.

URI: I can't let you, Itzhak. I can't.

(Without warning, ITZHAK punches URI, violently. URI reels backwards. ITZHAK punches him again. URI drops to ground, his gun falls from his hands. ITZHAK kicks gun aside.)

ITZHAK: I'm sorry, Uri. I'm sorry.

(ITZHAK walks past URI, exits. URI crawls to his gun, stands, quickly, calls out to ITZHAK.)

URI: ITZHAK! STOP! ITZHAK! ITZI! STOP! PLEASE STOP!

(URI takes aim, shoots offstage, two shots, killing Itzhak. Instantly, a flash of light and sound of Itzhak's body bomb exploding. URI, blown backwards, falls. Beat. HE rises to his knees, looks off, sobs. MUSIC: reprise of opening violin solo. And then . . . THE LIGHTS FADE TO BLACK.)

END OF PLAY

CLASS ACT, VERSION 379
(World Premiere)

HOLLY L. JENSEN

Original Production Information: Boston Theater Marathon
Sponsored by Turtle Lane Playhouse
Directed by James Tallach
Bailey . . . . Cameron James Reid
Stacy . . . . Gillian Gordon

Bailey and Stacy are high school sweethearts until the new kid in school and a Shakespearean sonnet test the boundaries of their love.

Class Act: Version 379 premiered at the Boston Theater Marathon and was produced at the Playwrights' Platform Summer Festival, where it received runner-up for best play. Recent productions include *Lizzy Izzy* at the 14th International Women's Playwriting Festival, Perishable Theater and *Vinum est Vita!* at the Infinite Story Festival, Exquisite Corps Theatre.

CHARACTERS
 BAILEY, 17, tough yet insecure
 STACY, 17, perky, wants to be liked

SETTING
 A high school classroom

TIME
 Now

. . .

Lights up. BAILEY and STACY are seated behind desks in a classroom. They remain perfectly quiet and still as the sound of a school alarm buzzes for five seconds.. After the buzzing ends, STACY jumps up from her seat and begins speaking energetically. BAILEY also stands, but he keeps his arms crossed and he looks annoyed to be there.

STACY: It looks exactly the same!

BAILEY: I barely remember.

STACY: Mrs. Johnson's desk was like in the exact same spot. She used to have a vase of daisies right at the edge.

BAILEY: I knocked it over once . . . by accident, of course.

STACY: And she used to like have a red cushion with gold flowers on her chair. *(STACY moves around to look and point at various things.)* Eric was here. Hilary was in front. No, that was Jackie? Yes, Jackie! And Thomas to the left. *(BAILEY cringes at the sound of THOMAS'S name.)* No, he was on the right. Next to you! Like how could I forget! And I was here. Like nothing's changed!

BAILEY: Always the same.

STACY: Even the book shelves. Crime and Punishment. Catch 22. Pride and Prejudice! My favorite! I mean, I didn't actually like read the book. I saw the movie. Like so romantic!

BAILEY: Pride and Prejudice and Zombies. Now that was a killer flick.

STACY: Bailey, he acts like he's not, ya know, into the whole like romance thing, but I know he really is.

BAILEY: Stace's my girl.

STACY: We met a couple years ago.

BAILEY: I was workin'. At PJ's Tavern.

STACY: Like such a cute little place, ya know.

BAILEY: A total dive.

STACY: At the foot of Mt. Minnow.

BAILEY: Middle of fuckin' nowhere.

STACY: Everyone was like so friendly.

BAILEY: A bunch of smelly drunks.

STACY: I was there with my two cousins . . . my older cousins. And there was a karaoke machine.

BAILEY: I hated that thing.

STACY: So we like decided to sing a few songs. 'Cuz like, we didn't know anyone. And we had a few wine coolers. Kiwi blackberry. Like so delicious. I remember, I was feelin' tipsy.

BAILEY: The thong song. That's what she sang.

STACY: First we sang Sweet Home Alabama. Then Vogue. And then . . . the thong song

BAILEY: She looked hot.

STACY: After we were done, Bailey, he like sent an empty plate over to my table that said . . .

BAILEY: Call me, 932-229-222

STACY: It was written in chocolate syrup! Isn't that sweet? We've been together 11 months now.

(A beat.)

BAILEY: Fuckin' homo.

STACY: I'm thinkin' we'll get married after graduation. We like talked about it a little.

BAILEY: I mean, did he really think he could get away with that shit? Not showin' up like that?

STACY: Thomas was our friend, ya know. I mean, he'd just moved here 'bout six months ago. His Dad's a doctor. Like a heart doctor or somethin'.

BAILEY: Ya can't mess with someone like that.

STACY: We hung out a few times. Ya know, like went to his house, played pool. Had a few beers. 'Cuz like his Dad was never home. They even had a horse. Like a real horse.

BAILEY: So he had money. Big fuckin' deal.

STACY: I wanna have a baby right away. I already told Bailey. I mean, we don't wanna be like old when we have kids, ya know. Those mothers who look like grandmothers.

BAILEY: Thomas, does he really think he's better than us? 'Cuz his Dad's a doctor? I fuckin' hate that. I hate doctors. I mean, who the hell made them God? Decidin' who lives, who dies? My Dad was a coal miner. Worked his whole fuckin' life in them mines. And when he wasn't there, he was drinkin'. Cirrhosis ain't no way to die. Ain't no doctor that coulda saved him.

STACY: My family, we own a chip factory. And I help out, ya know, like after school and weekends. But my Dad, he says I can work more after graduation. I'll be in charge of like processin' potatoes, keeping ahead of all of the orders that come in and makin' sure they go back out. It's a lot of responsibility. So like, it's totally perfect.

BAILEY: It was beautiful.

(A beat.)

STACY: Sometimes, Bail, he'd visit me at work.

BAILEY: Fuckin' beautiful.

STACY: The first time, he just wanted to hold it.

BAILEY: Heavy. It was heavy. But I was careful.

STACY: It was so heavy. I like had to use two hands. And so shiny. I helped polished it.

BAILEY: A locked-breech, semi-automatic, single-action, recoil-operated pistol.

STACY: It was my Dad's. He kept it at the factory. Just in case.

BAILEY: Browning Hi-Power Mk I. Uses a 13-round staggered magazine.

STACY: There was this one time. In English class. Mrs. Johnson, she had each of us choose a sonnet. From like Shakespeare or somethin'. And we had to read it out loud. In front of the whole class. And when it came to Thomas, he chose the really famous one . . .

BAILEY: I mean, what the fuck was he thinkin'?

(STACY recites the following Shakespearean sonnet as if she's trying to seduce BAILEY or the audience with the words.)

STACY: "Shall I compare thee to a Summer's day?
Thou art more lovely and more temperate.
Rough winds do shake the darling buds of May,
And Summer's lease hath all too short a date."

BAILEY: It was weird, he stood right in front of my row.

STACY: "Sometime too hot the eye of heaven shines,
And oft' is his *(STACY stresses the word "his")* gold complexion dimm'd."

BAILEY: Thomas, he looked right at me. When he was readin' that stupid poem.

STACY: "And every fair from fair sometime declines,
By chance or nature's changing course untrimm'd.
But thy eternal Summer shall not fade
Nor lose possession of that fair thou owest;
Nor shall Death brag thou wanderest in his shade."

BAILEY: And again. He looked at me again. I mean, what the fuck? Ain't that poem written to some douche bag? What's up with the "his"?

STACY: "When in eternal lines to time thou growest:
So long as men can breathe, or eyes can see.
So long lives this, and this gives life to thee."

BAILEY: Why the fuck's he keep starin' at me?

STACY: I know Bailey really loves me. I mean, a lot of guys say they love their girls. 'Cuz they wanna get in their pants and stuff. But not Bailey, he's different. I mean, he is so respectful. Like, not once has he tried to do that. He says he wants to wait, ya know. Wants it to be super special.

BAILEY: My stomach, it started turnin'. I took my pencil and started jammin' it in my notebook. Broke off the tip and just kept pushin' it through the paper . . . pretendin' it was Thomas's face.

STACY: Like this one time. I was at Bailey's. We were kissin' in his room and I was gettin' a little . . . ya know, hot. So I was like wantin' for him to do somethin'. And after a bit, I just couldn't take it no more. So I put his hand up my shirt. It was sweet, ya know. Like he didn't know what to do. And he just like grabbed my tit and held it. 'Cuz he was nervous, I guess.

BAILEY: Stacy, she was better friends with Thomas. And, I told her, told her I wanted to knock him out.

STACY: I don't know. I mean, Thomas, he was kinda shy. And Bailey, he wasn't, ya know. So maybe like Thomas kinda admired him for that. But Bailey, he like couldn't let it go . . . it was like he became totally obsessed.

BAILEY: She got on my nerves, always naggin' me to drop it. Tellin' me to forget the poem and shit, to ignore Thomas. But it wasn't just the poem . . .

STACY: I just . . . I just wanted him to forget it, ya know. Or just deal with it . . . talk to him. Find out if it was somethin'.

BAILEY: When I got that email . . .

STACY: That email.

BAILEY: I can't . . . can't even repeat what it said. It was fuckin' disgustin'.

STACY: The email, it was from Thomas. And Bailey, he wouldn't even show it to me. Said it was bad. Real bad . . . thought he was just gonna mess him up. Thomas, he was bein' stupid and ignorin' me anyways. I didn't care none. I don't know, I guess I was kinda pissed that he was hittin' on my guy. I mean, what's up with that?

BAILEY: Stacy, she let me borrow the gun.

STACY: He came by the factory one Friday after school. Said he just wanted to borrow it for the weekend . . . I didn't know . . .

BAILEY: I told her I just wanted to take it home. To show my cousin. *Bailey laughs.* I hid it in my gym bag.

STACY: On Monday, we were in English class. I remember, we were readin' Beowulf. I mean, we were really readin' it. Not like watchin' the movie with Angelina Jolie, who gets all naked in gold and stuff. And Bailey, he just like got up and walked outta class. Mrs. Johnson, she yelled after him. And I got up, but she told me to sit down . . . I keep wonderin' if things would've been different if I hadn't . . . anyways, a few minutes goes by and then there was this crash. And the classroom door flew open. And it was Bailey. And he looked weird. I mean, his eyes, they were all glassy and shit. Kinda zombie-like. And he had my Dad's gun in his hand.

BAILEY: I mean, I just planned to scare him. That's all. Just wanted to see Thomas . . . like react, ya know. Do somethin'. Say somethin'. He was fuckin' with me. So I like pointed the gun at his head and told everyone that he was a homo . . . and he didn't say shit. Just sat there starin' at me with them dark eyes. And I watched his piss draw a line down his pants. I thought, I don't wanna see this digustin' pig ever again. I thought, I can be the hero. Save our school from this homo, ya know . . . so I like shot him.

STACY: Sounded like a firecracker. Happened so fast.

BAILEY: Mrs. Johnson, she started screamin'. So fuckin' loud. And I just had to make it stop. Had to shut her up.

STACY: Mrs. Johnson, our teacher. She had young children. Pictures on her desk, ya know. She looked like one of them grandmother types.

BAILEY: Stacy man, she just stood up and she stared at me. With a strange look. Like she hated me. I was afraid, man. Like what if she didn't wanna be with me no more?

STACY: I didn't know he'd go like totally crazy. I just wanted to get his atten- tion. I mean, why didn't he realize that I sent him that email from Thom- as? I mean, I totally didn't expect . . . I just wanted to know . . . I mean, when Bailey responded, like what did that mean? I just didn't believe it, ya know. Like Bailey totally agreed to meet him. And he must've been so pissed when Thomas didn't show up . . . but what was I supposed to do? I didn't know . . .

BAILEY: She didn't even scream . . . just looked at me and said my name. Once. And . . . I shot her . . . Stacy, she fell backwards, over her desk. But her eyes were still open. Still lookin' at me with that horror . . . I couldn't see nothin' after that. Everythin' was loud and fuzzy . . . I, I didn't know what to do . . . so . . . I put the gun in my mouth.

(STACY and BAILEY freeze. They remain perfectly quiet and still as

the sound of a school alarm buzzes again for five seconds. After it stops, STACY begins speaking energetically, BAILEY crosses his arms and looks annoyed to be there, a repeat from the beginning.)

STACY: It looks exactly the same!

BAILEY: I barely remember.

STACY: Mrs. Johnson's desk was like in the exact same spot. She used to have a vase of daisies right at the edge.

BAILEY: I knocked it over once . . . by accident, of course.

STACY: And she used to like have a red cushion with gold flowers on her chair. *(STACY moves around to look and point at various things.)* Eric was here. Hilary was in front. No, that was Jackie? Yes, Jackie! And Thomas to the left. *(BAILEY cringes at the sound of THOMAS'S name.)* No, he was on the right. Next to you! Like how could I forget! And I was here. Like nothing's changed!

BAILEY: Always the same.

(Lights out.)

END OF PLAY

WAITING FOR GRETCHEN

Susan Kosoff

Waiting for Gretchen was originally produced for the Boston Theater Marathon XI, May 17, 2009, by the Wheelock Family Theatre, Boston, MA.

Directed by Susan Kosoff
Jane. . . . . Jane Staab
John . . . . John Davin
Gretchen. . . . . .Erin Jenkins

John is sure he knows what daughter Gretchen is coming to announce. He and wife Jane spar with sparks flying until Gretchen arrives to reveal her true intent.

Susan Kosoff is a producer, director, playwright, author, professor, and founder of the Wheelock Family Theatre. She has an extensive background in educational and theatrical consulting, and her plays have been performed on stages around the country. Her latest publication is *The Young Actor's Book of Improvisation* (with Sandra Caruso).

CHARACTERS
    JANE: a middle-aged woman
    JOHN: a middle-aged man
    GRETCHEN: their 24-year-old daughter

SETTING
    The kitchen

TIME
    Cocktail hour, the present

. . .

JOHN: Is it 5:00 yet?
JANE: Very close.
JOHN: I'm tired of working.
JANE: So stop.
JOHN: I like a reason other than that I'm tired. I know it's silly.
JANE: Quite. However, the fact is that it is now 5:00.
JOHN: Goodie. I'll wash up.
JANE: What will you have?
JOHN: What are you having?
JANE: I thought I might have a Cape Codder.
JOHN: Really?
JANE: Really. And you?
JOHN: Well, I was going to have a glass of wine, but I must say a Cape Codder sounds tasty.
JANE: Would you like me to do the honors?
JOHN: Oh, no. I'm happy to do it.
JANE: There's some munchies next to the sink you can bring over, too.
JOHN: I see. How nice. *(Making drinks.)* The Connolly family calls the cocktail hour attitude adjustment hour. I suspect they do a lot of attitude adjusting. Did I ever tell you that? *(Brings drinks.)* Here you go. Cheers.
JANE: Thank you. Cheers. Yes, many times.
JOHN: So I have. Here. Have some munchies?
JANE: I will. Just set them down. No need to rush. You're a retired man now.
JOHN: I'm a tired man now that I'm working for you. *(Sits.)* Ah, it is nice to put my feet up. I haven't stopped since lunch. *(Sighs.)* Oh, this is tasty.
JANE: Now that you've quit smoking you don't take as many breaks.
JOHN: I don't take any. There's nothing to do on a break if you don't smoke.
JANE: I'm glad you quit.

JOHN: You never said.

JANE: What good would it have done?

JOHN: I might have quit sooner.

JANE: I doubt it. Most people do things when they are ready and not a minute sooner. Besides, you only would have gotten stubborn about it. You always dig your heels in when somebody tells you what to do.

JOHN: I don't know about that. You're not just any old somebody. I might have taken what you had to say to heart.

JANE: Perhaps. We'll never know now.

JOHN: I suppose not. How's your drink?

JANE: Just fine, thank you. Did I tell you Gretchen was coming by?

JOHN: No.

JANE: Well, she is. Probably anytime now.

JOHN: For any special reason?

JANE: She said she wanted to talk to us.

JOHN: About?

JANE: She didn't say.

JOHN: Do you think she's going to tell us she's gay?

JANE: I assume she assumes we assume as much.

JOHN: Oh. Well, what then? That she's not gay?

JANE: Very funny. I don't know. Perhaps, unlike you, she has more on her mind than her sexual orientation.

JOHN: At her age? I doubt it. When did she say she'd be here?

JANE: After work.

JOHN: So here we sit waiting for Godot. I mean Gretchen.

JANE: We're not waiting for Gretchen. We're adjusting our attitudes and Gretchen is stopping by.

JOHN: I was trying to be funny.

JANE: I'm glad you told me. Was that something the Connollys used to say?

JOHN: All right. How's that drink?

JANE: Still fine, thank you.

JOHN: Seriously, why do you think she wants to talk with us?

JANE: Seriously, I don't have any idea. And what's more I don't know why it has you so agitated.

JOHN: You'll think I'm being foolish.

JANE: If I do, it won't be the first time or the last, I'm sure.

JOHN: I think she's going to tell us she wants to have a baby.

JANE: Really?

JOHN: Yes, really. And not the old-fashioned way.

JANE: Meaning?

JOHN: Meaning she wants to use artificial insemination.

JANE: What in heaven's name gives you that idea?

JOHN: She did. The last time she was here. Remember she came with her pregnant friend — what's her name — Karen?

JANE: Yes.

JOHN: There was something about the way she kept asking her questions. I can't say exactly. It wasn't even what she said but how and she kept looking at Karen's big belly.

JANE: Well, fancy that.

JOHN: Of course I could be wrong.

JANE: True.

JOHN: I certainly hope I am. Want a second?

JANE: Why?

JOHN: Because you've finished your first.

JANE: No. I mean, yes, I'd like another. But, why do you hope you're wrong? *(Takes glass.)* Easier on the vodka this time.

JOHN: I don't like the idea.

JANE: Which?

JOHN: Come to think of it, I'm not crazy about any of it. Single parenting is bad enough but artificial insemination is over the top.

JANE: You've chewed this one over a bit, haven't you?

JOHN: I guess I have. Here. Your Cape Codder, easy on the vodka. Cheers.

JANE: Cheers. I think you should just let Gretchen bring up what she wants to talk about.

JOHN: Of course.

JANE: You may be completely off base.

JOHN: We'll see.

JANE: Indeed. My, my, my.

JOHN: What if I happen to be right?

JANE: I don't know.

JOHN: Really?

JANE: Really. I have to think about it.

JOHN: You have to think about artificial insemination?

JANE: That's your male ego talking.

JOHN: What do you mean my male ego?

JANE: Just what I said.

JOHN: What about it?

JANE: Men just can't stand the idea they have become superfluous when it comes to making babies.

JOHN: You know I resent your lumping me into some grand generalization about all men. And, if I'm not mistaken, sperm is still a necessary ingredient in making babies.

JANE: That's my point.

JOHN: Which is what exactly?

JANE: Forget it. She'll be here soon enough.

JOHN: I don't want to forget it.

JANE: Well, I do.

(Long pause.)

JOHN: But what if I'm right?

JANE: What if you are?

JOHN: You're not going to go along with it, are you? I'm certainly not.

JANE: I don't think we have much to say on the matter.

JOHN: Well, I have a lot to say on the matter. We are still her parents. And I, for one, don't like the idea. Not one bit. I don't just not like it. I can't stand it. I won't stand it. And she is going to have to hear how I feel about it, whether she likes it or not. I'm telling you that now. I went along with the gay thing, but I'm going to put my foot down on this one.

JANE: Don't fracture your foot. You do feel strongly about this, dear. *(Doorbell rings several times.)* There she is. Now, let her talk first.

GRETCHEN: *(Entering, Starbucks in hand.)* Hello. Hello. Anybody home?

JANE: Hello, darling. We're in here.

(Gretchen kisses them both.)

JOHN: Hi, kiddo. Want a drink?

GRETCHEN: *(Sitting.)* No thanks. Karen and I stopped for coffee. How are you? How's the no smoking going?

JOHN: Karen?

JANE: You look good. You always look good to me. How's work?

JOHN: So, what's going on with Karen?

GRETCHEN: Whoa, slow down a minute, you two. Let me catch my breath.

JANE: Of course, you must be tired.

JOHN: We've been waiting for you.

JANE: Adjusting our attitudes.

GRETCHEN: With the Connollys, no doubt.

JANE: No doubt.

JOHN: Ha ha. Your mother said you wanted to talk with us.

JANE: As you can see your father has gotten himself in quite a tizzy about it.

GRETCHEN: Why?

JOHN: Why? Well, we'll see.

JANE: John . . . enough. How is Karen?

GRETCHEN: The baby is due any minute. What's up?

JOHN: Baby? What baby? Whose baby?

JANE: Nothing, dear. We're just happy to see you.

JOHN: Do you have something in particular you want to say?

GRETCHEN: Mostly, I wanted to see you and . . .

JOHN: And what? Because I do.

GRETCHEN: Do what?

JOHN: Have something to say.

JANE: Now, John.

JOHN: Now John nothing.

GRETCHEN: What's going on?

JANE: Why don't you tell us what you wanted to tell us before I murder your father?

GRETCHEN: I've decided with a lot of thought. It hasn't been a rash decision even though it could . . .

JOHN: Could what?

JANE: Of course not, dear.

GRETCHEN: Could seem rash.

JOHN: You can skip the preamble.

JANE: John.

GRETCHEN: No, I want you to know how deliberate I've been about this. I know that I can handle it, even though it won't be easy.

JOHN: What? What can you handle?

JANE: Please, will you let her talk?

JOHN: I am letting her talk.

GRETCHEN: I'm getting to it. It's a big change, that's all, and I want you to understand. I guess I want your blessing.

JOHN: Aha! What did I tell you?

JANE: *(Swats him.)* It might be best if you just told us what you've decided and then we can talk about it.

GRETCHEN: Right. Okay. Here goes. I'm going to quit my day job and move to New York. I want to put my acting career first.

JOHN: That's it?

GRETCHEN: That's it.

JANE: That's it.

JOHN: No baby?

GRETCHEN: Baby?

JANE: No baby.

END OF PLAY

JOAN, JOAN, JOAN AND HITLER

(World Premiere)

RYAN LANDRY

Sponsored by Gold Dust Orphans
Directed by Ryan Landry
Adolph Hitler . . . . Larry Coen
Joan Crawford. . . . . .Billy Hough
Joan Jett . . . . Scott Martino
Joan of Arc . . . . .Megan Love

"Joan, Joan, Joan and Hitler" is a short play with a lot on it's mind.
It's an exercise in futility, a wandering piece of space junk that landed
somewhere between my head and my heart while I was trying to
think of something more important. The reader must judge it as
they see fit and take comfort in the knowing that it's author would
probably feel exactly the same about their work, were he to take the
time to actually read it.

Ryan Landry is Ryan Landry.

CHARACTERS
Adolph Hitler
Joan Crawford
Joan Jett
Joan of Arc

. . .

*The actors enter and take their seats facing the audience. For a full 60
seconds they sit in silence watching the second hand of a really big electric
clock hanging above their heads. (Yes! You do need a clock.) They may
look through their papers, sip their sodas, clear their throats etc. but for
the most part there is silence. Finally . . .*

HITLER: *(Checking his watch: sighing.)* . . . Well, that's one more minute of your
lives you've wasted. Anyone . . . ? *(Joan Jett raises her hand.)* . . . Joan?

JETT: . . . When do we eat?

HITLER: Is food that important to you?

JETT: That and pussy! *(Laughing, looking at the clock.)* . . . But who the hell
serves pussy at this hour?
*(She thinks this is very funny. The others do not. Especially Joan
Crawford.)*

CRAWFORD: *(Indignant.)* . . . That mouth!

HITLER: *(Keeping things calm with a warning tone.)* . . . Miss Crawford, we've
been over this! . . . In this room, Miss Jett is allowed to speak her mind
regardless of it's content. She is free to voice what she feels in her heart
. . . her concerns, her joys as well as her most intimate fantasies. *(Crawford
starts.)* . . . WITHOUT judgment. After all we ARE among friends.

CRAWFORD: . . . She's a punk!

JETT: . . . EAT SHIT!

CRAWFORD: *(To Hitler.)* . . . You see?!!! *(To Jett.)* . . . THAT is precisely the sort
of language that landed you here in the first place!

HITLER: *(To Crawford: chuckling: like a father.)* . . . Joan! I'm surprised at you.
. . . You speak of this maximum security psychiatric prison lost somewhere between space, time and reality as if it were a bad thing.

CRAWFORD: *(Melodramatically: looking around.)* . . . It's hell is what it is.
*(Hitler now turns to Joan of Arc, who all the while has been praying/
mumbling to herself.)*

HITLER: . . . Why so quiet, Joan?

ARC: *(Coming out of it.)* . . . I'm sorry. It's these voices. They tell me to do one
thing and then you tell me to do another. I suppose I'm just confused.

CRAWFORD: *(Cold as ice.)* . . . Arn't we all?

HITLER: No. No, I'm afraid I don't agree. I certainly don't think that our studio audience is confused. *(Standing: addressing the audience.)* . . . Are you?

CRAWFORD: *(Flipping out: grabbing Hitler and sitting him back down.)* . . . STOP IT! STOP IT! DO NOT DO THAT!!!! You must NEVER break the fourth wall!

HITLER: And why not?

CRAWFORD: *(Like a broken doll.)* Because once the wall is broken you must let the people in! The wall breaks and the people crawl toward you like roaches! They want to touch you! Tempt you! Taste you! . . . Oh, sure, it's all fine and dandy to have a million fans jerking off to your every move when you're up there on the screen! On the screen you're indestructible. No'one can touch you! You're an architectural dream . . . made of iron and steel! . . . But on the stage, well . . . that's a different story. The stage can tear you down, turn the skyscraper to a tiny coffin made of glass, turn the big golden trophy to a cheap china cup. The slightest bump and then you crack!

JETT: Aw, shut your blow hole. Some people have real problems.

(Crawford leaps to her feet as does Jett.)

HITLER: *(Separating them.)* . . . Joans!!!

(They are about to go at it when Arc screams and collapses on the floor. She writhes and shakes on the floor as if she were having a SEVERE epileptic seizure. Jett is the only one who helps her. Hitler and Crawford just stand and stare at Arc as if she were an animal in the zoo.)

JETT: *(Holding Arc down on the floor.)* . . . She's having another one of her fits! Hold her head! I'll get the spoon. Don't let her swallow her tongue this time! I'll be right back!

(She exits. Arc continues to writhe on the floor. After a while she begins to moan softly as her seizure subsides. Hitler and Crawford watch enraptured. Without taking their eyes off Arc, they produce a TV tray that holds two cans of beer and a box of Cheeto's. They sit and snack and stare at Arc as if they are sitting and watching a drama on TV. Arc now lies still, her seizure having ended.)

HITLER: . . . Definitely not as good as last week.

CRAWFORD: You know these young actresses today. No conviction. Too busy twittering to give a real performance . . .

ARC: *(Getting up and storming off.)* . . . That's it!

CRAWFORD: Well you don't have to get all indignant! *(To Hitler.)* . . . In my day stars were stars. Young girls like that one either "had it" or they didn't. SHE definitely doesn't have "it".

HITLER: She's young.

CRAWFORD: So?! In this business you either fuck your way to the top or you're out on your can.

HITLER: What's that got to do with her performance?

CRAWFORD: Nothing, I suppose.

HITLER: Well, try being a little more patient. Remember, not every woman possesses your talent, beauty, charm or those beautiful tits.

CRAWFORD: That's what I love about you, Adolf. You tell it like it is. *(They kiss. Hitler pulls away and begins to weep softly. As if consoling a shy boy.)* . . . What is it?

HITLER: *(As Crawford wipes his tears away.)* . . . I don't know. It's just that . . . There's something rather liberating about this style of writing. It makes me feel sort of . . . Well . . . dare I say it? . . . "Joyful".

CRAWFORD: *(Smiling.)* . . . Adolf!

HITLER: I mean in the "real" world I am Adolf Hitler . . . the most hated man in show business. But now, because of one playwright's vision . . . here I am in the arms of a Hollywood legend . . . successfully posing as a modern day psychiatrist . . . with a heart of gold even! . . . Geez! Who woulda' thunk it?!

CRAWFORD: *(Throwing her head back, laughing.)* . . . "Viva La Difference!"
(Arc enters with Jett in her arms. She is dead.)

ARC: . . . She's gone. I couldn't save her.

CRAWFORD: Drug overdose no doubt.

HITLER: Wait a minute! I thought you were the one on the brink of a melodramatic death scene!

ARC: I don't know what you're talking about.

HITLER: Yes, you do! Now stop it. When we last saw her she was running to find a spoon for you . . . and when we last saw you, you were just coming out of a severe epileptic seizure! . . . You may also recall that Miss Crawford and I were kind enough to critique your performance in the most constructive way we could without laughing our heads off and how did you thank us? By storming off in a huff!

CRAWFORD: I don't remember that.

HITLER: . . . What?!

CRAWFORD: You can't have it both ways, "Dolfy". If this young girl says she's healthy we have no choice but to believe her. I think they call this style "existentialism" or "da da" or "surreal -adoo-da-dad", something like that. Anyway, whatever they call it, WE, meaning us . . . are supposed to believe everything the other actors tell us and just go along with it no matter what happens. We are not to question their words even when they make absolutely no sense to us whatsoever. It's a style that was very popular back in the 60's and 70's when writers were to lazy or high to come up with a plot. Samuel Beckett started it I think, though it might have been Pinter or Ionesco. Who knows? I suppose it doesn't really matter so long as I *say* it doesn't. As long as I say it with conviction. Anyway, the A.R.T. does it all the time so you know it's gotta be legit.

HITLER: I've never heard of anything so absurd!

CRAWFORD: Well, I distinctly remember you saying not more than two paragraphs ago, how much you enjoy this type of theater. How "liberating" it is to think outside the bun.

ARC: You mean the box.

CRAWFORD: *(Pointing her finger at Arc.)* . . . Aha! Another hypocrite!

JETT: *(Sitting up.)* . . . Time check.

CRAWFORD: *(Checking the clock.)* . . . CHRIST! Five minutes . . . and I'm already bored. *(To the audience.)* . . . Look, how about you just let us go?

HITLER: . . . You can't do that!

CRAWFORD: . . . And why not?

HITLER: *(Pouting.)* . . . Because I'm having fun! Plus the rest of us worked really hard memorizing these ridiculous lines . . . right girls? *(Arc and Jett agree.)* . . . C'mon, Joan, it's only ten minutes. Remember, not everybody's a big Hollywood legend who can just rattle off dialogue as easily as you can . . . as if it were everyday conversation! Some of us had to practice!

CRAWFORD: *(Glaring at the audience.)* Alright . . . But I can tell by the looks on their faces they're having a terrible time. *(Turning.)* . . . Oh, but I suppose if you were lounging in some cushy seat over at the Calderwood Pavillion . . . you'd be having the time of your lives! I suppose if we were all out in Cambridge squatting "indian style" among the Ivy League hippie elite you'd be shitting your pants with gratitude right now! . . . Well, you're not and we're not so FUCK this modern mumbo jumbo crap, let's get down to the nitty gritty, lay our cards on the table and stop all this pussyfootin' around! If indeed we MUST spend an entire ten minutes together lets at LEAST engage ourselves in some sort of intelligent conversation! And I don't mean some long juvenile pop culture "rap" either. I couldn't give two shits about Lindsay Lohan's latest black eye or how she got it, got it?! . . . I want serious answers to serious questions! I want to know . . . from you . . . the people . . . Are you for or against . . .

(Three gunshots. Crawford falls to floor. Arc holds the gun.)

ARC: *(Smiling.)* . . . How's that for "conviction"?

HITLER: *(Running to Crawford.)* . . . Joan! Are you hurt?!

CRAWFORD: *(Sarcastically.)* . . . No. I'm down here practicing yoga! . . . OF COURSE I'M HURT! That french punk just shot me . . . three times . . . in the back!

HITLER: . . . How could you do this?!

ARC: Don't look at me. I only do what my voices tell me to.

HITLER: I thought you were a saint!

ARC: . . . Since when did you get all "Catholic"?!

CRAWFORD: You'll burn for this!

ARC: Too late!

HITLER: *(Back to Crawford.)* Joan! You can't really be dying. After all, you said yourself . . . this isn't reality . . . it's just a style . . .

CRAWFORD: I also said my daughters book would flop . . . and look where that got me. *(Poetically.)* . . . And now . . . as I lay dying . . . who will mourn the worst mother of all time?

HITLER: *(Tenderly.)* . . . You're remembered by the gays. At least the gays love you. No'one loves me.

CRAWFORD: Don't be foolish. And stop trying to hog all the sympathy for yourself. This is my death scene and if that little bitch is gonna shoot me in the back I should at least show her how to die!

HITLER: Your body may die but I swear to you that "Pepsi" will go on forever.

CRAWFORD: . . . Thank you. What a lovely sentiment. *(As she dies.)* . . . Now please . . . stop talking.

(Hitler breaks down and cries over the body. Arc then shoots Hitler three times. Jett and Arc now stand over the bodies.)

JETT: *(Blase.)* . . . Another one bites the dust.

ARC: *(Sighing.)* . . . I suppose he was nice enough once you got to know him. But who has time for intimacy these days.

JETT: *(Kicking at the bodies.)* . . . How do we know they're really dead? People come back to life all the time in these plays.

ARC: Let's watch and wait. That should at least eat up another minute.

JETT: O.K. *(Beat.)* . . . . Did you ever wonder what it's really all about?

ARC: What's that?

JETT: I mean this ridiculous existence. This "life" or what people call a life. Where are we really? And what the fuck are we really doing here?

ARC: *(Hearing her "voices".)* . . . Shhh. Listen . . .

JETT: . . . I don't hear anything.

ARC: . . . You will.

(The lights fade as Jett and Arc listen to what their voices tell them.)

END OF PLAY

NOT FUNNY
Original Production

CHRISTOPHER LOCKHEARDT

Sponsored by Metro Stage Company
Directed by Lisa Rafferty
Brad . . . . Jeff Mahoney
Emily . . . . Aimee Doherty

Laugh and the world laughs with you. Unless you're **bleeding on its floor.**

Christopher Lockheardt writes short plays because he can only concentrate on making one point at a time. To date he has made a dozen points 64 times in 40 theaters.

CHARACTERS
   BRAD, Man, any marriageable age
   EMILY, Woman, similar age

SETTING
   A kitchen

TIME
   Now

.   .   .

At center stage, facing each other, stands EMILY and BRAD. They are both staring in befuddlement at a steak knife whose handle is protruding from Brad's abdomen. Blood from the wound is soaking into his shirt. After a beat, they look up at each other, Brad with an expression of pale bemusement, Emily with one of horror.

BRAD: I think I get your point.
   (He sinks to his knees. Emily rushes to his aid.)
EMILY: Oh my god! Brad, I'm so sorry! I didn't mean to —
   (She stops and straightens up.)
EMILY: Wait. Was that a joke?
   (Brad smiles weakly up at her.)
EMILY: That was a joke, wasn't it? You just made a joke. I stabbed you in the stomach with a steak knife and you made a joke about it.
BRAD: Not funny?
EMILY: I stabbed you! In the stomach! With a steak knife! With one of my good steak knives!
BRAD: I think the knife's okay.
EMILY: I stabbed you! And you made a joke about it!
BRAD: Sorry.
EMILY: See? This is exactly what I was talking about!
BRAD: You were talking about stabbing me in the stomach?
EMILY: No!
BRAD: I was about to say, I should have been paying better attention then.
EMILY: You're still joking!
BRAD: I'm sorry! It's keeping my mind off the bleeding!
EMILY: You do this with everything! Everything! I try to talk to you, to tell you

things that are important to me, things that should be important to you. And what do you do?

BRAD: Bleed?

EMILY: Joke! Make wisecracks! Sweep it all under the funny ha-ha rug!

BRAD: The what?

EMILY: Why can't you ever take anything seriously? Why can't you ever take me seriously?

BRAD: I do take you seriously!

EMILY: No! You don't!

BRAD: You just stabbed me in the stomach with a steak knife! How can I not take you seriously?

(Pause.)

EMILY: I'm sorry I stabbed you.

BRAD: That's okay.

EMILY: I didn't think I was going to do it.

BRAD: I didn't think you were either.

EMILY: I just wanted you to listen to me.

BRAD: I was listening to you.

EMILY: You were not!

BRAD: Of course I was!

EMILY: What was I saying then?

BRAD: Ummm . . . You know, the whole . . . the whole ummm . . .

EMILY: See? You weren't listening!

BRAD: Well, I was distracted by the knife! And the spit flying out of your mouth.

EMILY: I was not spitting!

BRAD: You were. You're kind of a spitter.

EMILY: I am not a — Stop it! This is what you do! This is exactly what you do! I try to tell you something important, something very important to me, and you do everything you can to distract me, to throw me off my —

(Brad collapses onto his side.)

EMILY: Oh my god! Are you okay?

BRAD: I feel a little dizzy.

EMILY: Oh my god, I'm so sorry. I . . . I just get so mad, and then you . . . you . . . and it just all gets so —

BRAD: I know, I know. I understand. It's hard for you.

Pause.

BRAD: You know, Emily, I've been thinking. Maybe we could, you know, we could . . .

EMILY: *(Excited that he is at last trying to communicate with her.)* What, sweetie? What could we do?

BRAD: If it's not too late . . .

EMILY: What? Anything!

BRAD: Maybe we could call 911?

(Confused pause.)

EMILY: What?

BRAD: 911? I'm feeling really lightheaded.

EMILY: Oh! Right! I'm . . . Oh my god! You *are* bleeding!

BRAD: Yeah. Sorry about that.

EMILY: Oh my god! I'm so sorry! I don't what I could have been — The phone! My phone!

BRAD: In your pocket, hon.

EMILY: Right, right.

(She takes phone out of her pocket.)

EMILY: What . . . What's the number?

BRAD: 911?

EMILY: Right, right. I'm just so . . . Okay, okay.

She dials the phone.

BRAD: That's it, hon. I knew I could count on you to stay calm and collected.

EMILY: Yes, operator, we have a serious accident at —

(She suddenly looks at Brad.)

EMILY: What did you just say?

BRAD: Nothing.

EMILY: You made another joke.

BRAD: No, I didn't!

EMILY: Yes, you did! I can not believe you!

BRAD: I didn't! Look, will you just tell them to come get me already?

EMILY: Why? So you can tell them a funny joke too? Here you go. Tell them a funny joke, Mr. Funny Joke Man.

(She throws phone at him.)

BRAD: Oh, you've got to be —

(He grabs phone.)

BRAD: Hello? Yes, operator, we need — . . . No, that was just my — . . . Yes, we do need help. There's been a stabbing.

EMILY: *(Snorts.)* "There's been a stabbing." You can never just come out and say something! You always have to talk around it! "There's been a stabbing. There's been a misunderstanding. There's been this girl at the office."

BRAD: I'm sorry, operator. Can you repeat that question? There's someone talking loudly in the background. . . . Yes, a stabbing.

EMILY: Just tell her! Tell her who's been stabbed!

BRAD: I've been stabbed.

EMILY: Tell her who stabbed you!

BRAD: My . . . somebody stabbed me.

EMILY: Tell her!

BRAD: My wife stabbed me.

EMILY: Tell her what you did when your wife stabbed you!

BRAD: I'm sorry, ma'am. Could you repeat that?

EMILY: Tell her what you did!

BRAD: (*To Emily*). Not you! (*To operator.*) No, not you, ma'am. I was talking to
— . . . No, she's okay. She just a little — What? . . . Oh, it's not important. She's just — . . . No, she just wants me to tell you something. . . .
What I did after she stabbed me. . . . I didn't do anything! I just made a
joke! . . . Ummm, I said, "I think I get your point"? . . . No, ma'am. No,
it wasn't very funny. . . . No, I perfectly understand why that might make
her mad. Do you think you might — . . . No, ma'am. I shouldn't have
— . . . Yes, ma'am, men can be very — . . . I will. I will definitely be sure
to — . . . .Ma'am, I'm starting to worry about blood loss. My head feels
very — . . . No, ma'am. I don't blame her. I can really be very — . . . Men
really just don't get it sometimes, I know, yes. Can I ask if an ambulance
is coming? . . . An ambulance? . . . 54 High Plain. Brown house on the
corner. . . . Yes, ma'am. . . . I will, ma'am. . . . Thank you, ma'am.

(He drops the phone as he falls back onto the floor.)

EMILY: She agreed with me, didn't she?

(Brad nods.)

EMILY: She knew exactly what I was talking about, didn't she?

(Brad nods.)

EMILY: I bet her husband does the exact same thing. Just finds her button and
pushes it and pushes it and pushes it. Anything to keep from actually
listening to her.

(Brad nods.)

EMILY: Why is that so hard? Why is it so hard to just shut up and really listen
without putting up this huge wall of wisecracks and jokes? Is that really
so hard?

(Brad shakes his head).

EMILY: I swear, it's like you'd rather get stabbed in the gut! Somehow that's
easier for you to face. You can understand that! "Oh, look! A six-inch
steak knife is sticking out of my stomach! I know just what to do! I saw it
in a Rambo movie!" But a woman with a broken heart, a woman lost and
hurt? Aieeee, run! Flee! Hide! Blood? Easy! Tears? Panic! Isn't that right?

(Brad lies still.)

EMILY: C'mon, admit it. That's exactly how it is, isn't it?

(Brad lies still. As Emily questions his still form, the lights slowly and ominously fade.)

EMILY: Isn't it?

(Brad lies still.)

EMILY: Brad?

(Brad lies still.)

EMILY: Are you okay?

(Brad lies still.)

EMILY: Brad?

(Brad lies still.)

EMILY: Is this a joke?

(Brad lies still. Emily creeps closer to him.)

EMILY: This is a joke, isn't it?

(Brad lies still. Emily creeps closer to him.)

EMILY: Is this a joke?

(Brad lies still. Emily leans over him, concerned.)

EMILY: Is this a joke?

(Brad lies still. Emily leans right down over him.)

EMILY: Is this a joke?

BRAD: *(Suddenly opens his eyes.)* HA!

(Emily screams in fright. Pause.)

BRAD: Not funny?

(Curtain.)

END OF PLAY

SARASOTA
(World Premiere)

Melinda Lopez

BOSTON THEATER MARATHON XI
May 17, 2009
Sponsored by Public Theatre
Directed by Diego Arciniegas
Murray .... Steve Barkhimer
Tony .... Gabriel Kuttner

Sarasota is a brief meeting between an old school doctor and a new school doctor. Murray, a gruff senior physician considering retirement might get a new kind of medicine from his junior colleague. Funny and sweet.

Melinda Lopez is the author of *Sonia Flew, Gary, Alexandros,* and *Caroline In Jersey.* Ms. Lopez is also an actress and has appeared in regional theaters across the US as well as film and radio. Melinda makes her home in Boston.

CHARACTERS

MURRAY, *GP. Old school. Works too hard, cares too much. 70's*
TONY, *Plastic surgeon. Pretty. Glib and clever. 50's*

SETTING

Murray's office.

TIME

Now

. . .

TONY: You look like hell.

MURRAY: You look fourteen.

TONY: Injectibles. Very natural. The things we can do with collagen —

MURRAY: What do you need?

TONY: A favor.

MURRAY: Is it the kids?

TONY: Sleeping like babies — where does that expression come from? Babies don't sleep. They scream all night long.

MURRAY: What the hell are you doing with twin newborns at your age?

TONY: Angie goes back to work next month — We asked her mom to come down and help us out. Jean. From Boston. Angie wants family to watch the girls.

MURRAY: Lavender and Cinnamon. What the hell kind of a name is Cinnamon?

TONY: We're adding an in-law apartment onto the house. So that's where the favor comes in.

MURRAY: I've got a great contractor.

TONY: She needs a GP

MURRAY: Grandma?

TONY: — She's leaving her HMO behind — and she can't find a new doctor.

MURRAY: We aren't taking any new patients.

TONY: Her health is very good. She walks three miles every day. Does the *New York Times* crossword in pen.

MURRAY: Pen?

TONY: She terrifies me.

MURRAY: Blood pressure?

TONY: So –so.

MURRAY: What does that mean?

TONY: Borderline. Some arthritis.

MURRAY: You're killing me.

TONY: Only when it rains — and it never rains in Sarasota!

MURRAY: Only in the rainy season!

TONY: No family history of cancer or heart disease. She's going to live forever. A mammogram here — bone density scan there —

MURRAY: Last year Medicare paid me $133 for a bone density test — This year, I'll get $79. You know what my losses are?

TONY: The cuts hurt me too.

MURRAY: Come on — your patients pay cash for collagen.

TONY: We need her. We begged her to come — and now we can't get her settled. I had to promise her central air and a wet bar. And now I can't find her a GP? She's called twenty-five doctors already. They all say the same thing — no new patients. What they mean is —

MURRAY: You're killing me.

TONY: No new Medicare patients.

MURRAY: There's payroll, employee health insurance and malpractice insurance. And they all go up every year. My payments have been cut 40 percent. I lose money every time I see one new patient. What am I supposed to do — not insure the building? When I started out, people stood up when a Doctor walked in the room. Now we're pencil pushers. It's not why I went into medicine.

TONY: Old school.

MURRAY: Look, I can't take grandma as a new patient. The truth is, I'm putting in for my own retirement.

TONY: Seriously?

MURRAY: I haven't run the paperwork, but I am going to.

TONY: Something happened? You look like hell.

MURRAY: Thank you.

TONY: When was the last time you had a physical?

MURRAY: Don't start with that —

TONY: Just answer the question, Doctor.

MURRAY: You ever wonder — I had a patient last week. Heart attack. Young guy, mid fifties. DOA in the emergency room. We resuscitated. Put on the gear, paddles, jumped him, I had three nurses and two interns, a whole staff full of people. We did everything. We did what we were trained to do. We made a miracle, there in the ER. Guys heart starts up. He's alive. For about five minutes. Flatlines again. We bring him back again. But. I know — Tony. I'm there, and I know I have to do it. It's what I have sworn to do. And if it was my kid, I'd want the doctor doing the same thing. But if it was me?

TONY: What?

MURRAY: If it was me — I don't know.

TONY: You fill out some paper work — I promise I'll never hook those paddles up.

MURRAY: He lived another five minutes. Beautiful wife. Waiting for him to come home.

TONY: You'll never get used to it.

MURRAY: I love being a doctor, but I hate practicing medicine.

TONY: Old school.

MURRAY: I got into it for love you know. I fell in love with a nurse, and that was it.

TONY: Lillian?

MURRAY: My mother.

TONY: Your mother was a nurse too?

MURRAY: Best damn nurse I ever knew. Until I met my wife.

TONY: Lilly was the best.

MURRAY: It was a lot easier when I had her to come home to at the end of the day,

TONY: She's been gone, what, four years?

MURRAY: Seven.

TONY: I'm worried about you.

MURRAY: You're a plastic surgeon, not a psychiatrist.

TONY: You should talk to a doctor —

MURRAY: I'm talking to a doctor right now.

TONY: You sleeping all right?

MURRAY: I see their faces at night.

TONY: What the hell. I haven't slept in six months. I'll probably never sleep again.

MURRAY: I'm supposed to be traveling the Greek Islands with my wife. We were going to see every one of the Cyclades.

TONY: How many Cyclades are there?

MURRAY: About a two hundred.

TONY: That would take a while.

MURRAY: The rest of your life.

TONY: Listen. About Jean.

MURRAY: You want to see my books?

TONY: She's seventy- two. Retired school teacher. Eighth grade English. Buy her dinner.

MURRAY: I thought this lady needed a GP?

TONY: So treat her.

MURRAY: I can't afford to treat her.

TONY: So date her.

MURRAY: You're the one who needs psychiatric care. You're a nut job.

TONY: You choose.

MURRAY: This isn't going to fix the problem you know. Taking one more patient isn't going to fix anything.

TONY: Say yes.

MURRAY: She uses a pen? On the Times crossword?

TONY: Scouts honor.

MURRAY: That's classy. None of that Sudoku. I hate that Sudoku.

TONY: So you'll take a new patient?

MURRAY: I'm a damn fool.

TONY: I can't fix that. But I can make you look better.

MURRAY: Collagen. I know. But I don't have the cash.

END OF PLAY

THE INTERVIEW

Scott Malia

The Interview was produced by Emerson Stage, May 19, 2009 as part of the Eleventh Annual Boston Theater Marathon.
Directed by Courtney O'Connor
May Ellen . . . . Lisa Tucker
Del . . . . Grant MacDermott

The Interview is a comedy about Del, a Midwestern golden boy, who wants to date May-Ellen's daughter; however neither of them is what they first appear to be.

Scott Malia is a playwright, director, actor, and teacher with a PhD. in Drama from Tufts University. Scott is currently an Andrew W. Mellon Postdoctoral teaching fellow at College of the Holy Cross in Worcester. He has also written the full-length play, *Untitled by Jack*, which he also directed.

CHARACTERS

May ELLEN CHADWICK, A pert, old-fashioned, no-n
her late forties or early fifties with a pronounced Mi
DEL MATTON, A handsome, all-American boy of eigh
lar athlete at the local high school.

SETTING

The Chadwick's living room

TIME

The present

.   .   .

A simple, middle-class house in the Midwest. The decor leans towards country, but there is nothing garish about it. We are in a small living room. SR is a door leading to the kitchen. USL is an archway leading into a hallway — the rest of the house. MAY-ELLEN CHADWICK enters from the kitchen holding a plate of freshly made cookies and humming to herself. She is in her late forties/early fifties and while her look is not retro, she definitely seems like she could have stepped out of the 1960s. She is pert, practical, and has a thick Midwestern accent. She sets the cookies on the counter and starts arranging them to maximize their presentation. With her back to the hall, she does not see DEL MATTON enter from the hallway. He is eighteen, all-American good-looking, and seems very nervous. He waits for MAY-ELLEN to notice him, which she does not. He clears his throat.

MAY-ELLEN: *(Not turning around.)* I did know you were in the room, dear, I'm just not finished here.

DEL: Oh, uh, I'm sorry . . .

MAY-ELLEN: Not to fret, grab a seat. Mr. Chadwick took Heather out for ice cream, so it'll be just the two of us for the next forty-five minutes or so. *(He sits. She brings him a cookie on a napkin.)* You must be Del, aren't you just the cutest little thing I ever did see, I'm May-Ellen Chadwick, no Mrs. Chadwick, just May-Ellen'll do, I'm Heather's mom, but you already knew that, have a cookie, they're oatmeal raisin, hot 'n fresh.

DEL: *(Taking it.)* Thank you.

MAY-ELLEN: Have as many as you want. I'm on Weight Watchers, Mr. Chadwick has high cholesterol and I couldn't get Heather to eat something with carbs if I drugged her and used a crowbar.

y-Ellen laughs and holds the plate closer to DEL. DEL takes another one even though he's barely started the first one. MAY-ELLEN just looks at him as he chews. He is very uncomfortable.)

DEL: *(choking down his mouthful of cookie)* You have a lovely hom —

MAY-ELLEN: *(As if he hadn't been speaking.)* SOOOOOOO. I understand you have something to ask me?

(DEL swallows his cookie and collects himself.)

DEL: Yes, well, Mrs. Chadwick — *(she starts to protest)* — May-Ellen. Since, well, Heather and I aren't formally dating, I just thought it was only proper for me to ask your permission to take her to the Senior Prom. *(MAY-ELLEN still listens intently, smiling. DEL feels he has to speak more.)* Well, I, um, I have a great deal of respect for your daughter and I think she's . . . quite a young lady, so I would really be very honored to escort her. To the prom. *(May-Ellen is still all smiles, but does not yet respond.)* It's supposed to be a very nice, uh, event. The theme is. . . . a deserted island. Tropical. Probably lots of pineapple and coconuts. In the punch, anyway. Lots of nice leis. *(Realizing that phrase could be misconstrued.)* The flowered necklaces, with the. . . . from Hawaii . . .

(MAY-ELLEN is still silent for a bit. Then finally:)

MAY-ELLEN: Del, honey, are you quite nervous?

DEL: Unbelievably.

MAY-ELLEN: Well, don't be, because you have nothing to worry about.

DEL: Really?

MAY-ELLEN: Really. 'nother cookie?

DEL: I'm good. *(MAY-ELLEN gets up and goes to a nearby shelf and pulls out a photo album.)* So, is that a yes, then?

MAY-ELLEN: *(Not answering his question.)* Now, Heather would kill me if she knew I was showing this to you.

DEL: Baby pictures?

MAY-ELLEN: You have to promise not to tell her.

DEL: Scout's honor.

MAY-ELLEN: Are you a scout?

DEL: Uh. . . . no.

MAY-ELLEN: *(A moment of disappointment. She shrugs it off and places the large album firmly in his lap. He tries to mask his discomfort.)* Go ahead. Start flipping through.

DEL: *(He opens it up and looks at the first photos.)* Oh wow! What a cutie. Very sweet.

MAY-ELLEN: Del, have you dated many girls?

DEL: *(not expecting this)* Well . . . no, I'm a bit on the shy side.

MAY-ELLEN: Huh. Strapping thing like you. Big athlete. Popular. Seems kind of funny.

DEL: *(Uncomfortable and probably offended.)* Oh..well . . . yeah, I guess it is. . . .

MAY-ELLEN: Not gay, are ya?

DEL: Wha — No! I mean, no. . . . no, I'm not.

MAY-ELLEN: Acey-deucey, maybe? Try both sides of the salad bar, if you hear what I'm talkin'?

DEL: Mrs. Chad —

MAY-ELLEN: — May-Ell —

DEL: — May-Ellen. I'm very uncomfortable with this. You asked me if I date a lot and I don't. Any other questions are, well, too personal.

MAY-ELLEN: *(After seeming to reflect a beat.)* Gosh. . . . Well, gosh you're right. Hey, I'm sorry Del. I'm so worried about protecting my little girl that I forget that you're just a boy yourself. Kind of innocent, too? Aren't you? You know what I mean? Pure? —

DEL: — May-Ellen, I am a gentleman. That's all you need to know.

MAY-ELLEN: Well, I'll take you at your word. Hey, let's forget all this awkward nonsense. I've got more pictures in here that I'll think you'll like.

DEL: *(Turning the page.)* I'll bet. Heather was the cutest little — *(He looks down.)* — HOLY FUCKIN' SHIT!!! *(He nearly jumps out of his seat. May-Ellen stays him. She looks at him calmly.)* — Wh-wh-what is THAT?

MAY-ELLEN: *(Getting up and crossing to the bar.)* Oh, that? That's a snapshot of you with your dingdong in some prostitute's pooper. *(Pouring from a pitcher.)* How about a glass of iced tea?

DEL: What is . . . ? I. . . .

MAY-ELLEN: Almost like you forgot how to use your tongue, isn't it? Which isn't the case in this next photo —

DEL: — No, please, I don't want to see any more. What . . . what do you want?

MAY-ELLEN: Not a thing, punkin.

DEL: Where did you get those?

MAY-ELLEN: P.I. Not so expensive, either. Want his card?

DEL: So, I guess the prom's off?

MAY-ELLEN: No, no, it's still on. You just won't be going.

DEL: With your daughter?

MAY-ELLEN: With anyone's daughter. . . . or son, because I'm still not convinced that's not of interest to you, Mr. Backdoor Burglar.

DEL: So, you're blackmailing me into not going to the prom? Threatening to show these pictures? To who? I'd show them off myself.

MAY-ELLEN: *Still sunny.)* Ah, there it is. See Del, I didn't buy that whole aw-shucks, Jimmy-Stewart thing you were doing.

DEL: Oh no? 'cause it's working really well with your daughter so far.

MAY-ELLEN: Perhaps. But she's very young. . . . and you haven't ruined her yet. Yet. So I'm going to cut you off at the pass before you do.

DEL: Blackmail doesn't scare me. Do you know who my father is?

MAY-ELLEN: Sure do. Wanna see his album?

DEL: Right.

MAY-ELLEN: I'm not blackmailing you, Del.

DEL: Then what is this, scaring me straight?

MAY-ELLEN: No, this is murdering you.

DEL: Go ahead and try, lady, I can bench press more than you weigh. What did you do, poison the oatmeal cookies? *(A pause. May-Ellen says nothing.)* Yeah, right. Why don't I shove one down your throat just to see if you're bluffing?

MAY-ELLEN: Why don't you?

DEL: You're lying. And crazier than shit.

MAY-ELLEN: *(Takes out a gun from behind a couch pillow.)* And you, Prom King, are not a good boy.

DEL: Jesus, Mary and Joseph! I'm sorry, I'm really sorry, May-Ellen. I haven't touched your daughter, I swear.

MAY-ELLEN: *(Cocking the gun.)* And you're not going to.

DEL: Wait! I'll do anything! Anything!

MAY-ELLEN: Oh, I know, hon. I've seen the rest of your snapshots.

DEL: Please don't. Think of what Heather will think! Pleaseohplease. I'm begging you.

MAY-ELLEN: Gosh, you're right. She's in love, isn't she? She'll be devastated.

DEL: *(He starts backing towards the hallway.)* She will!

MAY-ELLEN: And you're young. This will teach you a lesson, won't it?

DEL: *(Gaining confidence.)* It will. It has.

MAY-ELLEN: You're sorry for what you've done.

DEL: *(Laying the sincerity on thick.)* I am. Deeply.

MAY-ELLEN: *(Starting to lower the gun.)* Ah. Well, that's a huge relief. Now I have a clean slate. *(She suddenly raises the gun and shoots him. He drops dead.)* And a messy rug.

(She picks up a cookie and sips her iced tea. She sighs contentedly and keeps eating her cookie as the lights fade.)

END OF PLAY

MISSED EXIT

Nina Mansfield

Missed Exit was originally produced by the Parish Players in the, February 13–22, 2009 as part of the Parish Players' Third Annual Ten Minute Play Festival.
Directed by Nora Jacobson.

Bob . . . . Paul Hunt
Rose . . . . Marc Chabot
Cheryl . . . . .Melody Blake
Donna . . . . Lillian Schley
Joe . . . . Joe Scaro
GPS . . . . .Becky Bailey and Pat Langille
Set and Lights . . . . David Ferm and Alex Cherington

Missed Exit was produced by the SpeakEasy Stage Company on May 17, 2009 as part of the Boston Theater Marathon XI.
Directed by James Fagen.

Bob . . . . Bob Murphy
Rose . . . . .Mary Callanan
Cheryl . . . . Philana Gratowski
Donna . . . . Jackie McCoy
Joe . . . . .Joe Lanza
GPS . . . . Carolyn Charpie

Missed Exit is a ten-minute comedy about a family of five trapped inside a compact car on their way to a wedding. After one too many wrong turns, the GPS comes to life.

Nina Mansfield's plays include *No Epilogue, Crash Bound, Smile, Missed Exit, Text Misdirected, Clean, The Tea Exercise* and *Pedestrian Casualty: Bronx, USA.* Her plays have been produced throughout the United States and in Canada. Her fiction has appeared in *Ellery Queen Mystery Magazine.* She is a member of the Dramatists Guild.

CHARACTERS

BOB, The Driver. 50s–60s. Rose's husband. Father of Cheryl and Donna. He wears glasses.

ROSE, Cheryl and Donna's mother. She sits in the passenger's seat. 50s–60s.

CHERYL, She sits in the back seat, in the middle. 20s–30s.

DONNA, Cheryl's little sister. Early 20s.

JOE, Cheryl's husband. Late 20s–30s. A peacemaker.

GPS, The Global Positioning System. A woman with a lovely voice. (Off-Stage Voice.)

SETTING

A compact car on the way to a wedding

TIME

The present

. . .

Lights up on a compact car. Five passengers are squeezed in. Bob drives. Rose sits in the passenger's seat. Cheryl sits in the middle in back, with Joe and Donna on either side of her. They are dressed for a wedding. The GPS system is attached to the dashboard.

GPS: Go .2 miles. Exit left onto ramp. Then bear right.

ROSE: So you go .2 miles. Then you are going to exit left onto the ramp. Then bear right.

CHERYL: Mom, he heard it the first time.

BOB: These windows keep fogging up.

ROSE: I think you have to turn up the heat.

DONNA: It's a million degrees in here.

CHERYL: That's 'cause you are hung over.

GPS: Go .1 miles. Exit left onto ramp. Then bear right.

ROSE: Over there, you have to exit left.

BOB: It said right.

ROSE/CHERYL/DONNA/JOE: It said left.

ROSE: Then bear right. Exit left, bear right.

JOE: Why don't we let him just read it.

BOB: That's a good —

ROSE: Because the last time he —

GPS: Exit left. Then bear right.

ROSE: Left, left!

BOB: I see it.

DONNA: No dad, the exit's left!

CHERYL: Left!

GPS: Recalculating.

DONNA: Shit.

ROSE: The last time I let him read it, he missed the exit.

JOE: It is confusing.

(Cheryl elbows Joe.)

JOE: What?

DONNA: Wake me when we get there.

GPS: Go .3 miles. Then turn right.

ROSE: .3 miles. Then turn —

CHERYL: He heard it mom.

ROSE: Then you're going to go .1 miles and turn right again. Then .3 and bear right onto ramp.

BOB: One step at a —

JOE: Basically, you're back tracking.

CHERYL: Could everyone stop giving directions?

DONNA: I told you we should have taken your car.

CHERYL: I thought you were sleeping.

JOE: She has a point.

CHERYL: Stupid me didn't want to get lost.

DONNA: She didn't want to waste gas.

CHERYL: Is there something wrong because I'm eco-friendly.

DONNA: You mean cheap?

(Joe and Donna exchange a look. Cheryl glares at Joe and he looks down.)

GPS: Go .1 miles. Then turn right.

ROSE: So, you're going to turn —

BOB: I heard it!

CHERYL/DONNA/JOE: *(At the same time as Bob.)* He heard it!

ROSE: Fine. You don't want my help. Fine. Fine. You don't have to be nasty. I'm just trying to help.

CHERYL: We are never going to get there. I'm going to be stuck in this car for the rest of my life.

GPS: Recalculating.

DONNA: Shit.

BOB: I just need some quiet. That's all I need.

JOE: That sounds like a good idea.

CHERYL: Dad, you're going the wrong —

JOE: Shhh!

CHERYL: Don't shush me.

GPS: Go .2 miles. Then bear left.

ROSE: Left Bob.

BOB: Here?

ROSE/CHERYL/DONNA/JOE: No!

JOE: What time does this thing start?

CHERYL: What do you care? You didn't even want to go to this wedding!

DONNA: Dear Lord. *(She pops open a can of beer.)*

CHERYL: You never want to do anything with my family.

DONNA: I wonder why?

GPS: Bear right. Then bear left.

JOE: I never said that. I just didn't see why we had to come all this way to —

CHERYL: *(To Donna.)* Are you drinking beer?

GPS: Bear left. Then stay right.

DONNA: No.

CHERYL: Real mature.

BOB: This looks familiar.

ROSE: We're back to where we started.

JOE: *(To Donna.)* Where'd you get the . . .

DONNA: Mini-bar.

JOE: Ahhh.

CHERYL: Could you try not to spill it on my dress.

DONNA: I'm not gonna spill it on your dress.

GPS: We'll see about that.

(All look around, not sure who just made the last comment.)

GPS: In .3 miles bear right. Then stay left.

JOE: What's with all these ramps?

DONNA: How far away are we?

CHERYL: Like, two miles. So close, yet so far away.

ROSE: Bear right, then stay left.

BOB: I know, I know.

CHERYL: There dad. You have to turn —

DONNA: No, not yet!

JOE: Just follow the purple line. See that purple line? It tells you where to —

GPS: Bear right. Then stay left.

JOE: I think you have to —

ROSE: Bob, you have to —

GPS: Stay left.

ROSE: Stay left.

CHERYL: I think I am going to shoot myself.

GPS: Now there's a thought.

(Cheryl glares at Donna. Donna shrugs. Rose looks around confused.)

GPS: In .1 miles, turn right.

JOE: *(To Cheryl. Conciliatory.)* We're almost there sweetie.

CHERYL: Don't call me sweetie.

DONNA: Thank God.

GPS: Turn right.

BOB: So now what?

ROSE/CHERYL/DONNA/JOE: Go straight!

GPS: Travel 1.1 miles. Then arrive at destination.

(A unified sigh of relief.)

JOE: I still don't understand whose wedding this is.

CHERYL: I told you. My cousin.

DONNA: Second cousin.

ROSE: My second cousin. Your second cousin once removed.

JOE: So you're related how?

ROSE: On my mother's side. I was really close to my Aunt Elizabeth, who died, but this is her husband's —

CHERYL: Mom, he doesn't care.

BOB: So I just keep going straight.

ROSE/CHERYL/DONNA/JOE: Yes!

BOB: Just checking.

(They drive in silence. Then Donna belches.)

DONNA: Whoops.

CHERYL: Lovely.

ROSE: Is my hair OK?

CHERYL/DONNA: Yes!

JOE: Actually, you have a hair just out of —

(Joe reaches over Cheryl to fix the stray hair for Rose.)

CHERYL: Great.

ROSE: Better?

CHERYL: It's fine mom.

ROSE: I didn't ask you.

GPS: Arriving at destination.

ROSE: Parking lot's right over there —

BOB: I see, I see.

(He makes a too sharp turn into the parking lot. Donna almost spills her beer on Cheryl.)

CHERYL: I told you to watch it.

ROSE: This doesn't look right.

CHERYL: Could we just get out of the car.

GPS: Finally, someone has a little sense here. Good idea.

(Silence. They all look at the GPS.)

DONNA: Did it just —

GPS: Yes, I did. Go on. Get out of the car. You can do it. Yes you can. *(No one moves.)* Or not.

ROSE: It's telling us to get out of the —

GPS: They heard me Rose. You need to trust me. I mean, you've got serious, serious control issues. What is it? Low self- esteem? Childhood abuse maybe? Dementia?

ROSE: Trust you . . . ?

GPS: And Bob, you need to get a new prescription. You're blind as a fucking bat. And that's an understatement. *(Silence. They stare at machine.)* Donna, keep drinking like you do, and your liver will be shot it oh, two years max. Probably sooner. Plus, has anyone ever told you that you're a slut.

DONNA: Excuse me —

GPS: And Cheryl, you're pregnant. *(Pause. Everyone looks at Cheryl.)* Sorry Joe. You aren't the father. *(Silence)* Just kidding. You're not pregnant. But she is cheating on you Joe. *(Pause.)* Hah, not really. But you are kind of a bitch Cheryl. How the hell do you take it Joe? I mean, seriously? You need to grow some balls. Wear the pants in the family.

(Uncomfortable silence.)

ROSE: I think we should . . .

DONNA: Yeah, why don't we . . .

(They start to get out.)

GPS: I'm just kidding folks. Sense of humor anyone? Have fun at the wedding. It's not gonna last. This marriage I mean. The wedding — it's just going to go on, and on, and on . . . .

JOE: Could we not use the GPS on the way —

BOB: I think that's probably a good idea.

(They all start to walk away.)

GPS: Oh, come on. Sense of humor folks. Hello? Hello? Is anyone there? I was just kidding? Oh come on, you can't seriously think I meant all those things . . . Anyone there?

(Lights Fade.)

END OF PLAY

HER EYES

Scott McCrea

Sponsored by Cape Repertory Theatre
Directed by Steve Reynolds
Arthur.....................................Art Devine
Sue .... Vicki Summers

A man believes the soul of his dead wife may still be alive in the recipient of her donated eyes.

Scott McCrea received his M.F.A. from Columbia University. His plays, short and long, have been presented at theaters throughout the country. Currently, he teaches at the State University of New York's Purchase College. His book *The Case for Shakespeare: The End of the Authorship Question* is published by Praeger.

CHARACTERS
ARTHUR, 40's. He wears a business suit.
SUE, 40's

SETTING
Sue's front yard

TIME
The present

. . .

ARTHUR is sitting on the ground, with his head between his knees.
SUE enters, brandishing a hammer.

SUE: I called the police. You gonna get the hell out or not? *(Silence. He stares at her.)* This is my front yard! You get the hell out! *(Silence.)* What do you want from me? What do you want? You been followin' me around all fuckin' day. Ya scared the hell out a' me, you know that? I mean, ya look harmless enough, but you been followin' me. I don't wanna be followed. *(Silence.)* I called the police! *(She turns to go.)*
ARTHUR: Don't go.
SUE: Why the hell not?
ARTHUR: You have my wife's eyes. *(Pause.)* I don't mean they look like hers —
SUE: I know what you mean . . . Your wife, huh?
ARTHUR: Yes.
SUE: Well, I guess they hadda be somebody's. *(Pause.)* So why 're ya followin' me? Ya want 'em back? *(Silence.)* That was a joke.
ARTHUR: I know; it's just that, I do in a way. Want them back. I wish she could
    — . . .
    (Pause.)
SUE: What'd she die of?
ARTHUR: Car accident.
SUE: That's funny, that's how I lost mine. My husband. He lost his life, I lost my eyes. They oughta' make tougher windshields, don't ya think?
ARTHUR: I thought — I don't know why — I thought — you would look like her.
SUE: You did, huh?
ARTHUR: Not exactly, but similar. The same type. I thought, at least around the eyes . . .

SUE: They don't look the same?

ARTHUR: Hers were closer together. They were set differently in the face . . . How do they feel?

SUE: They feel like eyeballs; how do you think they feel? . . . What's your name?

ARTHUR: Arthur Prowse.

SUE: They feel like eyeballs, Arthur.

ARTHUR: May I look at them?

SUE: What, up close?

ARTHUR: Yes. *(Pause.)*

SUE: Lemme see your hands. *(He turns out his palms.)* Lemme see under your coat. *(He opens his suitcoat.)* Take it off. *(He does.)* Now turn around . . . All right. I'm sorry, Arthur, but you been followin' me all day an' I think you're some kind a' nut.

ARTHUR: I understand.

SUE: You can come near me, but not too close.

(He slowly moves toward her, then stops.)

ARTHUR: *(bursting into tears)* Oh my God!

SUE: That's close enough.

ARTHUR: I saw your eyes in her face. I mean, her eyes in — . . .

SUE: Yeah. I know.

ARTHUR: Why can't she just die! I want to be free! *(Pause.)*

SUE: You didn't have any children, did ya?

ARTHUR: No.

SUE: See, you wouldn't be this way if you had kids. People without kids get too close. Spend all their love on each other. Become like one person. Then one dies, ya lose half your soul.

ARTHUR: Did you have children?

SUE: No.

ARTHUR: *(Pause.)* How long were you blind?

SUE: Three years.

ARTHUR: How did you live?

SUE: With my sister.

ARTHUR: You must be . . . relieved to see again.

SUE: It's easier.

ARTHUR: My wife would have been glad to know she helped you.

SUE: I think she knows.

ARTHUR: How?

SUE: Somehow.

ARTHUR: *(Pause.)* Can I ask you something?

SUE: Like what?

ARTHUR: Are you right-handed or left-handed? *(She laughs.)* What's the matter?

SUE: Of all the questions, Arthur, I didn't see that one comin'!

ARTHUR: I'm sorry, I — . . .

SUE: No, that's all right. If ya really want to know, I'm right-handed.

ARTHUR: Would you say you were very right-handed or . . . closer to ambidextrous?

SUE: I'm real right-handed.

ARTHUR: What about recently? Do you find you're using your left hand more?

SUE: *(Pause.)* Well, that's the damn'dest thing, Arthur. Come to think of it, I have been openin' doors with my left hand. You a doctor?

ARTHUR: No. I'm a vice-president. Of an insurance company.

SUE: Shouldn't you be at work?

ARTHUR: They don't miss me. I'm a vice-president. *(He chuckles.)* I could go to Paris and nobody would notice . . . Have you ever been? To Paris?

SUE: Never.

ARTHUR: There's a creperie near Notre Dame. Do you like crepes?

SUE: What are they?

ARTHUR: They're like very thin pancakes. Near Notre Dame, there's a creperie. Guess what they put inside them.

SUE: How would I know?

ARTHUR: Guess.

SUE: Wait a minute, I can taste it. I can taste it, it's — . . . it's — . . .

ARTHUR: Strawberries and chocolate?

SUE: *(Pause.)* Yeah.

ARTHUR: It was my wife's favorite.

SUE: Well, I always liked strawberries and chocolate. Always. I liked dipping 'em in melted chocolate. I liked strawberry and chocolate ice cream together. Always.

ARTHUR: It was my wife's favorite.

SUE: It was a lucky guess. Or maybe I read your mind or somethin'. It doesn't prove anything. She's not in here, Arthur.

ARTHUR: Do you find yourself watching football?

SUE: *(overlapping "football")* No. No more a this.

ARTHUR: Please! *(He grabs her wrist.)*

SUE: *(pulls away)* Don't touch me! Get away from me!

ARTHUR: I'm sorry! I'm sorry! I didn't mean to — !

SUE: Awright, awright, just don't touch me.

ARTHUR: I'm sorry.

SUE: *(Pause.)* She liked football?

ARTHUR: Yes.

SUE: I saw a game last Sunday. But, you know, I'll watch anything 'cause a' my new eyes. It's a coincidence, Arthur. Nothin' else.

ARTHUR: You don't believe that yourself.

SUE: Ya wanna know what I believe? I'll tell ya what I believe. I believe your wife is dead. I believe our body is a shell. An' when we die, we leave this shell. An' what remains is not us. These are not your wife's eyes, these are mine. She used to see through 'em, now I do. But they're not her. She's gone.

ARTHUR: What if she's not?

SUE: No . . .

ARTHUR: What if we inhabit what ever part of us is still alive?

SUE: That's not possible.

ARTHUR: How do we know?

SUE: *(Pause.)* So you're sayin' there might be two of us in here?

ARTHUR: Yes.

SUE: What if there are?

ARTHUR: I'd want to be . . . with her.

SUE: You'd wanna kiss her?

ARTHUR: *(Pause.)* Yes.

SUE: *(Pause.)* Awright. You come over here very carefully. *(He approaches, gingerly takes her in his arms and kisses her.)* Not half bad, Arthur.

ARTHUR: It wasn't the same.

SUE: Well, it wouldn't be. I'm in here too, ya know.

ARTHUR: I thought I'd . . . sense her somehow.

SUE: You didn't?

ARTHUR: No.

SUE: Well, maybe next time. Tell me more about her.

ARTHUR: *(suspicious)* No, you tell me.

SUE: Tell you what?

ARTHUR: Why do you think she's in you?

SUE: *(Pause.)* Well . . . When I first saw you, ya looked familiar. That's why I wasn't afraid of ya.

ARTHUR: What else?

SUE: I knew your name was Arthur. I just knew it, even before ya told me. I thought I could hear a voice . . .

ARTHUR: What else?

SUE: I don't know. I don't know. I'm sorry.

ARTHUR: It's all right. Take your time.

SUE: *(Pause.)* I can't do this to ya, Arthur. I just can't. I thought I could, but- . . . Look. I didn't hear no voice. An' I didn't taste no strawberries and chocolate.

ARTHUR: You said you did.

SUE: I'm sorry.

ARTHUR: But she's here.

SUE: No, Arthur. I'm alone. An' I've been alone. For a long time. I've been a burden to people for years. And then here you were, a nice-lookin' man, followin' me to my front yard . . . I don't even open doors with my left hand.

ARTHUR: You're lying.

SUE: No, Arthur.

ARTHUR: You're afraid of the truth.

SUE: I'm sorry.

ARTHUR: *(grabs her around the neck and chokes her.)* Jenny! Jenny, I'm here! I'm here!

(She drops her hammer. She falls to the ground, pulling him down with her. On the ground, she retrieves the hammer.)

ARTHUR: Jenny! . . . Jenny! *(She hits him on the side of the head. He rolls away from her onto his back and lies motionless. Pause. She catches her breath.)*

SUE: Oh God . . . Can ya hear me, Arthur? I'm callin' the police now. Can you hear me? *(Pause.)* I never loved nobody like that, Arthur. And nobody ever loved me like that . . . But I'm callin' the police now. *(She crawls to her feet and suddenly freezes.)* Oh my God . . . Oh my God, I can see her. I can see her, Arthur. She's in a red dress. And she has long dark hair . . . She's lookin' at me . . . She's lookin' at me like she's curious or somethin'. She's got head cocked to the side and she's lookin' at me . . . She has such beautiful eyes.

(The lights fade.)

END OF PLAY

NO SKATING

Dana Biscotti Myskowski

No Skating was originally produced by Actors' Shakespeare Project
Boston Theater Marathon XI, May 16-17, 2009
Directed by Courtney O'Connor
Mom................................ Sarah Newhouse
Son .... Sean Garahan

In *No Skating* a troubled teen faces the toughest trick yet: how to
skate past Mom; it is part of *Joint Accounts,* a play in ten-minute
moments for four actors.

Dana Biscotti Myskowski, screenwriter, playwright, professor, producer, & mom, launched Smoky Quartz Productions for the premiere 7 Day PSA Competition, is in pre-production on her short
screenplay *The Provider,* and began *Green Chair Reader,* an on-line
review of striking short screenplays. Dana can be found at: green-
chairpictures.blogspot.com

CHARACTERS

MOM, 40's, Determined, loving, and independent.
SON, 17, Drug dependent, but still his mother's son.

SETTING

Son's bedroom. (Staging note: can be black box, with only a few simple props to suggest the room.)

TIME

Present Day. Morning. Late for an adult, early for a teen.

PROPS

Magazine, pillow, blanket, cup, skateboard, wrench, laundry basket, clothes, a chair, and (optional) spray-painted sign that reads: "Fuck you! You can't tell me what to do!"

. . .

Lights up.

Enter Mom with a laundry basket. Son sleeps beneath a spray-painted sign that reads: "Fuck you! You can't tell me what to do." Mom studies Son a moment, her face revealing her profound sadness. She straightens up a notch, paints on a fake smile, and picks up scattered clothes.

MOM: *(sing-song voice, happy)* Time to wakey-wakey, sleepy head.
SON: Fuck you.
MOM: *(cheery, as if she's saying "Good morning" in response to his "good morning")* Fuck you, too, dear.
(This gets the teen's attention; he peeks at Mom as she checks the pockets of his jeans.)
SON: What the hell are you doing?
MOM: Laundry.
SON: I don't need you to do my fucking laundry.
MOM: If you say so, dear.
(Mom drops the laundry basket — THUD!)
SON: Ouch! I have a fucking headache.
MOM: So do I, dear.
(Mom leaves; Son rolls over, searches for sleep. Mom enters with a cup of water and aspirin.)

MOM: Here. Take these. You'll feel better in the morning.

(Son groans and hunkers in deeper into his blankets. Mom shrugs and takes the aspirin, drinks the water, sets down the cup, and opens the curtains.)

SON: Fuck! Do you mind? I'm trying to sleep here.

MOM: Actually, I do mind . . . I want you out of bed and taking control of your life.

SON: Fuck you!

MOM: You, too, dear.

(Mom picks up a skateboarding magazine, sits, and flips through the pages.)

MOM: What time did you get in last night?

SON: Late.

MOM: See Jenny?

SON: Fuck Jenny!

MOM: I hope not.

SON: And her fucking mom and dad.

(Son looks at his Mom.)

SON: What the hell are you doing now?

MOM: What does it look like: *(holds up the magazine)* reading your skate boarding magazine.

SON: Can't you just fucking leave already?

MOM: *(still cheery)* No, I fucking can't. Not until you're fucking out of bed.

SON: Most people fuck in the bed.

MOM: *(leafing through the magazine, overly cheery)* Or in the kitchen, or the living room, or the shower. . . .

SON: *(covering his head with the pillow)* Ewwww. Gross.

MOM: Oh, please. You're a teenager. Hormones raging. Sex is on your brain twenty-four-seven.

SON: Talking about it even vaguely with my mom somehow takes the sexiness out of it.

MOM: *(to no one)* Ah, hear that?

(Son looks around: who is she talking to?)

MOM: He actually speaks human, after all.

SON: Who the hell are you talking to?

MOM: The air. Same as usual.

SON: Can you please leave? I need some privacy.

MOM: Not until you're up.

SON: I sleep in the raw.

MOM: Then pull your blanket around you when you get up.

(Son whips the blanket off and stands. He sleeps in his jeans and t-shirt from the day before.)

SON: You didn't even turn away.

MOM: Honey, you ain't got nothing new I ain't seen before.

SON: Double negative.

MOM: Was it? I wasn't counting.

SON: Why is it so important I get up today? I told you I'm never going to school again.

MOM: And I told you that was fine. So long as you don't hang out here all day. I have work to do.

SON: I know you. You have some devious plan, don't you.

MOM: If by devious, you mean I'm planning to take you to the rehab clinic, then yes, I do.

SON: Fuck you! I already told you I'm not going.

MOM: And I already told you . . . you are going. *(smiles, cheerily)* So fuck you, too.

(Son makes a decision: fuck her. If he has to go to the clinic, then he's going to have one last score. Here. Now. In front of her. He reaches for his stash hidden below his mattress. It's not there.)

SON: What the fuck?

(Son scurries to the other side of the bed, reaches under.)

SON: Fuck.

(It's still not there. He reaches into his jeans' pockets. Nope. Not there either.)

SON: Where the hell is it?

MOM: *(reading from the magazine)* I flushed it.

SON: *(a visceral, drug-induced rage fills his face)* You WHAT?!

(Mom looks up into his face. She feels the first pang of fear. She tries to hide it, as she ducks behind the pages of the magazine.)

MOM: That stuff will kill you.

(Son looks around: he's a caged beast whose last great meal has been taken away unfairly. He finds his skateboard, picks it up, casts it aside and grabs the large wrench hidden there; he lifts it. He looks like he could kill his own mother . . . or the drugs could. Now Mom is afraid. She tries not to reveal just how much. She swallows some courage, casts aside the magazine, and stands, quasi-challenging him).

MOM: What are you going to do? Kill me?

(They stare at each other. It's a showdown. In this moment Mom does not recognize her only Son. She's rethinking every decision she's ever made. But Son recognizes his Mom. Thank God. He lowers his arm. Mom

relaxes a smidgen, but no more. Son turns, cocks, and throws the wrench as hard as he can into the darkness of the back of his room. Mom heads for the door as nonchalantly as possible.)

MOM: I'll be in the car waiting.

SON: You'll have to wait a long time if you're waiting for me.

MOM: *(stopping)* I already have.

(Mom steps toward the door.)

SON: I hate you!

MOM: *(it is "I love you, too")* I hate you, too, dear.

(MOM EXITS.)

SON: FUCK!

(Son throws his pillow, blanket, magazine, the plastic cup.)

SON: Fuck!

(Son kicks the laundry basket and beats the air with his fists. Venom and props exhausted, Son grabs his skateboard and heads for the door.)

SON: Fuck.

(Son exits.)

(Black out.)

END OF PLAY

TALKBACK

Jack Neary

Produced in May, 2009 by the Boston Theater Marathon, and presented by New Century Theatre, Sam Rush, Artistic Director.
Director: Jack Neary

Bill . . . . Andrew Dolan
Voice. . . . . Shaine Carney
Mary. . . . . Ann Marie Shea
Franklin . . . . Robert Murphy
Carolyn. . . . . Ellen Colton
Roberta. . . . . Sheriden Thomas
Sharon . . . . Maggie Nichols
Natalie . . . . Kathy St. George
Edward. . . . . James Bodge
Paul. . . . . Jerry Bisantz

Note: Other than "Bill" and the "Voice," the remaining characters are audience plants. At the BTM, the cast members were not listed in the playbill, to add to the surprise factor. The playwright recommends this approach.

A playwright oversees an audience talkback after a performance of his new play.

Jack Neary is the author of *The Porch, Jerry Finnegan's Sister, First Night* and *Kong's Night Out*, which was produced in 2009 by the Meadow Brook Theatre, and featured Cindy Williams. Mr. Neary has also written adaptations of *The Fall of the House Of Usher* and *The Turn of the Screw*. His most recent play is entitled *Auld Lang Syne*.

SETTING
A theater stage

. . .

At rise, there is a simple, empty chair on stage. After a brief moment,
there is a VOICE OVER. It's a cheery female voice.

VOICE: Thank you, so much, all of you, for coming to the show today and for
staying around for the talk back with the playwright and director. Who
happens to be the same person! So without further ado, here he is, Bill
Hanrahan.
(Bill enters. He's just a guy in his thirties or forties. A guy who has writ-
ten and directed a play. Just a guy. There is a scattering of applause.)
BILL: Thanks. Thanks a lot. Thanks. Thanks for being here. Thank you. *(sits)*
So . . . what can I help you with? *(silence)* Anything you want to know?
Any questions about anything? *(long beat)* Hands? *(another long beat)*
Nobody? *(sees a hand; points)* Yes! There! Right there!
(The actors playing the audience members who participate are scat-
tered all over the place. So any character who is not Bill is sitting in the
audience.)
MARY: *(a sweet lady)* Well, thank you for writing that play.
BILL: You're welcome.
MARY: *(beat)* It gave us something to do today.
BILL: Well, that's what I'm here for. *(nothing)* Is that all? *(beat; to the room)*
Anything else?
MARY: It's nice to have something to do.
BILL: I'm sure it is. Anything else from anybody? *(points)* Yes. You. Yes.
FRANK: Frank Deeble. Actor.
BILL: Yes. Frank. Hi. Thanks for coming.
FRANK: Just did Sidney Bruhl. DEATHTRAP. With the Players. You know
them, right? Up in Lowell? The Players?
BILL: Uh . . . DEATHTRAP. Good play.
FRANK: Yeah. We're thinkin' IRNE's.
BILL: That's nice.
FRANK: Those are awards.
BILL: That's nice.
FRANK: Played Sidney.
BILL: Yes, you said.
FRANK: Didn't do it gay, though.
BILL: Ah. I see. What?

FRANK: Didn't play him gay. Made a choice, you know? Actor's choice. Made him straight.

BILL: You did. You did. And . . . how did that . . . work out . . . for . . . for . . . the story?

FRANK: What do you mean?

BILL: Never mind. You have a question?

FRANK : Okay. So. . . . in your play there . . . the psychiatrist.

BILL: Yes. Doctor Lorden. Uh huh.

FRANKLIN: You think you really need him?

BILL: Need him?

FRANKLIN: In the play.

BILL: He's . . . he's the leading character.

FRANKLIN: I don't know . . . seemed . . . extraneous.

BILL: Well, Lorden is pretty much the protagonist, and . . . his attempted suicide sets the whole play into motion, and when the . . .

FRANKLIN: You know what?

BILL: What?

FRANKLIN: The suicide?

BILL: Yeah?

FRANKLIN: Forget the attempted. Go with it.

BILL: Well . . . if I . . . go with it . . . then who is the play about?

FRANKLIN: I don't know. You're the playwright.

BILL: *(beat; looks elsewhere; points)* Yes?

CAROLYN: You know what really, really impressed me about this show?

BILL: Tell me.

CAROLYN: I mean really. It almost, sort of, blew me away, it was so amazing.

BILL: What? I can't wait! Gee. . . .

CAROLYN: The facial expressions.

BILL: Oh.

CAROLYN: I mean the way they made their faces do those . . . expressions.

BILL: Yeah. The actors are good at that.

CAROLYN: *(demonstrating):* The . . . nose scrinching . . . and the way they . . . they make their eyes . . . kinda . . . you know, bulge out that way, and . . .

BILL: The facial expressions, yes.

CAROLYN: How do they do that? The way they make those expressions, you know, with . . . with their. . . . their . . .

BILL: Faces.

CAROLYN: Yes! Blew me away!

BILL: Well, you know, they . . . they read the play, and they work with the director to find the truth behind the story and the characters and the words, and when all that comes together in their . . . minds, you know, their bodies and their . . . their faces pretty much react the way anybody's bodies and faces would react. To the truth. They . . . express . . . this reaction . . . in their minds . . . and their faces . . . follow right along.

CAROLYN: Really?

BILL: Really.

CAROLYN: You mean, they don't just . . . make those faces up while they're out there?

BILL: Well, yes and no. but it's important for you to realize that there's a cognitive process that makes it all happen.

CAROLYN: *(beat):* The facial expressions?

BILL: Yes.

CAROLYN: *(longish beat)* Well, you know, when you see them, just tell them I thought their facial expressions were amazing.

BILL: I will.

CAROLYN: Best thing in the play.

BILL: You bet. *(looks; sees; points)* Next!

ROBERTA: I have a question about the curtain speech.

BILL: The curtain speech?

ROBERTA: Yes, the speech. . . . what's his name made before the show. Went on about ten minutes.

BILL: The curtain speech, yes.

ROBERTA: Or, as I call it, Act One. Too long.

BILL: I'm with you on that.

ROBERTA: But what really annoyed me was that . . . screed about the candy wrappers.

BILL: Screed?

ROBERT: Yes. Screed. Look it up. I was absolutely insulted that I was being admonished, as if I were four, to not open a piece of candy during the show. I mean, since when is that his business?

BILL: Well, that's interesting, because there's actually a good reason behind that . . .

ROBERTA: Good reason? It's a piece a' candy!

BILL: It's not the candy that's the problem. It's the wrapper.

ROBERTA: The wrapper?

BILL: Yes . . . the actors . . . you know, they work very, very hard to stay in character in the play . . .

ROBERTA: Well, I'm not arguing with that. I mean, those facial expressions . . .

BILL: Yes.

ROBERTA: *(in awe)* My God . . .

BILL: Well, in order . . . for their faces . . . to express . . . the actors need to concentrate . . . and when they hear a candy wrapper being opened in the audience, it affects their concentration.

ROBERTA: Well, don't you think I know that?

BILL: Do you?

ROBERTA: Of course I do! And that's why . . . when I open my piece of candy . . . I open it slowly. *(demonstrates with a candy wrapper)* Very. . . . very. . . . very. . . . very . . . slowly. So that I don't jar the actors.

BILL: *(she's still unwrapping)* See . . . see . . . it's . . . it's the slowly . . . that does the jarring.

ROBERTA: Oh, please . . .

BILL: No, really. The slower you open the candy, the more disturbing it is for the actors. STOP UNWRAPPING THE CANDY!

ROBERTA: Well, that is just stupid.

BILL: Maybe. But true.

ROBERTA: *(sits)* I give up.

BILL: *(breathes, looks; points)* Yes . . . Yes, the very pretty girl in the red blouse.

ROBERTA: *(from her seat)* What am I, chopped liver?

BILL: *(to girl)* Yes!

SHARON: Hi . . . uh . . . sorry, I'm a little nervous . . .

BILL: Relax. We're friends here.

ROBERTA: Yeah, relax Red Blouse. Have a piece a' candy!

BILL: *(to Roberta)* Ma'am! *(to girl)* Go ahead.

SHARON: Uh . . . how long did it take you to write that play?

BILL: Well, that's an interesting question. I started writing that play six years ago.

SHARON: THAT play?

BILL: Yes.

SHARON: Really?

BILL: Really.

SHARON: *(beat)* Wow. Unbelievable.

BILL: Well, writing a play is really a long and exhaustive process.

SHARON: Yeah. But . . . THAT play?

BILL: *(looks)* Next?

SHARON: Six years?

BILL: Next!

SHARON: Wow.

BILL: Lady in the back, there.

NATALIE: You're a Catholic.

BILL: Uh . . . well, I was raised Catholic, yes.

NATALIE: So you're lapsed.

BILL: Well . . . I suppose, I . . .

NATALIE: You write like you're lapsed.

BILL: I do?

NATALIE: Do you have any idea how many times you use the Lord's name in vain in that play of yours?

BILL: Uh . . . no, I don't.

NATALIE: Sixty-one.

BILL: Really? Jeez.

NATALIE: Okay, that's sixty-two.

BILL: How could you possibly know that?

NATALIE: *(takes out a notebook)* Thirteen Gods. Twenty-three Jesuses. Nine Christs. Twelve God damns. And four Jesus Christs. Which I count separate from the Jesuses and the Christs.

BILL: And that . . . bothers you?

NATALIE: Deeply.

BILL: What about the fucks? Got to be five fucks in the play.

NATALIE: I don't give a shit about the fucks.

BILL: *(looks and points)* Guy, there. You.

EDWARD: *(he is about a hundred)* Your play . . . reminded me a great deal . . . of a play . . . I saw . . . here in town . . . when it came through . . . town . . . here . . . in tryouts . . . in '47.

BILL: Really?

EDWARD: And that play . . . was called . . . DEATH OF A SALESMAN.

BILL: My God.

NATALIE: Sixty-three.

BILL: *(ignores her, to Edward)* Thank you so much. My play reminds you of DEATH OF A SALESMAN?

EDWARD: *(beat)* What play is that?

BILL: My play. The one you saw here today.

EDWARD: What about it?

BILL: You said it reminds you of DEATH OF A SALESMAN.

EDWARD: Oh. No. It remind*ed* me of DEATH OF A SALESMAN. I don't know why. I think maybe it was the pants with the suspenders the old fella wore in the second act.

BILL: Oh.

EDWARD: DEATH OF A SALESMAN was good.

(Bill sits, frozen, speechless. He puts his head into his hands, and lowers his head to his knees. After a moment, he rises, his face red. He takes a deep breath, then speaks.)

BILL: You know . . . you people . . . you come to a play . . . a PREVIEW, by the way . . . and you sit here . . . and you . . . you . . . you don't even bother to . . .

VOICE: Thank you, all, for sharing your thoughts with Bill here today.

BILL: Thoughts? Are you telling me anything this. . . . this . . . bowling league had to say involved thinking?

VOICE: Thank you!

(Instantly, the lights BLACK OUT. But Bill will not concede.)

BILL: Hey! HEY! Don't you turn out the lights on me! Put 'em back on! COME ON! I want to take one reasonable question from these people before I go home. Let's GO! HEY! LIGHTS! NOW!!!

(The LIGHTS come back on. Bill, breathing heavily, looks to the audience).

BILL: *(cont'd)* All right. Look. I'm giving you one last chance. I want one of you to ask me a cogent, pertinent, intelligent question about my play. I don't care if you loved it, hated it, or if you don't give a shit one way or the other. Just . . . ask me something that will leave me with the notion that there is at least one sane, book-learned individual in this audience here today. One question. One good question. Just one. Please. Ask.

(Long beat. But he sees a hand.)

BILL: (cont'd) Yes. You. Please. Please don't let me down.

PAUL: Why do you do this?

BILL: Why do I do . . . what?

PAUL: Why do you write plays? There's no money in it. You write something honest and funny and real and the audience loves it but the newspapers send critics who have never written a play or set foot on stage in their lives and nine times out of ten they crap all over you so the audience stops coming. The theater makes you sit on stage after a preview and answer questions which is a form of torture not even Jack Bauer could come up with. Takes you a minimum of a year from the time you sit down to write it to the time you finish the first draft and then you send it to some theater where it's read by a 19 year old intern whose frame of artistic reference is Dancing With The Stars. Why do you do it? Why do you write plays?

(Bill is frozen. There is a long, long, long moment of frozen nothing. Finally, without moving a muscle, he speaks.)

BILL: Lights.

(BLACKOUT.)

END OF PLAY

HEADBANGER

Ronan Noone

In Boston Theater Marathon May 09 —
Directed by Bridget Kathleen O'Leary for New Repetory Theatre
Phil . . . . Christopher James Webb
Woman . . . . Jessica Webb

Phil is a writer battling with his inner demon on the way to finding the word, the exact word, he needs to finish his story.

Ronan Noone's plays, *The Lepers of Baile Baiste, The Blowin of Baile Gall, The Atheist, Brendan, and Little Black Dress* have played in theaters across the United States and London. He is published by Samuel French, Ltd, Baker's Plays, Dramatist's Play Service, Ltd, and the Princeton University Library Chronicle. He has won three Independent Reviewers of New England (IRNE) Best New Play awards, an Elliot Norton outstanding script award and a National Playwriting award.

CHARACTERS
   A Man, Phil, Mid to late Twenties
   A Woman, Mid to late Twenties

SETTING
   Here

TIME
   Now

. . .

A man is banging his head slowly and rhythmically off the side wall. We see a woman at the front and centre.

WOMAN: This is Phil. Phil is a writer. He writes poems, short stories, novella's, novels, screenplays and regular plays. He is a published writer. He doesn't make a lot of money from his writing but, nevertheless
   (Pause. Phil stops and contemplates the word. He likes it.)
PHIL: Nevertheless
   (He returns to his head banging.)
WOMAN: He continues to write. It is a compulsion, he says. Anytime he is asked about writing by people who want to write, he says
PHIL: It is a vocation.
WOMAN: Sometimes he says
PHIL: I hear a voice in my head and I have to put it down or there is a line I hear and that line can suddenly spark an image and that image — well, I have to explore it.
WOMAN: These statements on writing are given to people who are fascinated by the process of writing or not — who ever will listen, really.
PHIL: It is a compulsion.
   (She looks at Phil. He stops. He begins again.)
WOMAN: So, Phil regularly brings these old saws out from under the covers to who ever will listen, and, of course, not using the same line every time, changing syntax, structure and words, yet always maintaining the meaning
PHIL: Let them have it.
WOMAN: For instance he will say
PHIL: I write because it is a compulsion
WOMAN: To the old ladies book club. But the school children he will say

PHIL: I write because I need to write

WOMAN: Note the word "need" is more accessible to children rather then

PHIL: Compulsion.

WOMAN: And to the reporter who sometimes, although rarely, may want an interview, and let's be frank here — talking to a reporter is more often imagined by Phil rather then having ever occurred. Nevertheless - *(Phil stops banging.)*

PHIL: I have never talked to a reporter.

(Woman pauses and is annoyed at the interruption. He bangs again.)

WOMAN: Nevertheless -

(Pause. Phil stops banging.)

WOMAN: To the reporter he will say —

(Pause. Phil returns to banging.)

WOMAN: Go ahead.

(Hesitantly, he stops banging. He makes his way to the middle of the stage.)

PHIL: I write because I have been given a gift and, although -

WOMAN: Note his use of "Although."

PHIL: I am an Atheist, nevertheless -

WOMAN: Atheist adds a sliver of controversy to the article, he thinks.

PHIL: You finished?

WOMAN: Sorry.

PHIL: Nevertheless, the spiritual side of my nature realizes that there is nothing worse than wasting a gift.

WOMAN: He will then go on to give an example from the bible, a proverb, or a . . . . . a . . . What's the word you're looking for?

PHIL: A proverb.

WOMAN: I just said that, you know the stories in the bible like when the son who is bad comes home —

PHIL: The son who is bad comes home . . . The prodigal son -

WOMAN: Yes. What do you call that kind of story?

PHIL: Yes. I know the word I'm looking for — the son who is bad comes home. The son who is bad comes home. The son who issss -

WOMAN: Parable.

PHIL: PARABLE. I got it.

WOMAN: He will then go on to give the reporter an example from the bible, a proverb, a parable on wasting gifts. That will assuredly-

PHIL: "Assuredly"

WOMAN: Give his pronouncements on writing -

PHIL: HEFT.

WOMAN: He will pause, allowing the reporter, older woman, student to digest this information and as he watches their face -

PHIL: Studies their face.

WOMAN: Excuse me. Studies their face as they digest the writers morsel from the philosophy of writing, Phil will study the scene because Phil will then create a line, a sentence, a piece of dialogue in his mind to describe the scene in which Phil is now instrumental in creating and in actual fact partaking in. Phil will say -

PHIL: The student is digesting my words -

WOMAN: And Phil will say -

PHIL: The student is allowing my words to ferment like a good wine because words are like grapes.

WOMAN: And then Phil will say -

PHIL: The student will pour out my wine of words.

WOMAN: Wine of words!

(She laughs. Phil looks at her, saddened. She stops.)

PHIL: The student will pour out my words like wine from his mind which is a bottle, and LINK the PARABLE that I told him to their own inspired thoughts on writing.

WOMAN: And Phil will take solace in some small way that Phil has gained immortality because to Phil, the student will be quoting Phil's wine of words on writing.

PHIL: Sometimes I simply use a quote from Shakespeare.

(He states this declaratively.)

PHIL: "Neither a borrower OR a lender be"

WOMAN: Nor a lender. NOR a lender

PHIL: That can be quite effective too, although, the bible example has more HEFT. I think.

WOMA: Now the reason Phil is banging his head against the wall — well.

PHIL: It is one of the side effects of being a writer

WOMA: Or someone who thinks they are a writer.

PHIL: *(Hurt)* Oh — .

WOMAN: Yes.

PHIL: *(Meditating)* I AM CONFIDENT. I AM STRONG. one, two, three, it's good to be me. Four, five it's good to be alive. I AM THE MAN. *(Woman will interject as Phil meditates.)* One, two three, it's good to be me, four, five it's good to be alive. I AM THE MAN.

WOMAN: And when the reporter comes around again Phil will tell the reporter that -

PHIL: Once I spent a whole day banging my head against a wall trying to come

up with an ending that worked. An ending that fit, an ending that seam-
lessly lacked. . . . that seamlessly lacked . . .
(She looks to Phil to answer. He doesn't know the word he's looking for.)
WOMAN: Phil can't find the word he wants.
PHIL: I'll find it.
WOMAN: And when the reporter laughs Phil will tell the reporter that -
PHIL: An ending that seamlessly lacked . . . .
WOMAN: And the reporter will say "You actually banged your head against the
wall, — literally — and Phil will laugh — And Phil WILL LAUGH.
(Phil laughs, a theatrical bombastic laugh, and cuts deadpan into —)
WOMAN: And Phil will tell the reporter —
PHIL: For an ending that seamlessly lacked. . . . . SHIT.
WOMAN: WHAT IS PHIL GOING TO TELL THE REPORTER —
PHIL: It is a metaphor.
WOMAN: YES! Yes!
PHIL: *(anguish)* I can't find the word.
WOMAN: The reporter will smile. But the real truth, the truth, THE TRUTH
is Phil did spend the day banging his head against the wall, looking not
for the ending of a story that never came, but because his compulsion,
his need, his love of words told him to bang his head against the wall,
and like all those other writers that he has read and to which he owes,
undoubtedly.
PHIL: UNDOUBTEDLY.
WOMAN: His gratitude, and, of course, on who's words and stories he has
digested and let ferment, pouring out of him like a good "wine of words",
a bottle labelled Phil the writer, AKA,the Fat bastard,
PHIL: Stop it.
WOMAN: Useless So and So, pretender, hypocrite, phoney, loser –
PHIL: That's unfair
WOMAN: Vintage 2009, because words are like grapes and he can not remem-
ber exactly if his words are fresh, or a paraphrase, or an exact quote he
picked up from a real writer.
PHIL: Stop it.
WOMAN: Although, Phil thinks if he speaks, just speaks a quote with the con-
viction that he created the quote, then, it will sound like his own freshly
squeezed quote and will, of course, give him HEFT. And, well, if he is
corrected he can always laugh it off -
(Phil cries terribly.)
WOMAN: with, with, with, with —
PHIL: *(Through the tears.)* "We writers never borrow we steal."

(He suddenly stops crying.)

WOMAN: Epilogue

(Pause. Phil returns to his banging.)

WOMAN: The real reason Phil is banging his head against the wall, well, he read recently about writers who had epiphanies and out of these epiphanies the writer became fresh, original, inspired, immortal. And with that in mind Phil decided to bang his head against the wall intentionally and with frequency hoping to cause brain damage. Nothing too serious,

PHIL: Minor.

WOMAN: Minor brain damage and he believes that when this minor brain damage becomes permanent he may begin to see the world in a new light.

PHIL: It will remove the staleness from every new thing.

WOMAN: Another quote he stole from some writer, which one he doesn't remember, but he expects this approach to improve his imagery by acquiring a slant, a fresh slant, giving him a fresh perspective of the world, and in so doing inaugurate

(Phil stops.)

PHIL: *(Very Happy.)* Inaugurate. Inaugurate. I thought I forgot that word!

WOMAN: Inaugurate his position as the new go to writer with the freshest voice, the freshest grapes if you will.

PHIL: Yes.

(He smiles.)

WOMAN: Nevertheless, I continue to argue with Phil about his latest misadventure in seeking immortality. But he sees no difference between what he is doing and what many writers down through the years have accomplished through an abuse of alcohol and drugs. *(Pause.)* And, well, I can't argue with that, can I? *(Pause.)* So, now, as to Phil and whether his new writerly approach will catch on or not — all we can do is wait and see.

(The woman walks off as Phil keeps on banging. Suddenly he stops. Eureka!)

PHIL: CONTRIVANCE that's the word. I got it. An ending that seamlessly lacks contrivance.

(He is pleased. He smiles. He returns to the banging. Curtain.)

END OF PLAY

IF AT FIRST . . .

John Edward O'Brien

If at First . . . was originally produced by Mill 6 Collaborative as part of the Boston Theater Marathon XI, May 17, 2009
Directed by Dawn M. Simmons

The Writer.	David Josef Hansen
The Guy	Alan White
The Lady	Ally Tully
The Waiter	Rodney Raftery
The Muse	Hannah Husband
The Other Writer	Lonnie McAdoo

A writer, over tired and under deadline, attempts to forge dramatic gold with no help from his characters, his imagination or his muse.

John is an original company member of Mill 6 and currently the Artistic Director. His plays have been performed in Boston, New York, Cambridge, Provincetown and Ashland Oregon. He would like to thank his parents, his Mill 6 colleagues and Ernest. He is a graduate of Fordham University, College at Lincoln Center. www.mill6.org

CHARACTERS

THE WRITER, Male (20's-30's) A blocked playwright.

THE GUY, Male (20's-30's) A character in his play. He is a little bit slow.

THE LADY, Female (20's-30's) A character in his play. She is a little bit feisty.

THE WAITER, Male (20's-60's) A character in his play. He is a little bit sarcastic.

THE MUSE, Female (20's-60's) The writer's muse who is short on inspiration.

THE OTHER WRITER (20's-30's should be close in age to The Writer) A more successful playwright.

THE OFFSTAGE VOICES at the beginning can be double cast with any of the actors aside from the Writer.

SETTING/TIME

The play takes place late at night in the Writer's apartment, his imagination and somewhere in between.

. . .

(Lights up very tight on the Writer. He is in a narrow pool of light at his writing desk laptop before him. He is staring intensely at it. He does not move. Lights dim. Lights up again tight as before. The Writer looking more intense than before. He is clearly thinking of his next line. His next word. His next letter. Suddenly a flicker of an idea. He moves to start to type and then . . . the idea leaves him. He slinks down in his chair. Lights dim. Lights up tight again. The Writer is holding his head in his hands.)

WRITER: Think. Think. Think. Think. Think. Think. Think. Think.
(Lights dim. Lights up again. Still tight.)

WRITER: OK. Ten minute play. A setting. A couple of characters. Some dialog. A little conflict. A resolution. Not difficult. You've done it before. No pressure. No pressure.
(A figure emerges in the half shadow. A Ghostly female muse.)

MUSE: Scripts must be typed in standard format.

WRITER: No pressure.

MUSE: A separate title page will be the only place your name can appear.

WRITER: No pressure.

MUSEE: Scripts must be postmarked by the 15th in order to be considered for the festival.

WRITER: OK! A certain amount of pressure.

(Lights down. Lights up again still tight on the writer.)

WRITER: So, let's see what we have so far. *(Reading)* Lights up.

(The lights come up upstage behind him showing an empty space.)

WRITER: Good start. *(Pause.)* And at the moment my ending as well. So lights up and then . . . something happens. *(Pause.)* Or. *(Retypes or deletes.)* No lights up *(The upstage lights go out.)* and the first line in darkness. Hmmm. Yes very dramatic. A voice in the darkness says — *(Types as the voice says.)*

VOICE IN DARKNESS: *(Very loud and imposing.)* Hello.

WRITER: *(Retypes.)* No. No. *(Retypes as voice says:)*

VOICE IN DARKNESS: Let there be light!

WRITER: Too Biblical. *(Retypes.)*

VOICE IN DARKNESS: Who goes there?

WRITER: Better. Yes. A question. A mystery. It worked for Hamlet. Uhh . . . so who goes there? Uhh . . . Bill, no. Umm the Queen! No. Uhh Jesus? Biblical again. OK. Scrap it. *(Types.)* Lights up on a small café table.

(The upstage lights come up and there is indeed now a small table and two chairs.)

WRITER: OK. Characters. A nice respectable young lady.

(A Nice Respectable Young Lady emerges from out of the shadow.)

WRITER: Hmm. Just a Young Lady. *(The Lady let's her hair down, or throws away her glasses — something to be a little less "nice").* OK and a guy. My alter ego.

(A very handsome and studly "representation" of the writer emerges. The GUY and the LADY stand on either side of the table.)

LADY: So, why did you ask me here, Reginald?

WRITER: Too British.

LADY: Francisco.

WRITER: Too gigolo.

LADY: Bill.

WRITER: Jeez, I've got to remember to pay the phone bill. It keeps cluttering my mind.

LADY: Bob. So, why did you ask me here, Bob?

GUY: Jessica –

WRITER: Good one. First time too.

GUY: Jessica, I have something very important to tell you.

LADY: What is it, Bob? Tell me!

GUY: I have cancer.

LADY: Oh, no, Bob! *(She swoons.)*

WRITER: No. Been done.

GUY: I'm gay.

LADY: Oh, no, Bob! *(She swoons.)*

WRITER: No. Not my alter ego.

GUY: I didn't ask you here. You asked me.

WRITER: Hah. In your face, Jessica. *(Pause — realizes this does not exactly solve the problem).* Oh yeah . . . .

LADY: That's right I did. Because I need to tell you that —

WRITER: Hmmm. Something pressing. Something current.

LADY: I need to tell you that I cannot continue seeing you until you divest from Sudan.

WRITER: Too large a topic for 10 minutes. Something more "everyday."

LADY: I need to tell you I cannot continue seeing you until you return those late library books.

WRITER: OK. Move on. Fix it in revision.

GUY: But I have dyslexia and I need longer to read them.

WRITER: Maybe it will work.

LADY: That's always your excuse. You just like having those books line your book shelves. And you're too cheap to buy them.

GUY: An arborist's money can only go so far.

LADY: But if you invested more wisely, say in a long term CD. Your money would start working for you.

GUY: I don't even have enough money to pay the phone bill.

WRITER: Boy these two are dry. *(An idea)* Ah ha. Enter Jesus.

(Another Actor enters dressed as Jesus.)

LADY: Sweet Jesus!

WRITER: *(Retyping)* Enter Jessica's Father.

(The actor pulls off his Jesus robe and is dressed in a business suit underneath.)

LADY: Daddy!

WRITER: *(Retypes.)* Enter a waiter.

(The actor pulls off his suit coat. He is wearing typical waiter garb — white shirt, tie, black pants now.)

LADY: May we see the wine list?

WAITER: *(to Lady and Guy)* If this continues much longer it's going to be "Enter a Nudist".

(They all chuckle.)

WRITER: Huh? *(Then quickly)* OK. Focus.

WAITER: Our specials today include –

WRITER: *(Thinking)* Umm. *(Types.)*

WAITER: Steak. Some kind of fancy fish I will look up later. And rhubarb and rutabaga.

LADY: Oh, so many choices.

GUY: What was the first one again?

WAITER: It was steak, Bill.

GUY: Bob.

WAITER: Whatever. You're both ordering the steak because it's the only real option.

WRITER: Wha —

WAITER: I mean really. "Some kind of fancy fish I will look up later"? He couldn't write filet of sole?

LADY: Oh that sounds nice.

WAITER: We don't have any.

WRITER: Hey, Buddy, I'll worry about the details later. I need to get the arc sorted out.

WAITER: Well, my arc involves me having some plausible lines.

WRITER: The play is not about you, Waiter. I can set it on a park bench and ditch you. In fact that would probably make it more producible. Fewer characters.

WAITER: You were bored when it was just these two.

LADY: Yes, that's right.

WRITER: I said you were dry.

GUY: Hey, I have a question. What the hell is an arborist?

WAITER: A tree surgeon.

GUY: I'm a doctor? Cool.

LADY: No. You can't be a doctor. You have no money. That's why you keep the library books. Oh, and I liked it better when he had cancer.

WRITER: No one asked you what you liked.

LADY: Don't get quick with me. I'll just walk out of here.

WRITER: Oh you will? I don't think so.

LADY: Just watch me.

(She starts to exit. The Writer starts typing furiously. She races back and kneels at the Guy's feet and wraps her arms around him.)

LADY: I will never never leave you. Ever. Ever! EVER!!

WAITER: Three evers?

LADY: That's a cheap parlor trick.

WRITER: Cheap or not you are my characters and will do what I want you to do. Now you *(to Lady)* sit down. You *(to Guy)* order the steak. And you *(to Waiter)* take their order.

WAITER: Steak? An excellent choice Monsieur.

GUY: Is it a French Restaurant?

WAITER: I don't know.

WRITER: Yes!

GUY: Are we in France?

WRITER: No!

LADY: Is anything going to happen beyond the ordering of food?

WRITER: You want something to happen?

LADY: I bet the audience would appreciate that.

WRITER: Fine.

(Types as the Guy quickly pulls out a gun and shoots the Lady. She drops to the floor.)

WAITER: That's your answer? And why would the dyslexic arborist have a gun?

WRITER: Who cares?

WAITER: Fans of logic?

GUY: Hey maybe I'm an arborist in a rough neighborhood and I carry the gun for protection.

WRITER: There you go.

WAITER: Protection from what?

GUY: *(as writer types)* Some kind of threat, which I will look up later.

WAITER: OK. Now the gloves are off. You *(to Guy)* do not shoot her. You do not even have a gun. You have kept the library books out long past their due date to get the attention of the head librarian *(indicates lady on the floor)*. You were too shy to ask her out, so you came up with this plan to get her to notice you. She falls for your simple charm and the waiter brings you a delicious chocolate torte, which you share.

WRITER: Hey, that's not bad. Ok so *(retyping)* lose the gun. *(more typing)* Not dead.

LADY: *(sitting up)* Oh, I'm still in this play? I liked it better when I was dead.

WRITER: Oh, just you wait. It's going to be good.

WAITER: Correction. It was good.

WRITER: What do you mean was? I haven't written it yet.

WAITER: But someone else did. This story isn't familiar? Your freshman writing class? "Overdue Romance" by Larry DesSharnes.

LADY: Who the hell is Larry —

WRITER: Larry DesSharnes. He was a machine. He would churn out one act plays about three a week.

LADY: And you stole this from him?

GUY: For shame. That's plagiarism.

WRITER: Oh my God. I'm so stressed about writing something that I must have borrowed –

GUY: Plagiarized.

WRITER: One of Larry's ideas. Okay. So that's easy to fix. It's not library books. It's DVD rentals.

WAITER: Oh, come on . . . .

WRITER: I know which character is going to get shot in this version.

WAITER: OK. Why don't you sort it out? And we'll sit here and wait.

WRITER: All right. Muse of Drama, I need you. I need some droplet of inspiration. Muse of Poetry, I need some sort of fire ignited. Where are these muses? Hello?!? Is there any muse available? Muse of Commercial Jingles. Anyone?!

(There is a sound of a heavenly choir. The lights flicker. The characters all stand up and look in the direction of the Writer. A beautiful woman enters. She carries a large torch [or flashlight or some other means of illumination]. She approaches the Writer.)

WRITER: Are you -. Are you my muse?

MUSE: Yes.

WRITER: Did you bring me some inspiration?

MUSE: No. I brought the harsh light of reality. *(She shines the light in his face).* I'm here to tell you to pack it in and call it a night. Start working on next year's contest tomorrow.

(The Writer pulls out a gun and shoots her.)

LADY: You're going to get a reputation as a writer who doesn't like women.

WRITER: I don't care! I don't care what that reputation is. I want any reputation as a writer. Anything other than a wannabe writer.

WAITER: Well you can start by writing a list of decent specials I can offer people.

WRITER: Do you know what I am going to do?

GUY: Shoot someone else?

WRITER: Do you know what I am going to do?

WAITER AND LADY: No.

WRITER: Do you know — ?

LADY: Just tell us!

WRITER: I am going to — I am going to — I am going to –

(Lights up on the far extreme side of the stage where ANOTHER WRITER sits typing.)

ANOTHER WRITER: Jeez. What can he do? I hate when I write myself into these corners. *(Inspiration)* Ah-ha! *(he types)*
(The Writer and the Lady pair off and the Guy and the Waiter pair off and both couples begin to tango. The Muse rises and extends her arm to dance to The Other Writer.)
ANOTHER WRITER: Perfect! *(Takes her hand).* And Lights down.
(The lights go down.)

END OF PLAY

TROFIMOV, A STUDENT

WILLIAM OREM

Trofimov, a Student was originally produced at the Boston Theater
Marathon XI and sponsored by Image Theatre, May 2009
Directed by Anne Garvin
Professor Kirkland . . . . Jerry Bisantz
Mark Shrive . . . . Ryan Garvin

An English professor teaching a class on Chekhov is visited by a
disgruntled student who brings a gun into his office.

William Orem writes in multiple genres, including, fiction, poetry, and drama. His plays have been performed in Miami, Ft. Lau-
derdale, Louisville, Buffalo, and Boston, with a staged reading at
Urban Stages in Manhattan. Currently he is a Writer-In-Residence
at Emerson College.

CHARACTERS

KIRKLAND, A university professor. Attractively middle-aged, neither stodgy nor immature. HIS hair is perhaps a bit long. HE can be arrogant, but only as a result of the seriousness of his commitment; in a world of musty gatekeepers, HE is the rare academic who actually should be in the profession.

MARK SHRIVE, Around twenty, short-cropped or shaved head, wearing a leather jacket. HE is immediately imposing, moreso for being psychologically aggressive than physically large. HE is in the cul-de-sac of development some young men get into where HE is not fully in control of HIS tone, and struggles between appropriate self assertion and hostility — a struggle that does not lessen HIS menace.

SETTING

KIRKLAND's university office. A paper-strewn desk, shelves on all sides, jacket on a coat rack, a green reading lamp. A room where serious work is done, old-school style. Dog-eared books crowd the shelves, suggesting the kind of hands-on passion for literature that brings with it a certain lack of concern for outward form.

TIME

Present day

. . .

At Rise: KIRKLAND is seated behind his desk, reading. One foot is up in a relaxed gesture. SHRIVE enters without knocking.

SHRIVE: Professor Kirkland.
KIRKLAND: *(attempting to point out HIS rudeness)* Come on in.
SHRIVE: *(missing this)* I'm Mark Shrive . . . I'm in your Chekhov. Your Introduction of Chekhov class.
KIRKLAND: Really? I don't recognize your face.
SHRIVE: Is that supposed to be funny?
(KIRKLAND registers the remark, sits up now more formally.)
SHRIVE: *(realizing his mistake — fluster)* I mean, I know I missed a couple of classes . . . it wasn't my fault.
KIRKLAND: What can I do for you, Mister Shrive.
SHRIVE: I know I missed a couple.

KIRKLAND: A couple? That means two. Be careful with your words.

SHRIVE: A few.

KIRKLAND: When I say I don't recognize you, I am not "trying to be funny." How many times have you been absent this semester?

SHRIVE: Three times.

KIRKLAND: Mind if I check? *(KIRKLAND looks for book among a tumble of student papers on HIS desk. The desk is a mess.)*

SHRIVE: Don't you know where you own grade book is?

(KIRKLAND stiffens. Then HE opens the desk drawer, removes book.)

KIRKLAND: Shrive. Shrive. Mark Shrive. *Introduction to the Plays of Anton Chekhov.* Tuesdays and Thursdays, 9:15. Six absences. And two major papers missed.

SHRIVE: It was only four absences.

KIRKLAND: I have them marked down.

SHRIVE: You must have counted wrong.

KIRKLAND: *Excuse* me?

SHRIVE: I mean, you could have.

KIRKLAND: *(recognizing)* You're the fellow who came without a book. I remember you now. We had a discussion over the pointlessness of coming to my class when you hadn't bothered to buy the book.

SHRIVE: I have it now.

KIRKLAND: Now? This is the seventh week of the semester. You have been absent at least six times. Frankly, there have probably been more. I stopped counting at six.

SHRIVE: You said we could have three absences before it affected our grade.

KIRKLAND: Three *excused* absences are . . .

SHRIVE: So if it's only four, that would mean I was still passing, because . . .

KIRKLAND: Excuse me, Mister Shrive, this isn't a matter of debate. You don't come to class, I write it down. You don't come to my office hours, I . . .

SHRIVE: Okay, you say it's six. You're going to stick to that, whatever. I can let that pass. So then if three absences are okay before it affects my grade . . .

KIRKLAND: Hold on, I am not asking you to *let anything pass.* Did you . . . *(HIS temper breaking.)* For God's sake, what do you think this is?

SHRIVE: Is that one of those . . . am I supposed to answer that?

KIRKLAND: *(pause; collecting HIMSELF)* The word you want is 'rhetorical.' The question was merely rhetorical. Now I have an apodictic question . . . a literal one . . . one I would like you to answer.

SHRIVE: . . . okay . . .

KIRKLAND: *(hard, but with sympathy)* Mark . . . what are you doing in college?

(Beat.)

SHRIVE: Sorry?

(KIRKLAND thinks about how to proceed, then enters a general muse more directed toward HIMSELF than anything else. Years of frustration behind this.)

KIRKLAND: I see so many of you. After a solid decade of teaching . . . of trying . . . it's only gotten worse. Young people, smart people, who think the purpose of an undergraduate education is to find a way undiscovered through four years of inactivity. To walk out with a stolen degree, a piece of paper that claims a false merit, something ostensibly earned through effort when in fact you have shown no initiative except in the art of personal evasion. Children from a new generation, who feel a professor is a kind of television set, something you can watch or not watch, that a bachelor's degree is a commodity, already purchased with the admission fees. Frankly, I'm astonished at the temerity . . . *(As KIRKLAND is speaking SHRIVE unzips his backpack and begins removing books. After a book or two he removes a large black pistol. KIRKLAND falls silent.)* . . . What is that?

SHRIVE: *(putting the pistol down on KIRKLAND'S desk while HE continues to rummage slowly, methodically, through HIS backpack)* I have it.

KIRKLAND: You aren't allowed to carry something like that.

SHRIVE: *(producing a textbook from the bag)* Here's my textbook. Do you want to see it?

(Beat.)

KIRKLAND: What are you doing here?

SHRIVE: What am I doing? I'm showing it to you. *(Pause.)* You said I hadn't even bought the text. Well, here it is. I'm showing it to you. *(Pause.)* Do you see it, professor Kirkland? *(Pause.)* I want you to understand that I have it. The book, I mean. Your book. And I keep it with me. All the time. In my backpack. During your classes. When I pass you in the hall. When I see you walking home at night. I have it all the time. *(Beat.)* Do you understand what I'm saying?

KIRKLAND: . . . I think I do . . . yes . . .

SHRIVE: You think you do? Be careful with your words.

KIRKLAND: . . . I do . . .

SHRIVE: You do? You do understand.

KIRKLAND: Yes.

SHRIVE: See, now I don't know whether you really do or not.

Let me help you.

I have it all the time. That means I have it during your boring ass lectures. During every stinking day of your boring ass lectures, where you stand up like a fucking prostitute fag, begging the students to suck your dick. Isn't that right?

KIRKLAND: *(pause, looking at the gun, still within Shrive's reach)* That's right.

SHRIVE: What is? What's right?

KIRKLAND: That I'm a . . . that I'm a fag prostitute.

SHRIVE: Oh you are? A fag prostitute who does what on the weekends?

KIRKLAND: I . . . on the weekends I . . .

SHRIVE: On the weekends you do what?

KIRKLAND: I suck dick. I suck big fag dick.

SHRIVE: Big! You added the word big. I didn't say the word big.

KIRKLAND: No. Not big.

SHRIVE: I don't know if they're big or not. Maybe you suck tiny little baby dicks. I'm just saying I didn't say the word big. I'm just saying you got to pay attention to words, Professor Kirkland. A little thing like that. It can reveal a lot.

(Beat. SHRIVE packs up HIS books slowly, replaces HIS gun last, zips the bag and throws it over HIS shoulder.)

SHRIVE: Okay, so I'm glad we had this talk. *(Pause.)* Now you know what you have to do. Don't you? *(Something dawns on Kirkland's face. SHRIVE goes to door.)* Oh, Professor Kirkland.

KIRKLAND: Yes.

SHRIVE: *(pleasant)* What's my grade? I've been meaning to ask.

KIRKLAND: Your grade.

SHRIVE: Yeah, my grade. I'm just wondering what grade I'm going to get in "Introduction of Chekhov."

(Significant beat.)

KIRKLAND: Why . . . you're going to get an F.

(Beat.)

SHRIVE: Excuse me? *(Incredulous.)* Excuse me?

KIRKLAND: *(measured)* I said you're going to get an F in *Introduction to the Plays of Anton Chehkov.* You have missed more classes than I find acceptable. Your papers, as you deign to call them, have been downloaded, incoherent, or simply failed to appear. The state of your mind is pitiable, and unworthy of either a commendation from a professor in particular or a degree from this institution in general. Further, I am going to recommend to the Dean that you be placed on Academic Probation.

(Pause.)

SHRIVE: *(trying to save HIS cockiness)* Is that it?

KIRKLAND: *(calm)* Oh, no. You can also take that self-loading Glock nine millimeter semi-automatic you have in your bag, ram it as far as you can up your tight little rectum, and pull the trigger. *(Pause. Then, real anger:)* Boy, do you think you frighten me? Do you think I'm more afraid of you than I am of Madame Liubov Ranevskaya? If so, you are badly mistaken. Did you really expect I might be more impressed by you than I am by Leonid Gayev and Yermolai Lopakhin? If you believed you and your ridiculous weapon would mean anything to a man who has known Ivanov, a man who has known Gurov, then I weep for the paucity of your thought. *(Detente. KIRKLAND stands suddenly.)* God damn you, I am trying to save your life. Don't you dare wave that ridiculous metal penis in here. This is a church to the gods. Chekov would eat the soul of a sniveling creature like you. You cannot withstand him without me. And without Chekhov you will not survive. Do you undertstand me? You. Will. Not. Survive. *(Pause. Sits.)* You think you can frighten me, Mark? *(From what HE had been reading.)* "Well, good-bye, old man. It's time to go. Here we stand pulling one another's noses, but life goes its own way all the time. When I work for a long time, and I don't get tired, then I think more easily, and I think I get to understand why I exist. And there are so many people in Russia, brother, who live for nothing at all." *(Pause.)* That frightens me, Mark. That should frighten you. That should *terrify* you.

SHRIVE: *(moving toward the door)* Yeah . . . well . . .

KIRKLAND: I'm not finished. *(SHRIVE stops.)* You have homework. Go home and read *Uncle Vanya*. I don't mean some of it. I don't mean the Cliffs Notes. I don't mean some internet trash. Read it. All of it. If you don't understand parts of what you read, read other things about those parts until you do. Learn it. *Understand it.* Get down on your knees to that play like your god damned short life depended on it, because you can bet your skinny ass it does. Then, Shrive — then — *then* you can come back in here and talk to me about what men like you . . . and men like me . . . *have to do* in order to stay alive.

(Stunned — or is he inspired? — SHRIVE goes to door. KIRKLAND stands.) Mark. *(SHRIVE turns.)* I *will* see you in class.

SHRIVE: Yes . . . *(With HIS first pride.)* Yes, sir.

(The two men face each other.)
(BLACKOUT)

END OF PLAY

PLEASE REPORT ANY SUSPICIOUS ACTIVITY

RICK PARK

Sponsored by Phoenix Theatre
Directed by Giselle Ty
Antonio. . . . . Matt Spano
Dirk . . . . Matt Wood
Man . . . . Art Hennessey

As the announcer on the Blue Line subway asks riders to "please report any suspicious activity", one rider wonders what to do when two gay dolphins enter his car and begin to have a lover's quarrel.

Rick Park is an actor and playwright in Boston. His 10-minute plays have been performed throughout the US. Rick is also the author of several one-act and full length plays. His most current project was the critically acclaimed "THE SUPERHEROINE MONOLOGUES: A Parody of Epic Proportions", co-written by John Kuntz, produced twice in Boston.

CHARACTERS

MAN, 30–50, Just a regular guy
ANTONIO, A dolphin
DIRK, A dolphin and Antonio's boyfriend

SETTING

Subway car on an MBTA Blue Line train in Boston.

. . .

Subway car on the MBTA Blue Line (Boston). MAN sitting alone in middle of seats, reading a magazine. We hear the recorded announcement as lights come up.

ANNOUNCEMENT: And please report any suspicious activity to the nearest MBTA employee.
(MAN looks up as the announcement is played and then back to his book.)
ANNOUNCEMENT: Next stop: Aquarium. Doors open on your right.
(After a few seconds, the train stops and the doors open. Enter ANTONIO and DIRK, two dolphins. DIRK enters and sits on the MAN's right hand side. ANTONIO pauses, glares at DIRK and deliberately chooses to sit on the MAN's left side. They all ride in silence for a minute. The MAN doesn't quite know what to do with the idea that two dolphins just got on the train. He is trying hard NOT to stare but sneaks sideways glances when he can. Finally:)
DIRK: *(Starts to say something but is cut off.)* Anto . . .
ANTONIO: Don't.
(Beat.)
DIRK: Antonio?
(ANTONIO puts his finger up as if to silence DIRK.)
ANTONIO: I said "don't" . . . *(ANTONIO notices the MAN staring at him. ANTONIO stares back.)* What? You?ve never seen a dolphin on the train before? Jesus!
(ANTONIO slides down one more seat.)
DIRK: This is stupid.
ANTONIO: So now I'm stupid. Is that what you're saying?
DIRK: Of course not.
ANTONIO: Did you think I was so stupid that I would actually ENJOY this little trip to the aquarium??

DIRK: Antonio.

(ANTONIO addresses the MAN on his next line.)

ANTONIO: He thought I would enjoy it.

DIRK: I didn't know.

ANTONIO: You didn't know? You didn't know? *(ANTONIO laughs, the high pitched whistles of a dolphin, followed by some clicks.)* That is rich. That is downright affluent!

DIRK: Why would I have brought you there if I had known?

ANTONIO: I gave up trying to figure out why you do anything a long time ago.

DIRK: I didn't know!

ANTONIO: Yeah, well that and learning to propel yourself backwards will get you a sardine.

(Beat.)

DIRK: I'm sorry. *(Beat.)* I said I'm sorry. *(Beat.)* Did you hear me?

ANTONIO: Yes, I heard you. My echolocation equipment is working just fine, thank you.

(MAN looks surreptiously from DIRK to ANTONIO and back. ANTONIO catches him and he turns back to his book. ANTONIO addresses the MAN.)

ANTONIO: He took me to the aquarium.

DIRK: Antonio . . .

ANTONIO: For our anniversary.

DIRK: Stop.

ANTONIO: Two months today.

DIRK: Antonio . . .

ANTONIO: The same aquarium . . .

DIRK: He doesn't care about this . . .

ANTONIO: That his ex-boyfriend . . .

DIRK: Jesus Christ . . .

(ANTONIO is now addressing DIRK. He is getting a bit loud.)

ANTONIO: Where his EX-boyfriend just happens to be the star of the newest exhibit!

DIRK: Antonio . . .

ANTONIO: Queen of the Giant Ocean Tank!

DIRK: Jesus!

ANTONIO: The Matthew McConaghy of the selachimorphas . . .

DIRK: Shhhh . . .

ANTONIO: Oh, I'm sorry! *(ANTONIO is addressing DIRK but referring to the MAN.)* Do you think he's too stupid to know scientific classifications of sealife? (*ANTONIO looks at the MAN, who gives him a shrug. ANTONIO proceeds to rattle off the following:*) Kingdom Animalia. Phylum Chordata. Subphylum Vertebrata. Class Chondrichthyes. Subclass Elasmobranchii. Superorder Selachmorpha.

DIRK: Tony, please?

ANTONIO: His ex is a fucking shark!

DIRK: Antonio . . .

ANTONIO: A fucking shark! He was dating his own species sworn enemy.

(At this point, both ANTONIO and DIRK are talking to the MAN.)

DIRK: It wasn't like that.

ANTONIO: What kind of self-loathing does a grown-ass dolphin have to have to date a shark???

DIRK: Don't psychoanalyze me . . . you know I hate that . . .

ANTONIO: And a hammerhead shark to boot!

DIRK : Rusty is not a hammerhead . . . his eyes are just . . . really far apart.

ANTONIO: Rusty!

DIRK: (*To MAN*) That's his name. My ex . . .

ANTONIO: RUSTY!

DIRK: It was a long time ago . . .

ANTONIO: You dated a *shark* named *RUSTY*!

DIRK: What do you want me to say?

ANTONIO: Our sworn enemy!?

DIRK: I was young . . .

ANTONIO: Oh, you were young?

DIRK: I was!

ANTONIO: Like that's a good excuse?

DIRK: We were young and . . . impressionable . . .

ANTONIO: Like right out of a movie!

DIRK: And in love . . .

ANTONIO: Like a fucking underwater West Side Story!

DIRK: I was being rebellious . . .

ANTONIO: Or maybe "Sea Side Story"!

(ANTONIO laughs his dolphin laugh.)

DIRK: I wanted to try something different . . .

ANTONIO: (*Singing to the tune of "Tonight".*) Tuna, tuna . . .

DIRK: I mean, is it a crime to want to date outside your pod?

ANTONIO: (*Singing to the tune of "A Boy Like That".*) A fish like that, he'll eat your brother! A fish like that will eat your mother! Stick to your own school, swim with your own school . . .

DIRK: I was trying to figure out who I was and what I wanted . . .

ANTONIO: *(Singing to the tune of "When You're A Jet".)* When you're a shark, you're a shark all the way. From your big pointy teeth to your skin, rough and grey!

DIRK: STOP IT! JUST . . . stop it! *(Beat.)* Stop it. This isn't funny, Antonio. It's not a joke.

(Beat.)

ANTONIO: I know.

DIRK: Just stop.

ANTONIO: I know it isn't.

(Beat.)

DIRK: I didn't know he would be there.

(Beat.)

ANTONIO: I know.

DIRK: I didn't know.

ANTONIO: It just . . . hurt.

DIRK: I know.

ANTONIO: You know? How do you think I felt, walking around that corner and seeing him in that giant tank? All those people watching him, taking pictures, pointing?

DIRK: I know.

ANTONIO: And then . . . then he looked at you and I saw it. The spark in his cold grey eyes. The way he did another lap around the tank and came right back to look at you. Smiling with those 4 rows of teeth. Sharing something with you that no one else would know. And then he looked at me. Those dead shark eyes. Sized me up with that one look.."Wow . . . Dirk's dating HER?" The scornful fluttering of his gills. The mocking sneer. Even the suckerfish attached to his underbelly was laughing and . . . I couldn't breathe. All those people in the dark, all around me and the bright lights in the tank and I could feel my blowhole closing up and I could see your face reflected in the glass and I had to get out of there.

DIRK: Tony?

ANTONIO: I had to get out of there . . .

DIRK: I know.

(DIRK stands and looks at the MAN. After a beat, the MAN understands and scoots down one seat so that DIRK and ANTONIO can sit together.)

ANTONIO: I'm sorry. I'm sorry if I caused a scene back there.

DIRK: I'm sure it's nothing they havent seen before.

ANTONIO: Do you hate me?

(DIRK puts his arm around ANTONIO.)

DIRK: How could I hate my Tony-Baloney?

ANTONIO: Because he's an ass?

DIRK: He's just a dolphin who wears his heart on his fluke. (*He gently rubs Antonio's fin.*) And a mighty sexy fluke it is, I might add . . .

ANTONIO: Oh, Dirk!

(*He laughs his dolphin laugh.*)

ANNOUNCEMENT: Next stop: Maverick Station.

DIRK: Whattaya say we get off at the next stop and I buy you a couple of slices at Santarpio's?

ANTONIO: With anchovies?

DIRK: I wouldn't want it any other way!

(*DIRK gives ANTONIO a kiss.*)

ANNOUNCEMENT: Entering Maverick. Doors open on your left.

(*Doors open and DIRK and ANTONIO exit. The MAN watches them.*)

ANNOUNCEMENT: Help keep the T safe. Please report any suspicious activity to the nearest MBTA employee.

(*The MAN looks at the seats just occupied by the dolphins and looks around the car. Then he picks up his book and continues to read. LIGHTS OUT.*)

END OF PLAY

FAMILY FIRST

Regina Eliot Ramsey

Family First" had its Premiere on May 17, 2009, at Boston Theater Marathon XI, held at the Stanford Calderwood Pavilion, Boston Center for the Arts. The producer was Playwrights' Platform of Boston

Director: James Tallach

Joey. . . . . Jonathan Popp
Vince . . . . Bobbie Trask

On the eve of receiving an award for heroism, Joey confides to his older brother, Vince, that he can't accept the award because he committed a reprehensible act.

Regina Eliot-Ramsey is a playwright, director, and producer. Her plays were featured in the 2007 and 2008 Playwrights' Platform Summer Festivals, Boston, MA, and three have been produced by Image Theatre, Lowell, MA. Her short play, *Family First*, was selected for the 2009 Boston Theater Marathon. *Impasto*, a full length-play, received a staged reading at the Whistler Museum in Lowell, produced by Image Theater. Her most recent play, *Pretty in Pink*, was featured in the Turtle Lane Playhouse Young Actors' Winter Festival.

CHARACTERS

JOEY, A young man in his twenties. Joey is immature and unsure of himself. He looks to his older brother for advise and approval.

VINCE, A man in his late thirties. Vince is Joey's older brother. A big bear of a man, Vince is devoted to his family.

SETTING

Vince's living room. The room has a sofa, a chair, and an end table.

TIME

Present — late evening

. . .

AT RISE: The lights come up on Vince's living room. It is late evening. The door bell rings. Vince enters stage left and goes to answer the door stage right. Joey enters.

VINCE: Hey, Joey, come in. I just got off the phone with mom. She and dad are real excited about tomorrow. You know the whole family's coming to the ceremony. Even our cousins from New Jersey are driving up to see you get the award.
(Vince puts his arm around his brother and hugs him.)
My brother, the hero.
(Joey pulls away.)
JOEY: Stop it, Vince. I'm not a hero.
VINCE: Sure you are, Joey. You saved that girl's life.
JOEY: You call that a life. She's lying in a hospital bed, hooked up to a bunch of machines. She'd be better off dead.
VINCE: Joey, you gotta stop beating up yourself. You did a good thing. If it wasn't for you those three animals would have got away.
(Joey appears nervous.)
JOEY: Is Marion home?
VINCE: No, she's out with her girlfriends. It's her bowling night.
JOEY: I gotta talk to you, Vince.
VINCE: What's the matter, Joey? You're a nervous wreck.
JOEY: Vince, I can't go through with the ceremony tomorrow. I can't accept the award.
VINCE: You have to accept the award. Mom and dad are looking forward to it. You can't disappoint them.

JOEY: I can't accept it, Vince. Don't you understand? I can't accept something I don't deserve.

VINCE: What are you talking about, don't deserve? You ID'd those three guys. Most people wouldn't have had the guts to do that.

JOEY: Vince, I'm telling you I can't accept the award. It isn't right.

VINCE: Joey, you're not making any sense. Look, you're just nervous about tomorrow. Sit down. I'll get you a drink.

(Vince starts to walk toward stage left.)

JOEY: I don't want a drink. What I have to say, I gotta say sober.

(Vince stops and turns to Joey.)

VINCE: Okay, Joey, if something's bothering you, get if off your chest.

JOEY: *(hesitantly)* I lied to the police. It didn't go down the way I said it did.

VINCE: You mean you didn't see those three guys rape that girl?

JOEY: No, I saw them rape her *(Joey hesitates)* but. . . .

VINCE: But what?

JOEY: It didn't go down the way I said.

VINCE: Tell me, Joey. How did it go down?

JOEY: I was coming from Donna's. We had an argument and she got mad and threw me out. I was so freakin' pissed. I must have walked up and down the street in front of her apartment building for half an hour until I decided to forget about it and go home. I was going to my car when I heard the screams coming from the alley. They had the girl down on the ground. She was kicking and putting up a fight. Then one of the guys slammed her head into the ground real hard and she went quiet after that. When they were done, they just walked away. They didn't even look back to see how she was. They just walked away.

VINCE: What the hell, Joey? Why didn't you call the police when you saw what they were doing?

JOEY: I don't know. I guess it didn't seem real. It was like I was watching a movie or a show on television. It just didn't seem real.

VINCE: Jesus, Joey, that girl might not be in a coma now if you'd called the police right away.

JOEY: Don't you think I know that? Why do you think I don't want to accept the award?

VINCE: Have you told anybody else about this?

JOEY: Shit no.

VINCE: Then everything's okay.

JOEY: Jesus Christ, Vince. How do you figure everything's okay? I lied to the police.

VINCE: Wait a minute, Joey. Let's think this through. So you didn't call the police right away. That doesn't change anything. You still had the guts to pick those guys out of a lineup. A lot of people wouldn't do that. They'd be too scared.

JOEY: Vince, it's not right. I gotta tell the police.

VINCE: Joey, listen to me. No one has to know how it went down but you and me.

JOEY: It's not right people thinking I'm some kind of hero.

VINCE: The girl's in a coma. There's nothing you can do. Telling the truth isn't gonna change anything. Just let it go.

JOEY: I can't let it go. Not after what I did.

VINCE: Joey, is there something you're not telling me?

(Pause)

JOEY: Vince, have you ever wanted a woman so bad you just wanted to take her? It didn't matter whether she wanted it or not. You just wanted to take her. I wanted Donna that night. We hadn't had sex for such a long time. She always had some excuse. She was busy with her job or she had a headache or some shit women give you when they don't want to have sex. I was so pissed when she threw me out. I wanted to go back in there and take her but I didn't have the nerve. Maybe if I had things might have gone down different.

VINCE: What do you mean things might have gone down different?

JOEY: She was lying there on the ground. God, she was beautiful. She had a body like those models you see on the cover of Sports Illustrated — long legs, perfect tits. I could wait my whole life and never get a chance to be with a woman like that. But there she was lying on the ground right in front of me and there was no one to stop me. It was just her and me. For a while I just stood there, looking at her. She was so beautiful. I wanted her. I wanted her like I never wanted anything in my life, and then I remembered I had a condom in my wallet. I had bought it to use with Donna but she threw me out.

VINCE: You had sex with that girl? Is that what you're telling me, Joey?

JOEY: Vince, she was beautiful. I might never get another chance to be with a girl like that?

VINCE: Jesus Christ, Joey, you raped that girl? What the hell was going through your head?

JOEY: I wanted to have sex with Donna but she threw me out and this girl was just lying there. She was like a gift from heaven, Vince. Don't you understand? She was like a gift from heaven.

VINCE: You had a fight with your girlfriend so you rape a girl in a coma? Is that your excuse?

JOEY: How the fuck was I supposed to know she was in a coma? I'm not a fuckin' doctor.

VINCE: Christ, Joey. What freakin' difference does it make? You raped her.

JOEY: Jesus, Vince, it's not like I planned it. It just happened.

VINCE: That's bull shit, Joey. Things like that don't just happen.

JOEY: So what do you want me to do? Vince, you tell me what I should do to make it right.

(Vince gets up in Joey's face.)

VINCE: I'll tell you what you're gonna do. You're gonna go to city hall tomorrow and when the Mayor hands you that freakin' award, you're gonna smile and say thank you. Do you understand, Joey? You're gonna smile and say thank you, and no one but you and me are ever gonna know how this thing really went down.

JOEY: I can't do that, Vince. I can't accept the award.

VINCE: You're gonna accept it, Joey. I won't let you disappoint mom and dad and the rest of the family.

JOEY: Vince, I gotta make it right. There's gotta be something I can do to make it right.

VINCE: What do you want to do, Joey? Go to the police and tell them what a sick son of a bitch you are? Tell them that you watched those three guys rape that girl and then raped her yourself. Is that what you wanna do? Huh, Joey? Do you know what that will do to mom and dad? It will kill them. Do you wanna kill mom and dad?

JOEY: Jesus, Vince, what are you saying? You know I wouldn't do anything to hurt mom and dad.

VINCE: Then keep your mouth shut. For Christ's sake, Joey, be a man. Think of the family.

JOEY: And what about that girl's family? They're gonna be at the award ceremony tomorrow. How am I supposed to face them?

VINCE: I feel sorry for those people too but you got to think of your own family first. Think of mom and dad. Think of your sisters, your nieces and nephews. For Christ sake, think of me.

JOEY: What about me, Vince? How am I supposed to live with myself if I don't make thing's right?

VINCE: I don't know, Joey, but you got your whole life to figure it out. Now you better go before Marion comes home. I don't want her to know anything about this.

JOEY: I wish this never happened, Vince. I wish I'd never stopped to see what was goin' on in that alley.

VINCE: Just go home, Joey. You can stop by the church on your way to the award ceremony tomorrow. It'll make you feel better.

(Joey slowly goes to the door to exit. He opens the door then turns back to Vince.)

JOEY: Vince, are you mad at me?

VINCE: You're my brother, Joey. A man has to stick by his family no matter what.

JOEY: Family first, right Vince?

VINCE: Yeah Joey, family first.

(THE LIGHTS FADE TO BLACK.)

END OF PLAY

NESTING

KARMO SANDERS

NESTING was originally produced at the Calderwood Pavilion by Holland Productions, May 17th, 2009, as part of The Boston Theater Marathon XI.
Directed by Krista D'Agostino.
Young Girl . . . . Carolyn Charpie;
Young Boy . . . . Gideon Bautista

Karmo Sanders
One Briar Patch
Scarborough, Maine 04074
(207) 883-5774
Email: karmo@maine.rr.com

Two starry-eyed young punk rockers set up housekeeping together. Here they find themselves discovering their true natures, in a situation that is not exactly what it appears to be.

Actress and playwright Karmo's comedy *Humpin'Glory Bay* was produced by Boston Playwrights Theatre. She opened her first musical *Radical Radio* at Playhouse 91 in NYC, her latest musical is the *Gold Rush Girls*. Karmo wrote and tours her one-woman show "Birdie Googins, Maine's Only Supermodel and Un-Registered Maine Guide."

CHARACTERS

GIRL, Early twenties, uncomfortably pregnant. She's overly emotional, nervous, fidgety and colorful in a bold eccentric style. The girl is unable to leave her "nest" on the sofa. Brave in her own way, she doesn't whine or screech.

BOY, Early twenties, outrageous punked out colors on hair, clothing. Over the top behavior, he's a nice enough guy, but very intent on himself. Can't stop preening, fixing his hair, playing with his clothes.

SETTING

A room, with a small sofa covered in pillows. The room is actually a tree and the small sofa is a nest, and the boy and girl are birds. Their actions and voices occasionally depict this fact. Pillows on the sofa hide four blue speckled eggs.

TIME

The Present

. . .

The Boy is getting dressed, fixing his hair, getting himself ready to go out on the town. Constantly preening, looking at himself in the mirror. He whistles merrily while the Girl sits resigned on the couch. Unable to leave her perch, she watches him.

GIRL: I don't how you can do keep doing it. Preening, preening, preening like some kind of —
BOY: What?
GIRL: You're just like my father.
BOY: Oh please, no, no, no not your family again.
GIRL: I wish I coulda looked like him, 'stead of –
BOY: (*Sighs.*) Your mother.
GIRL: Drab little thing.
BOY: I thought she was beautiful. Sang like-
GIRL: A lark. I know everybody said so . . . who cares, to-whit, to-whee, to-whit, to-whee.
BOY: Too whit too whee. I love that expression. (*Tries to kiss her.*)
GIRL: (*Flusters out of his arms.*) Leave me alone.
BOY: (*Continues fussing with his hair.*) What's wrong with you?
GIRL: What's wrong with me? What's wrong with me? You have the nerve to

ask what's wrong with me? Look at me. (*Reveals pregnant belly.*) And it's all your fault. (*Teary.*) And don't start lecturing me on the birds and the bees, all right. I got it. I thought this was supposed to be a love nest.

BOY: Just saying.

GIRL: What?!

BOY: Just saying is all.

GIRL: What, are you just saying?

BOY: Not my fault.

GIRL: Not your fault. As I remember I was doing just fine, then you got all puffed up, started chasing me, flushing me to the ground.

BOY: (*Disgusted, shocked*) What are you saying? I took you by force?

GIRL: Well . . . .not exactly, I.

BOY: (*Sweet on her.*) I'll never forget that sweet afternoon, you twitching that cute little behind of yours, prancing around.

GIRL: You caught me off guard.

BOY: (*Fixing his hair.*) You should have stayed out of the game you didn't want to play catch.

GIRL: Where are you going anyway?

BOY: Just out with the boys. Maybe pick up a few more building supplies. Mud for those walls.

GIRL: Mud?

BOY: That's what they call that compound stuff you patch up those holes with. (*Beat*) You gonna' be all right.

GIRL: No.

BOY: (*Sighs.*) Why?

GIRL: I wish you and your friends would do something useful once in a while.

BOY: Like what?

GIRL: Like drive off those new neighbors. They're at it day and night. Yak-kity, yakkity, yakkity, yakkity. She can't shut up. I'd think she'd drive him nuts.

BOY: (*Sarcastic.*) You think?

GIRL: (*Teary again.*) Stop it. See how mean you are?

BOY: I'm not mean. It's my nature. Just — being my nature.

GIRL: Being your nature. That's a good one, is that why you're always posing? Standing on every perch and street corner singing into the wind.

BOY: It's what I do.

GIRL: I 'spose fat, what is that, just being my nature?

BOY: Is that a stupid question?

GIRL: Is that a stupid answer? I had dreams, hopes, I was going fly. Somewhere anywhere, NY City. I sing just as good as you.

BOY: Better.

GIRL: Now all I am, is tired, tired, tired.

BOY: Well, if you'd stop fidgeting around all the time, might help. Wear yourself out all that fidgeting.

GIRL: *(Picks up book)* It's called nesting.

BOY: Nesting? Well that's good then. *(Starts to leave,)*

GIRL: *(Fidgeting)* My mother made a beautiful nest.

BOY: Good for her. *(Again attempts to leave.)*

GIRL: I never understood that. How they wouldn't let me out of the house, then they kicked me out. *(Teary.)* One day they just kicked me out. And when I went back they were gone. Can you believe it?

BOY: Yes. Can I go now?

GIRL: If my mother'd been around.

BOY: Here we go again. Mymother, mymother, mymother, mymother.

GIRL: She would have warned me about fowls like you.

BOY: Foul? Now I'm foul? I can't cope with these mood swings.

GIRL: It's a kind of bird.

BOY: *(Guilty beat.)* Is there anything I can get you before I go?

GIRL: Are you coming back?

BOY: Of course I'm coming back.

GIRL: I just have such deep abandonment issues.

BOY: It was your upbringing.

GIRL: I'll never abandon my children.

BOY: Never say never.

GIRL: What do you mean by that? What are you saying? You'd abandon your children?

BOY: I'm just saying, eventually, someday, hopefully, you kick 'em out of the nest.

GIRL: I will never! Never-never-never-never-never-

BOY: Shh! Settle down, why don't you let me go get you something. Wouldn't just take me a second to go down there. What do you want? Crunchy? Sweet? A juicy snack before I go?

GIRL: Nothing. I don't want anything. Go. I don't want to look at you anymore. You look just like my father. He looked just like you. *(Covering her head with a pillow.)*

BOY: *(On his knees next to her.)* Look Robin.

GIRL: Don't call me Robin. I hate that name. Why did I have to get a stupid name like Robin. I want to be called Tiffie or Britney or Paris, Hilton, something clever. Instead it's just plain old Robin, that's me. (*Head back in pillow crying.*)

BOY: (*Totally at a loss.*) Dude. (*Beat, starts to creep out the door.*)

GIRL: (*Screechy voice.*) Ok then. Goodbye, goodbye, goh oh oh ooooh.

BOY: (*Leaving.*) Careful you're starting to sound like a hoot owl.

GIRL: Never, no! (*Jumps.*) Oh!

BOY: What!

GIRL: Oh my guh guh guh gudness, goodness goodness. (*Orgasm, laying an egg, audience doesn't see egg.*)

BOY: Whoa. (*Completely confused.*)

GIRL: Oh my gaaaahhh, (B*ig orgasm.*) Oh . . . oh. Yes. Yes. (*Lays another egg*) Oh . . . .

BOY: Tweetie, what's going on.

GIRL: Tweetie, I love that. You do love me. (*Takes his face in her hands.*) You do— Ah . . . (O*rgasm begins.*) Whoaoh.

BOY: Is it?

GIRL: Weee eee eeee . . . YES . . . .. (*Lays another egg.*)

BOY: Are you . . . done?

GIRL: I don't know.

BOY: Is it . . . ?

GIRL: I don't know

BOY: How many?

GIRL: Well there's, (*Moving around, counting the eggs with her butt.*) One, two, (*Surprised:*) three.

BOY: Can I see?

GIRL: No! They just got here!

BOY: (*Trying to see*) Just one little peek. Apeek, apeek, apeek! (*Getting louder and louder, flaunting his chest, proud, yelling at the neighbors*) Apeek. apeek, apeek.

GIRL: Oh just yell it to the whole neighborhood why don't you. (*Laughing, proud of him.*)

BOY: I'll yell it from the rooftops! (*Starts out the door.*)

GIRL: No! Don't go, don'tgo, don'tgo, don'tgo. It's (*Trying to lay another egg, painful:*) oooo, ahhh. Little son of a twit . . . .ahhhhhhhh . . . .

BOY: (*At her side.*) You can do it. (*Really uncomfortable in this situation*) Ah . . . ..

GIRL: I want my mother,

BOY: Me too.

GIRL: I wish you'd never been born.

BOY: Me too. Metoo, metoo, metoo, metoo, metoo, metoo–

GIRL: (*Builds*) Eeee Eeee Eee Eeeeee. (*Suddenly stops, silence, feeling something*)
BOY: Tweetie?
GIRL: That's funny. (*Fluffing herself up, settling back down,*) I guess.
BOY: You guess?
GIRL: I guess I've got it! (*Proud, feeling under her, peeking here and there.*) One, two, three — four is your boy . . . .
BOY: That's fine, one boy is good enough for me.
GIRL: Want to see?
BOY: (*Delighted, almost singing.*) Do I want to see? Absolutely, most definitely, count on me.
GIRL: Oh look at you, clever you, rhyming, rhyming-rhyming away. (*Pecks his cheek in a kiss, stands up, they both look at the eggs adoringly.*)
BOY: (*Thrilled*) They're blue! Did you do that just for me?
GIRL: I know. I know. Blue's your favorite color.
BOY: With those cute little specks, oh I love you! (*Kisses her*) Thank you. Thank you thankyouthankyouthankyou.
GIRL: I'll take that snack now. Bring me a worm, and maybe a couple of a crispy crickets, I like beetles too. And keep singing, just so I know where you are. (*Picks up needles, starts knitting, whistling.*)
BOY: Gotcha. I gotcha. I gotcha. I gotcha. (*Starts whistling, pecking around. Stops, cocking his head, listening, pecks up a worm. Flings it at her, they both whistle merrily.*)
(*Black Out.*)

END OF PLAY

SMALL WINDOW
A Ten Minute Comedy

George Sauer

Original production sponsored by Centastage
Directed by Amber Hitchison with the following cast;

Rick . . . . .Allen Phelps
Rob. . . . . James Shanda Hitchison
Brian. . . . . .Rick Park

Three men meet to finalize a scam involving a severed finger and a taco. Surprisingly, the meeting does not go as planned.

George Sauer's one-act plays have been presented at several festivals across the country. His full-length comedy *Heading For Eureka* was recently produced at the Boston Center for the Arts by Centastage. His ten-minute play *Horticultural Therapy* is published by Smith and Kraus.

CHARACTERS

RICK, Male. Twenty to thirty.

ROB, Male. Similar age.

BRIAN, Male. Similar age. A bit crazy.

SETTING

A shabby restaurant

TIME

The present

. . .

RICK and ROB sit facing one another at a small table. A plate with a sandwich is on the table.

RICK: (*Pushes plate towards ROB.*) Are ya gonna try it? (*Beat.*) It's getting cold.

ROB: Remind me why I'm doing this?

RICK: Why? How can I do it? I work there. I can't be the customer.

ROB: No. Remind me why I'm doing this *now*.

RICK: For practice. So you won't be sitting, staring, looking suspicious. People don't order food and then watch it.

ROB: Some people do.

RICK: Ya. Crazy people. And crazy people never collect. You have to be able to eat it as soon as I put it in front of you.

ROB: Why do I have to eat it? Can't I just . . . discover it?

RICK: No! You have to bite into it.

ROB: Oh, man. I'm getting cold —

RICK: What! No! We're way beyond second thoughts here. We have a very small window of opportunity to pull this off!

ROB: Then let me practice the scream first.

(Starts to scream.)

RICK: No! I'm not worried about the scream. I know you'll get the scream right. It's what activates the scream that needs work.

ROB: But if the scream is effective, I can fake the rest.

RICK: Fake the rest! You can't fake it! Or everyone would be doing this. We need teeth marks through it! There's no faking that!

ROB: Why can't they be your teeth marks?

RICK: My teeth marks?

ROB: Sure. You can bite it. Serve it to me. Then I pretend to bite it and scream.

RICK: But our teeth are different.

ROB: How different? You're not missing any. I'm not missing any. It's not like they're gonna call in a dentist.

RICK: They might. Dentists are trained to do stuff like that. Besides, then I'm doing all the work. The placement and the biting.

ROB: And I'm doing the discovery and the scream.

RICK: What? That's nothing.

ROB: Plus! Plus, the public humiliation. That's with me for life. I'm known as the guy who bit into someone's finger served in a taco.

RICK: Borrito.

ROB: Whatever. (*Pushes plate towards RICK.*) Go ahead. Remember that small window. (*RICK grabs sandwich and bites into it.*) Oh, dear god. That sound! I'm gonna spew!

RICK: See. Nothing to it. Mind over matter.

ROB: I don't believe you did that. Not for any amount of money!!

RICK: Relax. Do you think I have extra fingers for the practice run?

ROB: So what's in there?

RICK: Look.

ROB: What is it? A parsnip? What's this on the end?

RICK: Finger nail polish.

ROB: Nice touch but I think you can count me out of this project.

RICK: No! This project is about opportunity!

ROB: I thought it was about money?

RICK: Well, that too. But grasping that window of opportunity and throwing it wide open that's the American way. (*Reaches for cell phone in his pocket.*) Shit. There's the signal and we haven't settled anything.

ROB: I didn't hear your phone ring.

RICK: We're in a public place! I have it on manner mode. (*Answers phone.*) Ya, Brian. What's up? (*Beat.*) Here, waiting for you. Do you have it? (*Beat.*) I'm just asking. (*Beat.*) I know it's a rhetorical question. (*Beat.*) Okay, I apologize. (*Beat.*) "I am sorry I questioned your ability to come up with a finger." (*Beat.*) Sure. See ya soon. (*Hangs up phone.*) God, he is so difficult.

ROB: Who is?

RICK: Brian. Who did you think I was talking to?

ROB: How should I know? Remember, I don't know Brian.

RICK: I know you haven't had a formal introduction but I would think you could deduce who I was talking to.

ROB: Maybe I'm not in the mood to deduce.

RICK: Be in whatever fuckin' mood you want but keep your mouth shut around Brian.

ROB: Why?

RICK: Because Brian is fuckin' crazy. Not kinda crazy. Not a little-bit crazy. Not occasionally crazy. Brian is career-choice crazy!

ROB: Oh great!

RICK: And whatever you do, do not, might I repeat for emphasis, do not stare at his head.

ROB: What does that mean?

RICK: It means he doesn't like people to stare at his head.

ROB: Why? What's wrong with his head?

RICK: Nothing. . . . major.

ROB: So why does he —

RICK: I guess he thinks it's too big.

ROB: How big?

RICK: A little big but the point is *he* thinks it's too big.

ROB: Is it big like the Elephant Man's?

RICK: What?

ROB: You know that old movie. (*Imitates.*) "I think my head is too big because it is filled with dreams."

RICK: Dreams? No. He is nothing like the Elephant Man.

ROB: Good. I don't think I could handle that.

RICK: The Elephant Man was friendly.

ROB: Oh, great. How the hell did you get mixed-up with him?

RICK: He's just some guy I know at the gym. There are a lot of crazy guys like him at the gym.

ROB: Makes me glad I don't work out. So where did he come-up with a finger on demand?

RICK: An industrial accident. Apparently it happens all the time. We were bullshitting around the squat rack and the plan . . . materialized.

ROB: Sounds like something the Elephant Man would "dream"-up.

RICK: (*Amused.*) If he ever knew we were talking like that . . . (*BRIAN enters, behind RICK.*) he would slam both our heads together like cymbals.

BRIAN: What like cymbals?

RICK: Brian!

BRIAN: Slam what like cymbals? Like this? (*Slams his two hands together.*)

RICK: No. We were talking about symbolism.

BRIAN: Symbolism? Leave me right outa that conversation. (*Looks around.*) What a dump! I hope you don't expect me to eat here!

RICK: Brian —

BRIAN: Just two words, I'd like to float by you. "Easy Access." I have been fuckin' driving up and down the street looking for a parking place —

RICK: Brian —

BRIAN: How does a place like this survive? Not on the ambiance. (*Picks up plastic menu.*) Must be the fine cuisine. Bingo. Here it is. Buck's meatloaf. There's my answer. Rachel Ray, step aside. Buck wants your time slot.

ROB: Who the fuck is Rachel Ray?

(BRIAN grabs ROB in a head lock.)

BRIAN: She's only the reigning queen of the Food Channel. And an inspiration to all of us who don't have time to cook! Who the fuck are you??

RICK: This is Rob, Brian. He'll be biting into the finger so he's a vital part of this project so we really need his face especially his mouth to be in one piece. Isn't that right, Rob.

ROB: (*Srangled voice*): Yes. I'll be biting into the finger which I'm sure you've gone to a lot of effort to procure. The details of which I'd really rather not know.

(BRIAN releases ROB.)

BRIAN: It's a pleasure to make your aquaintance.

ROB: Likewise.

RICK: So, where is it?

BRIAN: Ah, there-in lies a story.

RICK: You don't have it?

BRIAN: Did I say that!!

RICK: No, I apologize, once again. Please go on with your story. At your own pace.

ROB: Dear god, don't tell us how you got it!

BRIAN: A little squeamish, are you? And you're the one doing the deed. This project is destined for disaster.

RICK: He'll be fine. (*To ROB.*) Just think about that window.

BRIAN: What window?

RICK: More symbolism. Please continue.

BRIAN: In deference to your friend, let's just say that a severed finger came into my posession coincidentally with your desire for one.

RICK: Good so far.

BRIAN: The complication is that other parties have suddenly shown an interest in the object.

RICK: What other parties would even know about it??

BRIAN: The owner for one.

ROB: The owner wants it back?

BRAIN: Yes. He's sobered-up and is considering reattachment. So we need to come to an arrangement pronto because the ice is melting.
(BRIAN takes out zip-lock bag and throws it on the table.)
ROB: That's it. I'm fainting!
(ROB collapses.)
RICK: So what it is you want from me?
BRIAN: Money up front.
RICK: What kind of money?
BRIAN: Not a lot really considering what it means to the owner. $10,000.
RICK: Are you —
BRIAN: Plus my third of the eventual legal settlement as previously discussed.
RICK: Like I was saying. Are you fucking crazy? We had an agreement!
BRIAN: You had an agreement, as you call it for me to produce a finger so you could scam a restaurant out of a ton of money. Who are you going to complain to? I'm the one with the options. I could sell it back to the owner, increasing the amount demanded as the hours tick away. Or I could do the scam myself. Why do I need you two losers? To show me where to find a restaurant? *(BRIAN starts to put the zip-lock bag away. RICK grabs for the bag. BRIAN grabs RICK's hand.)* I'd suggest you take your hand away when I release it.
RICK: Or what?
(BRIAN takes out knife.)
BRIAN: I'm beginnig to see a way around our impasse.
(BRIAN starts to cut RICK's finger.)
RICK: Ahhh!
ROB: Hey, Brian. What ya doin?
BRIAN: I'm persuading your friend to sign his organ donor card. That gonna make you pass out again?
ROB: Probably.
RICK: Rob! Do something!!
ROB: You know, Brian, it occurs to me, if you wore jackets with bigger shoulder pads, your head might not look so big.
(BRIAN lets go of RICK and goes after ROB.)
RICK: Run!!
ROB: I think that window has just shut.
(RICK and ROB exit. BRIAN takes two napkins from the table and shoves them as shoulder pads inside his jacket. Pleased with the result, BRIAN sits at the table.)
BRIAN: *(Shouts.)* Hey, Buck! I could use a meatloaf sandwich over here.

END OF PLAY

MIKEY D.

John Shea

Mikey D., was originally produced by the Orfeo Group, May 17, 2009 for the Boston Theater Marathon XI.
Directed by Daniel Berger-Jones.

Mikey . . . . Mike Dorval
Mike . . . . Brett Marks
Big D . . . . .Rich Arum

When everyone you know is named Mikey D, the world can be a very small place.

John Shea is a former playwriting fellow with Boston's Huntington Theatre Company, his work has been included in the National Playwright's Conference at the Eugene O'Neill Theatre Center, as well as the Williamstown Theatre Festival. His play *Junkie* was commissioned by the Stanford Calderwood Fund for New American Plays.

CHARACTERS

MIKEY, early-thirties, big, out of shape, loud and dumb.
MIKE, early-thirties, big, out of shape, loud and dumb.
BIG D., Early-thirties, trim, fit, quiet.

SETTING

A busy street corner in Magoun Square, Somerville, Massachusetts.

TIME

Yesterday. Early afternoon.

. . .

Light comes upon MIKE and MIKEY standing on a street corner, drinking coffee.

MIKE: Time is it?

MIKEY: Just past one-thirty.

MIKE: We should have got up earlier.

MIKEY: Will you relax.

MIKE: I want to be at the gym by three, that means I gotta get home, take a shower, change my clothes . . .

MIKEY: Coffee will do us good, get rid of our hangovers.

MIKE: Couple lines would help too, you know take the edge off.

MIKEY: *(Taking a flask from his back pocket.)* Want a shot, Mike?

MIKE: Oh yeah, good thinkin', good thinkin', Mikey, get us through the day.
(MIKEY uncaps the flask, pours a shot into each of their coffees, and returns the flask to his pocket. They sip, feeling more relaxed. After a moment, MIKEY speaks.)

MIKEY: *(Looking off.)* Jesus Christ, will you look at that?

MIKE: Look at that ass.

MIKEY: I could eat that for a week and never get full.

MIKE: Holy shit, another one.

MIKEY: Good for you, 'cause now you won't have to be left out.

MIKE: Right, like you really have a chance.

MIKEY: Oh what, like you do?

MIKE: I don't know, maybe.

MIKEY: With that gut?

MIKE: Look who's talkin'.

MIKEY: *(Pointing in the direction of the girls.)* Check it out, check it out.

MIKE: *(Looking off.)* What?

MIKEY: Over there, that fuckin' loser. What does he think, he's gonna pick those broads up?

MIKE: Yeah, what does he think, he's gonna pick those broads up?

MIKEY: *(Squinting.)* Wait a minute, isn't that Mikey D.?

MIKE: No, Mikey D. moved away with that chick from over the gas station.

MIKEY: You're fuckin' numb. Mikey D. still lives over the school with his mother.

MIKE: You're talkin' out of your ass. Mikey D. moved away after he married that girl, what was her name . . . Mary, after he knocked her up.

MIKEY: Oh, Mikey D'Onofrio, I'm talkin' about Mikey D'Orio. Isn't that him down there?

MIKE: Oh yeah, Mikey D. You're right. *(MIKEY lets out a loud, piercing whistle through his teeth. MIKE tries to hush him.)* Leave him alone, he's tryin' to score.

MIKEY: He ain't gonna score. *(MIKEY yells.)* Hey Mikey, save a piece for us.

MIKE: He's Eddie M.'s cousin, right?

MIKEY: Who, Eddie Mahoney?

MIKE: No. Eddie Mahoney is Mike D'Ambrosio's cousin.

MIKEY: That the Eddie M. goin' out with that chick, what's her name, Mary . . . somethin'?

MIKE: What, from over the donut shop?

MIKEY: No. from over Trum Park.

MIKE: No, she's not goin' out with Eddie Mahoney. The Eddie M. who's goin' out with Mary from over Trum Park, is Eddie Murray, Michael Di Fiorio's cousin.

MIKEY: Eddie Murray's not goin' out with Mary from over Trum Park. He's goin' with Mary from over the drug store. The Eddie M. who's goin' out with Mary from over Trum Park, is Eddie McKenna, Mike DiBenedetto's cousin. You know Mikey D., right?

MIKE: Eddie McKenna is not goin' out with Mary from over Trum Park, he's goin' out with Marie, from over on Sycamore, near where Mike DiPietrio got that apartment.

MIKEY: Mikey D. moved out of his mother's house?

MIKE: Yeah, got that apartment with Eddie Monaghan, Mike D'Angelo's cousin.

MIKEY: Isn't he that idiot almost blew his hand off with those firecrackers last Fourth of July,

HE WAS SO WASTED?

MIKE: That's the one.

(They silently sip their coffees.)

MIKEY: So Eddie M. is goin' out with Mary?

MIKE: That's what I hear.

MIKEY: I thought she had better sense than that.

MIKE: These broads always go for the stupid Irish guys. Think they'd know better. All the Irish have small dicks.

(They laugh and sip their coffees. After a slight pause, MIKEY continues.)

MIKEY: I'm gonna have to get a job soon.

MIKE: You're not collectin' no more?

MIKEY: They're cuttin' me off.

MIKE: That ain't right.

MIKEY: But I'm appealin'.

MIKE: You got the right. My cousin Eddie got like three extensions on his unemployment.

MIKEY: Fuckin' Irish guys know all the angles. I mean look at the Kennedys.

MIKE: Yeah, look at the Kennedys.

MIKEY: Besides, my mother's makin' me pay board.

MIKE: What are you gonna do?

MIKEY: What can you do? Mothers.

MIKE: Yeah, mothers.

(They sip. MIKEY points off excitedly.)

MIKEY: Holy shit . . . another one.

MIKE: Like a posse.

MIKEY: Pussy posse.

(They high five, impressed with their own cleverness.)

MIKE: Hey Mikey, give 'em one of your whistles.

(MIKEY lets out an ear-shattering wolf whistle. They laugh.)

MIKE: Do you believe that shit? They all turned around.

MIKEY: Cocky bitches.

MIKE: Yeah, cocky bitches.

(They stand silently for a moment. BIG D. enters.)

MIKEY: Michael D. Jesus, haven't seen you in a dog's age.

BIG D.: Mikey, good to see you.

(Handshakes all around.)

MIKE: Michael D., Big D., how the hell you doin'?

BIG D.: Doin' good, Mike, doin' good.

MIKEY: I thought you moved away.

BIG D.: Nah. Only over the square.

MIKEY: What are you doin' around here?

BIG D.: See my mother. Mary had the baby, so now I gotta visit more.

MIKEY: You still with Mary from over the projects?

BIG D.: Yeah. We got married. Didn't you know she was havin' a baby?

MIKEY: Yeah, but that don't mean you're still with her. I mean look at my brother, five kids and he's not with any of their mothers anymore.

MIKE: Shit, a kid. You workin'?

BIG D.: Yeah, over the Holiday Inn. *(MIKEY and MIKE shake their heads in disbelief and awe. BIG D. continues.)* What are you guys up to?

MIKEY: You know us, Big D., same old shit.

MIKE: Yeah, same old shit.

MIKEY: Hey, Big D., what are you doin' tonight? There's a party over at Michael D.'s later, interested?

BIG D.: Can't. Gotta have dinner with my mother, you know, with the new baby and shit.

MIKEY: Afterwards. We'll be there late. Me and Mike are gettin' a case after we go the gym.

MIKE: If we ever really get there.

MIKEY: And look. See those broads down there? They been checkin' us out all afternoon. There's one for you.

BIG D.: I'm a married man.

MIKEY: So?

MIKE: Yeah, so?

BIG D.: I don't do that shit anymore.

MIKEY: Fuckin' whipped.

MIKE: Yeah, whipped.

BIG D.: Besides, those girls can't be more than fifteen years old.

MIKEY: So?

MIKE: Yeah, so?

BIG D.: I gotta go. Mary's waitin' for me.

MIKEY: Where is she, your mother's?

BIG D.: Yeah, with Little Mikey, and I gotta get back.

MIKEY: Wow, I still can't believe you got like a kid and shit. That's wild.

MIKE: Yeah, wild.

BIG D.: Hey, good seein' you. Tell everyone I said, "Hi."

(BIG D. exits. MIKEY yells after him.)

MIKEY: Hey, give our regards to Mary. *(Confidentially to MIKE.)* Everyone else has.

(They watch BIG D. walk away.)

MIKE: He looks like shit.

MIKEY: What a fuckin' waste, workin' in a hotel.

MIKE: Prob'ly makin' like eight bucks an hour.

MIKEY: And what's with that shit, "Oh, I'm married."

MIKE: Yeah, thinks he's hot shit.

MIKEY: Big fuckin' man.

MIKE: Yeah, big, fuckin' man.

MIKEY: Imagine marryin' a girl from over the projects. Trash.

MIKE: Yeah, trash.

MIKEY: Let's go the bar.

MIKE: What about the gym?

MIKEY: We'll go tomorrow.

MIKE: Yeah, we'll go tomorrow. What about the broads?

MIKEY: Nothin' happenin'. Prob'ly lezzies anyway.

MIKE: Yeah, prob'ly lezzies.

MIKEY: Hey, maybe Mikey D.'s workin', let us drink on his tab.

MIKE: He's Eddie Maloney's cousin, right?

MIKEY: No, Eddie Mulroney's. The Mikey D. who's Eddie M.'s cousin, is Mike DeGregorio.

MIKE: What, from over the tracks?

MIKEY: No, from over the sub shop . . .

MIKE: Oh yeah, Mikey D. I know him.

(Light fades as they exit.)

END OF PLAY

NINE LIVES

Danielle Slepian

NINE LIVES was originally produced by Apollinaire Theatre Company as part of the Boston Theater Marathon XI on May 17th, 2009. Director: Paul S. Benford-Bruce, Steven — Richard Richards.

NINE LIVES is the story of Steven, an HIV+ man forced to decide the fate of his beloved Marilyn, the cat who's sustained his solitary life for nearly twenty years.

Danielle Slepian is a playwright from Jamaica Plain, MA. Her play, *Date #4*, was a finalist in SLAMBoston, and another piece, *Seven Little Days*, won 3rd place in the Center for New Words annual playwriting competition. Danielle holds an MFA in playwriting from Brandeis University and is a registered nurse.

CHARACTERS

    STEVEN, a fifty-three year old recovering addict/drama queen.

SETTING

    A veterinary clinic. Boston, Massachusetts.

TIME

    Daytime, May 2009

. . .

SCENE. STEVEN stands CENTER STAGE, holding an empty, old, plastic pet carrying case that is scratched and worn. HE speaks to the veterinarian (who is an OFFSTAGE presence), while looking at a piece of paper.

STEVEN: I know. Her numbers. You've got her numbers. I see what you've circled. Her numbers suck. *(Beat.)* Which is exactly why I brought her here to you. So, we can fix this. Sure, her kidneys are failing, her liver is failing, but her heart is *(speaking with a forced "Old World" accent)* strong like ox.
(Pause. Softly, almost begging –)
Come on. You're the Dr. Doolittle — you can perk her up a little — I've seen you work miracles with my own myopic eyes. And I know she's got at least one more round in the ring — she's a lover not a fighter — but she's not out for the count yet! She'd been doing really well up until today. She's been eating more — and moving around more. She's just having a bad day. We can't write her off just because she's had one measly, crappy morning — that wouldn't be fair. Like the Nazis shooting sick people in the work camps. "Hello? Na-zis? They're working for you-ou!"
(Pause.)
Look, I've been following your instructions to a tee. I've been feeding her with the syringe, just like you told me to — and it's worked! She's been taking her food *and* her medicine. She hasn't thrown up in a week. Even longer actually. She hasn't puked in ten days. You should weigh her. You'll see. She hasn't lost any weight.
(Beat.)
Of course, I know how old she is. But you yourself said, *"Old doesn't mean sick."*
(Correcting.)

No, she's not twenty yet — she's nineteen-and-a-half.
(Beat.)
No, I disagree. I don't think it's her time. Not today. *(Beat.)* Two weeks ago, a month ago, maybe then — when I saw her beginning to suffer. Or last year, when she didn't eat for five whole days — you didn't give up on her then — I brought her here and you gave her the IVs and I brought her home, and she was the old Marilyn.
(Beat.)
I know she's had all the IVs she can take, but maybe there's something else you can do.
(Irritated -)
No, I don't have any suggestions. That's why we're here.
(Nervously –)
She's still breathing, right?
(Relieved.)
Okay. So, your staff has her back there with you, you're all doing what you can. I'll just wait until there's a plan.
(Pause.)
I don't like that plan.
(Pause.)
I think she needs more time.
(Pause.)
No, I don't want her to suffer.
(Pause.)
I know. That is what we agreed upon. I just don't think that's what's happening now.
(Pause.)
We just talked about that. But, you know what? I don't care about the numbers.
(Holds up the piece of paper –)
I mean, what do these goddamn numbers mean anyway? They don't paint the whole Technicolor picture. My numbers haven't been good in years — I don't think anyone's called them "good" *ever* — and here I am. About eighteen years after they said I'd be dead and gone — they'd written me off — I was sure that by this year, 2009, the only memory of me would be in the form of a 6X6 square on a traveling quilt.
(Beat.)
I mean, I'm still here. A living, breathing, vibrant, handsome, *(mumbling)* hmm-hmm-three year old, ho-mo-sex-u-al, HIV positive, mostly former meth addict. It's terribly dull to be completely recovered from *anything*.

(Pause. In disbelief –)
You didn't know? Come on! Which of those things didn't you know?
(Pause.)
Oh, *that.* *(Beat.)* Really? You're shitting me.
(Pause.)
No, no, no! Please. Please. Don't be offended. I just thought you would know. I mean you have MD, or VD, or what the hell letters do they put after your name? I mean, don't I look like a cat with FIV?
(STEVEN does his cat impression.)
Seriously, I just figure people can tell. I used to be paranoid about it, but you know, you reach a certain age, you just can't give a shit about what other people think of you.
(Beat.)
Do you remember the T.V. show, "The Golden Girls?" That was my favorite show back in the day. Still is.
(Doing his impersonation of the character, Sophia:)
Picture it: Sicily. 1888.
(Beat.)
Okay, not Sicily, Boston. And not 1888, 1988. *(Beat.)* Nineteen-Eighty-Eight. That's the year I was diagnosed, just a few blocks from here. Before the Berlin Wall fell, way before 9/11, before the Big Dig. You know, at that time, when they diagnosed you, they basically said, "Go home; you have two or three years." So, I tried to read everything I could back then to make myself healthier. I thought, "I'm gonna defy the odds — I'm gonna live to see 1995." It seemed like a pretty ballsy goal at the time. *(Beat.)* I'd go to these healing workshops, and they'd say, take care of something, take care of an animal, if you have something, someone to look after, your energy will shift, and you'll have a purpose and you can connect with the life force of that animal and that force will transfer over to you, and you'll have a reason to stay alive.
(Beat.)
I got Marilyn in the fall of 1989, when she was just eight weeks old. I got her and her sister both, Marilyn Monroe and Norma Jeane — the movie star and the yet-to-be-discovered white trash beauty. Oh, they were so cute. They were like babies — you just wanted to shake the crap out of them. Like maracas!
(Beat.)
Don't look at me like that. *(Sarcastically.)* They *loved* it.
(Beat.)
Oh! They were adorable! I'd never really been a pet person; I don't like

dealing with another living thing's shit. Their physical-literal-fecal shit. But these two girls — they wooed me. I had a spiritual conversion.

(Beat.)

So, I had these two little fluff balls. And I'd just spend a lot of time with them, trying to soak up their chi; I was like the total opposite of my Colombian neighbor who thought that cats would suck out your breath and kill you. At night, I used to lie so close to these little three pound creatures, trying to suck *in* their breath, so that I'd be able to keep on living. Mostly, I just got a lot of cat hair up my nose. They'd curl up on my chest if I were lying down, or I'd carry them around on my head — sometimes both of them at once — I have this big, flat head — but usually just one at a time. I hated to be away from them. I was working downtown at one of the big hotels at the time, and I would come home every day on my lunch hour, so I could rejuvenate myself with my cats.

(Beat.)

And then a year later I had that PCP pneumonia, and I was in and out of the hospital and then when I was home, I'd be lying awake in my bed at night, clinging to the two of them and petting them, and I weighed like 112 pounds, and I was crying and crying because I was going to die and who was going to take care of my girls?

(Beat.)

That was the first of many battles for my sorry-ass immune system. It was like my cells were U.S. troops in Fallujah or Afghanistan — they were outnumbered ten to one, they didn't have enough support, and no one had sent the requisite number of tanks or armor.

(Beat.)

Then, around '97, when the meds finally started working and I was finally on the right cocktail, that's when I started thinking, "Hey! I'm actually living with this thing! I made it past '95." I was like an AIDS Olympian. I felt so *invigorated.*

(Beat.)

I re-pledged my love for Norma J. and Marilyn-lyn. I wanted them to be healthy and happy — I felt I owed them at least that — so I did what neurotic mothers have done for ages; I gave them all sorts of shit that, in reality, was really bad for them. I fed the cats lots of milk and table scraps, which, of course, made them sick — especially Norma — as you can imagine, she was the more delicate of the two; Marilyn had a much easier time in life. The cats got milk, and I treated myself to meth. Oh! My love affair with crystal meth. I was so thin and sexy. And productive. I could vacuum all night. I had one 5X7 rug in my whole apartment, and I would just vacuum and vacuum in straight, parallel rows, over and over and over. Norma and Marilyn saw it all. If I stayed up all night, they stayed up all night.

(Beat.)

But then, Norma got cancer. You remember when we put Norma down? I'm still not sure I made the right decision with her. Maybe that wasn't her time. Marilyn and I were both wrecks after that. We just moped around the house together, looking at all of Norma's old haunts: the bedroom radiator, the windowsills in the living room, the back of the linen closet.

(Beat.)

After she passed, I started worrying that I was pushing my luck, and maybe I should clean myself up a little. It's hard to go to work when you're tweaking and haven't slept in three days. Eventually, I was fired. Which made not going to work so much easier. I started going to this day program, trying to get clean. My sister, she's a nurse, came from Ohio and helped me out during that time. I wasn't doing great, but she said she knew I'd pull through. She told me, "A nuclear bomb could fall on Boston, and there'd be no known survivors, and then out of the rubble would climb you and Marilyn."

(Beat.)

The last couple of years have been pretty quiet — Marilyn's been enjoying her "Golden Girl Years," and I've been working for Winston Flowers, creating arrangements and generally surrounding myself with beauty.

(Beat.)

I'm either blessed or just one lucky fuck because there's no reason why I should still be here.

(Long pause.)

You know, I expected her to outlive me.

(Pleading)

How about one more week? I really think she can pull through this. She's done it before!

(Long pause.)

Okay. Okay.

(Pause.)

Yes, that is what I said.

(Pause.)

No, no suffering.

(Pause.)

That is what we agreed.

(Long pause.)

Yes, my decision. I don't want her to suffer.
(Pause.)
I understand.
(Pause.)
I know. We did this with Norma.
(Pause.)
Sure, I'll sign it. But could I please just see her now? Before we do anything else?
(Pause.)
You'll bring her here?
(Long pause. STEVEN waits. The sound of someone bringing a cat in a carrier over to HIM. STEVEN turns towards MARILYN.)
Hello, my beautiful, beautiful girl.
(STEVEN begins to cry.)
(LIGHTS FADE TO BLACK.)

END OF PLAY

THE PRE-NUP
A Ten Minute Play

Marisa Smith

Sponsored by Foothills Theatre Company
Directed by Christopher James Webb

Heather................................ Jessica Webb
Dephina .... Amy Barker
Lincoln .... Russell Garrett

Delphina, an aging movie star, visits a Beverly Hills funeral parlor to say goodbye to her husband Lincoln, escorted by Lincoln's assistant Heather.

Marisa Smith: After working in the theater as an actress, producer and theater book publisher (Smith and Kraus Publishers), Marisa wrote her first play in 2004 (*Book Group*). Since then she has written, *The Devine Comedy, The Lumpkin Sister's Christmas Caper, Queenie's Christmas, Kong's Reunion, Dog's Life, and Saving Kitty* (full lengths*)* and ten minute plays *The Dress Rehearsal* and *The Pre-Nup* (*BTM X1*). In 2009 *Saving Kitty* won Best Play from NH in the Clauder competition sponsored by Maine's Portland Stage. Marisa's plays have been produced in her home state of NH, VT, MA and Florida.

CHARACTERS
Dephina, Woman in her 40's
Heather, Woman in her 20's
Lincoln, A corpse

SETTING
A funeral home in Beverly Hills

. . .

A funeral home in Beverly Hills. A private room. Lots of flowers. There's a closed coffin on a platform in the room. A door opens and DELPHINA and HEATHER enter. DELPHINA is dressed all in black, with a big black floppy hat and sunglasses. She has a large black purse slung over her shoulder. HEATHER is dressed in jeans and a tight T-shirt and holds DELPHINA'S arm as they enter. DELPHINA'S head is bowed.

HEATHER: We're here, Delphina, you can lose the sunglasses and the hat now.

DELPHINA: This is it, this is where he is?

HEATHER: Yeah, he's here. Look, this is your only time to be alone with him. Nobody knows he's here but that can't last forever. C'mon, you gotta do this.

(Gently turns her around and takes off her glasses and her hat and starts walking her towards the coffin. DELPHINA covers her eyes.)

DELPHINA: *(Peeks between her fingers.)* Is he in there?

HEATHER: Yes! I'll show you! *(Starts to open coffin.)*

DELPHINA: *(Runs and throws herself on the closed coffin.)* No, no, not yet. Oh my God. Lincoln, Lincoln, are you there, are you really there? I can't believe it. *(To HEATHER.)* Is he really in there? *(Shaking HEATHER'S shoulders.)* How could this have happened Heather, how? He's been drug free for twenty years, alcohol free for ten, and he just stopped eating anything that wasn't in it's original form —

HEATHER: Listen, the frigging clock is ticking, Delphina. I should open it. Right now only you and me and well, Buddy knows, but soon —

DELPHINA: Buddy knows?

HEATHER: Buddy was with him when it happened.

DELPHINA: Tell me again.

HEATHER: They were working on the Darwin contract —

DELPHINA: Oh, the Darwin project, Lincoln would be a great Darwin. He loves evolution.

HEATHER: And all of a sudden he had this like freight train of a headache and so Buddy went to get some aspirin in the kitchen and by the time he came back Linc was —

DELPHINA: — end of movie.

HEATHER: Do you wanna see him or not?

DELPHINA: I wish I were Catholic. A Catholic would know what to do now.

HEATHER: I'm opening it *now*.

(HEATHER starts to raise the lid of the coffin.)

DELPHINA: No, no, not yet! Just give me a minute, I just need a minute!

HEATHER: Okay, one minute.

DELPHINA: I really loved him, Heather!

HEATHER: Yeah, I know.

DELPHINA: I mean, other women said they did, they threw themselves at him, but I really did, through everything, I loved him!

HEATHER: Chicks really dug him.

DELPHINA: Please.

HEATHER: I'm sorry, I shouldn't be talkin' like this —

DELPHINA: Oh, c'mon Heather, you're not saying anything that the entire world doesn't know!

HEATHER: No, I'm sorry —

DELPHINA: Stop saying you're sorry. Must we woman constantly say we're sorry? Don't be! Are you kidding? Do you know how many times I fantasized about renting Grauman's Chinese Theater and inviting every woman Lincoln slept with in the past twenty five years just to show them that I knew, that I knew all the time. Jesus, it would be standing room only. Everyone knows that Lincoln was the biggest womanizer this side of Attila the Hun, or Bill Clinton — *(She starts to hyperventilate.)* Oh, it's so unreal, so horrible. Okay, *(Motioning to coffin.)* you can do it.

(HEATHER slowly raises the lid and reveals LINCOLN'S prone body.)

DELPHINA: *(Gasps.)* Oh, he looks so lifelike.

HEATHER: Yeah, he looks really real, yeah.

DELPHINA: I love his nose.

HEATHER: Great nose. That was somethin' Delphina — -to put up with that for all those years. Like true fucking love. *(HEATHER remembers something she heard at school.)* Which, like, never did run smooth. *(DELPHINA stares at her, surprised.)* Yeah, Madonna said that I think. Once. Maybe.

DELPHINA: *(Condescendingly.)* The Bard, I believe, Heather.

HEATHER: But everybody says that you were faithful to *him*.

DELPHINA: Yes, I was, I was indeed.

HEATHER: So those rumors about you and Marco Vega —

DELPHINA: *(Walks away from the coffin, agitated.)* Marco is a fantastic actor, a brilliant Achilles. APOLLO'S ANGER is going to put him on the map.

HEATHER: *(Following her.)* And you're playing his — -

DELPHINA: Mother! *(Laughing wildly.)* Thetis, the sea goddess. I have the most fabulous costumes, like spun sugar and latte foam. *(Puts her hands to her cheeks.)*

HEATHER: Jesus Christ, you're blushin'! You're all frigging pink! So it's true! You and Marco.

DELPHINA: Don't be ridiculous, it's hot in here. I'm old enough to be his mother, and I am his mother, you know, in the movie. Oh God.

HEATHER: What a hunk, no shit.

DELPHINA: I have been faithful to Lincoln for twenty five years, since the day we were married! I'm practically an old crone now, in a few years no man will even look at me much less be attracted to me. God, one time, just one time, I deserved a little — Please on the body of my dear beloved husband, not one word, you caught me at a vulnerable moment, Heather. Please. Oh, Lincoln, Lincoln *(Throws herself on his body.)* you were my one true love, forgive me my sweet, forgive me —
(LINCOLN bolts upright from his prone position in the coffin, DEL- PHINA screams. LINCOLN holds up a small recording device.)

LINCOLN: Okay, that's all I need. Heather, you were great. Delphina, you've violated the terms of our pre-nup with your confession of adultery.

DELPHINA: Lincoln! Ohmygod, I'm having a heart attack! But I knew, I knew you couldn't be dead, I never really believed it. Ohmygod, you're alive, it's a miracle! Heather, Heather, it's a miracle, we witnessed a miracle.

HEATHER: *(Laughing hysterically.)* He's risen from the dead, woo, woo.

DELPHINA: *(Looking back and forth at them.)* Wait. Heather. You knew. You knew he was alive. You knew.

HEATHER: The look on your face, farfuckingout, too bad we didn't have a camera. You should get an Oscar, you crazy old diva — -

DELPHINA: *(Shakes HEATHER.)* You bitch! You *evil* bitch!

HEATHER: You hit me! She hit me! I'm callin' the cops!

LINCOLN: *(Climbing out of the casket.)* Girls, girls, calm down, no physical violence, please.

DELPHINA: *(To LINCOLN, furious.)* What kind of sick joke is this? Here I was, devastated, in total grief —

LINCOLN: Yet you couldn't wait to tell Heather about your *boyfriend.*

DELPHINA: How did you do this, what did you say to the funeral home?

LINCOLN: I told them we were rehearsing for my new movie —

HEATHER AND LINCOLN: DEATH TAKES A SABBATICAL.

DELPHINA: What did you say about the pre-nup before? What's going on here!

LINCOLN: I needed to know whether or not you violated the terms of our pre-nup. As you recall, if you commit adultery, I'm not obligated to give you anything, no monies, assets, or real estate. Nada. Bupkis. *Zilch.*

DELPHINA: You want a divorce?

HEATHER: Tell her, Linc.

DELPHINA: You want to marry her? Your little personal assistant? God, Lincoln, how unoriginal. You've had dozens of "Heathers."

HEATHER: Linc, let's go. We've got the tape. Let's get outa here, it's creepy.

DEPHINA: You think that tape will hold up?

LINCOLN: I think this little baby *(Holds up recorder.)* will do the trick. *(Gives tape to HEATHER.)*

DELPHINA: Fine, divorce me but that tape won't help you. Marco will deny that anything ever happened between us. He has to, he's got a new girlfriend, Sierra Nevada or something.

HEATHER: Sally Dakota, she was in AN INCOVENIENT HALF TRUTH.

DELPHINA: Yeah, and I'll make it worth his while to deny it.

LINCOLN: With my money.

DELPHINA: Our money. Go ahead, Lincoln, try it, when I'm done with you it will be MY money.

HEATHER: You said — all we need is what you have on the tape!

LINCOLN: Yeah, but what if she's right and the pre-nup doesn't hold up and that Achilles dude says that nothing happened, then she's gonna go whole hog Scotty. She's gonna sue me for every penny!

HEATHER: But that's not what you said. You said we could have *everything*!

DELPHINA: Hey, you've got *him* Heather, isn't that enough?

HEATHER: This is a completely ridiculous conversation —

LINCOLN: Yeah, if I had nothing, would you still want to be with me babe?

HEATHER: Of course I would —

LINCOLN: But would you, if I were *broke* —

HEATHER: *(Feeling trapped and near tears.)* I don't wanna play this stupid game. You promised, all we had to do was —

LINCOLN: *(Holding her by the shoulders.)* I need to know Heather, if I had absolutely nothing would you want to marry me?

HEATHER: *(Frustrated and crying.)* Yeah, yeah!!

LINCOLN: *(On his knees.)* Are you telling me the truth, SO HELP YOU GOD?

HEATHER: No, No, goddamnit, I'm not!

(HEATHER throws the tape at LINCOLN and runs towards the door.)

HEATHER: And I quit, I quit, you bastard! Find a new assistant to screw!

(LINCOLN and DELPHINA watch her exit and Lincoln calls after her.)

LINCOLN: *HEATHER! HEATHER! SCOTTY! SCOTTY! (Still holding the pre-nup.)* Anyway, she kept dropping my laptop and she made the *worst* coffee.

DELPHINA: Scotty?

LINCOLN: Heather, the moors, you know. *(Brandishing the pre-nup.)* I think this woulda held up actually.

DELPHINA: God, I totally forgot about that thing.

LINCOLN: I never thought you'd be unfaithful to me in a million years, Delph, I had to find out for sure.

DELPHINA: And you wanted to see how I'd react if I thought you were dead? That's terrible! That's sick!

LINCOLN: *(Grinning.)* You were really ripped.

DELPHINA: I was. I mean God knows how many times I've wanted you to die, but in reality it was horrible. Just horrible.

LINCOLN: Really? Really bad? Were you in total pain and agony?

DELPHINA: You got me this time.

LINCOLN: I know.

DELPHINA: Too bad you didn't film it.

(LINCOLN points to the camera in the corner of the ceiling.)

DELPHINA: Nooo.

(LINCOLN nods.)

DELPHINA: You are a *genius*.

LINCOLN: C'mon. It's kinda cozy in here. *(Helps her into the coffin.)*

DELPHINA: Oo, I've never been in a coffin before. I feel like a virgin again. *(Is halfway in the coffin.)*

LINCOLN: *(Rips up the pre-nup.)* I don't think we need this anymore. *(The pre-nup flutters to the ground.)*

DELPHINA: Lincoln, I really think you should *direct*.

LINCOLN: YEAH!

END OF PLAY

CLOSE YOUR EYES

Erin Striff

Close Your Eyes was first presented as part of the New Works New Britain Festival, February 27–March 1, 2009.
Directed by Enza Giannone
Marjory/Clara . . . . Deborah Walsh
Caroline . . . . Iris McQuillan-Grace
Paul. . . . . Kevin DeChello

Boston Theater Marathon
Sunday, May 17, 2009
Sponsored by Boston Actors Theater
Directed by Joey Pelletier with Danielle Leeber
Caroline . . . . Jenny Reagan
Clara. . . . . Julia Specht
Marjory. . . . . Megan Atkinson
Paul. . . . . Jonathan Overby

Close Your Eyes is about a woman who is tried for infanticide, exploring what happens when an ordinary woman commits an unspeakable act. It is based on actual events.

Erin Striff has several ten minute plays currently in development. Her full-length play, *Skint*, appeared at the Edinburgh Festival Fringe and the Sherman Theatre, Cardiff, UK. Her adaptation of *Trilby, Trilby & Svengali*, appeared at Chapter Arts Centre, Cardiff. She lives in Connecticut with her husband and three children.

NOTE: Some of the material in this play came from interviews conducted in a series of newspaper articles by Daniel Jeffreys which appeared in *The Independent* newspaper in London from February-November, 1995.

CHARACTERS

CAROLINE, 30 year old middle class Englishwoman with an RP accent. Her vulnerability makes her seem much younger than her years. "Normal."

CLARA, 28 year old American airport security guard. Sympathetic and watchful.

MARJORY, 37 year old American Assistant District Attorney. Professional and determined, she believes in justice for victims who can't speak for themselves.

PAUL, 32 year old Englishman. Unused to talking about his feelings. His accent is not quite as proper as Caroline's. Wants to be like everybody else.

SETTING

JFK International Airport, Rikers Island, The Queens County District Attorney's Office and London, England.

TIME

September 23, 1994

. . .

SCENE 1

CAROLINE *(In spotlight.)*: I've named her now. Olivia Ann. She has to have a name — she's not just a baby girl.

(JFK Airport. CAROLINE hovers nervously, wearing a zip up sweat-shirt and clutching it around her. CLARA wears the uniform of an airport security guard.)

CLARA *(Beckoning.)*: Come on through. There's a line of people waiting.

CAROLINE: Can I please not go through the detector?

CLARA: You have to. Everyone goes through. You'll miss your plane.

CAROLINE *(Agitated.)*: You don't understand. I'm pregnant. I don't want to do anything to hurt the baby.

CLARA: It's okay — a metal detector isn't going to hurt anybody. All the preg-nant ladies come through here, they're just fine. Their babies are fine.

CAROLINE: Please. Can we talk somewhere else? I don't want my boyfriend to hear.

(They stand aside.)

CLARA: What . . . What have you got there? What are you holding? *(Moves clos-er to CAROLINE.)* You're not pregnant — you've got something under your sweatshirt.

CAROLINE: No, I'm pregnant. I'm pregnant. *(CLARA reaches for her.)* Don't —

CLARA: *(Prodding the bump with her fingers.)* It's all right. Calm down, ma'am. What's your name?

CAROLINE: Caroline Hughes. I'm here with my boyfriend. He went through already, he's waiting. Please don't tell him. I don't want him to find out about the baby.

CLARA: Where are you going back to, England? I hear that accent. Is that where you're from?

CAROLINE: I'm flying back to London with my boyfriend and his brothers. I don't want to miss the flight.

CLARA: Look, I'm going to have to ask you to unzip your sweatshirt.

CAROLINE *(agitated)*: No.

CLARA: I have to see what you've got there. It's all right. Just let me see. *(CAROLINE becomes more placid. She takes off the sweatshirt and carefully removes a plastic bag with drawstrings she has looped over her shoulders.)* What do you have there?

CAROLINE: *(Holding up the bag by the bottom so the drawstrings are on top.)* This is my baby.

CLARA: Where's your baby?

CAROLINE: In the bag.

(CAROLINE holds out the bag for inspection. CLARA, not comprehending, pulls the drawstrings open — she is hit with a smell and looks in revulsion. Caroline takes the bag back by the strings.)

CLARA: *(Calling.)* Can I get some backup here?

CAROLINE: You can't let my boyfriend see. He didn't know I was pregnant. He'll be so upset. He'll be so angry.

CLARA: Sometimes they're born dead. It's not your fault. You need to get some help.

CAROLINE: *(Stepping forward and dropping the drawstring bag, which falls heavily.)* I don't want my boyfriend to know.

(Blackout.)

SCENE 2

(Caroline and Marjory are onstage. The two women are lit separately and do not initially speak directly to one another. Caroline is in a prison outfit; Marjory is in a tailored suit.)

MARJORY: Are you ready? *(Smiles grimly off camera.)* Sound bite time. I'm Marjory Friedman, Assistant District Attorney, Special Victims Branch, and

I'll be prosecuting this case. I represent the dead baby and the state of New York.

CAROLINE: They brought me here to Rikers Island. I've heard of it on the telly. Crime shows.

MARJORY: On September 23rd, 1994, Caroline Hughes was arrested as she boarded a plane bound for the UK. The dead baby's body was found inside a bag. Two days later she was charged with Murder Two. That's for acting with depraved indifference to human life.

CAROLINE: It's funny, I never got into any trouble before. Except for running up a credit card. Now, I'm sharing a cell with six girls — one killed her boyfriend and there's another who shot a taxi driver. Most of the girls here were caught for dealing drugs. I've even started smoking.

MARJORY: Murder Two is the maximum penalty for infanticide in the state of New York. If charged, she'll receive a minimum fifteen year sentence.

CAROLINE: I've been doing what they call therapeutic drawing. Better than seeing the prison psychologist. I've been making Mother's Day cards for all the girls.

MARJORY: The defense is trying to say that it was post-natal psychosis. But they're going to have a hard time proving that because it doesn't usually occur immediately after childbirth.

CAROLINE: Mum and Dad say that American laws are really medieval, that they aren't as advanced as what we have back home. If I had gone into labor the next day, if I had the baby in England, everything would have been all right.

MARJORY: I understand that in the U.K. there's an Infanticide Act which treats these cases more leniently. But in the United States, you don't get a free pass when you kill a baby instead of an adult.

CAROLINE: I could never hurt anything, certainly not my own baby. It was blue . . . it never breathed.

MARJORY: Even her boyfriend reports that although he was not aware she was pregnant, she was not acting in any way that indicated severe mental instability.

PAUL: *(Entering and stops as if responding to reporters.)* I just want to set the record straight. I don't like talking about it, but I don't like reading all those things people are saying about me, either. We were just on holiday. We tried to look forward to the trip, me and my two brothers. When we got there, Caroline was a bit of a pain really all week. Of course, now I know why.

CAROLINE: We did all the things tourists do, like going up all those really tall buildings.

PAUL: We were laughing and joking at the metal detectors. Our metal belt buckles kept setting off the alarm. Suddenly there was all this commotion. Caroline was being dragged away and I heard someone shout, "This woman's got a dead baby!" I thought it must belong to somebody else.

CAROLINE: I wanted children, but I was scared too. I didn't know what changes it would bring to my relationship with Paul.

PAUL: I've been coming to grips with the fact I would have been a dad. I can't look at a little girl without thinking of the baby. That was my baby too. I had a right to know she had our child.

CAROLINE: I can remember my mother baking a cake when I was ten. We were talking about something and she broke an egg without really looking at it. Out fell this . . . half-formed chick. It just dropped into the bowl with all the flour. My mum and I just stared at it.

PAUL: What I still don't understand is why she kept the baby's body with her.

CAROLINE: I just couldn't leave her behind.

PAUL: I still have nightmares about that night. I see Caroline being dragged away and there's all this blood.

CAROLINE: My best friend Alison was dying of breast cancer. It felt like, while her tumor grew, so did mine. I thought I was dying. I thought I had a tumor like my friend.

PAUL: We went to New York to get over the death of my brother's girlfriend. We were trying to move on with our lives. She didn't seem ill to us, she was just a bit withdrawn. She used to lie under the blanket all evening and go to bed early. You can see photos of her, taken just weeks before. She didn't even look pregnant.

CAROLINE: I felt so guilty. I couldn't tell anybody about the baby once I knew Alison would never be able to have children. All I know is I miss Alison so much. She would have known what to do.

PAUL: At first, I thought the link to Alison was absurd. There's no way most people would have said they were best friends . . . but now I think that was all part of the delusion.

MARJORY: Since the defense can't prove it was post-natal psychosis, they're trying to prove that she was clinically depressed before the baby was born. But because of their earlier tactics, they are having a tough time finding people who will say Caroline's behavior was abnormal.

PAUL: I can't believe anybody would think Caroline could deliberately harm a baby; she loves children. But I think of that night, I read the papers . . . I don't know what to believe.

MARJORY: Ms. Hughes, I understand that you wish to make a statement concerning the incident that occurred on the night of September 22nd, 1994 at the SoHo Hotel in Manhattan.

CAROLINE *(To MARJORY.)*: It was our last day in New York. We'd gone for a ferry cruise round the harbor but I felt sick at dinner and asked Paul to take me back to the hotel. He and his brothers went on to a bar.

PAUL *(To CAROLINE.)*: I told her that she and I couldn't go on the way we had been, but she said everything was fine. I let it go. We were on holiday. I had no idea about anything — I just went out drinking.

CAROLINE: At first I rested but as the night went on, the pain got worse so I went to the bathroom, I turned on the taps and climbed into the warm water. I felt as though my body was ripping apart. I remember crying out for Paul and I thought I was dying. While I was in the bath, the baby came. I saw it, I pulled it out.

MARJORY: Did the baby move?

CAROLINE: No. I didn't know what to do, I thought it was dead.

MARJORY: Was it a boy or a girl?

CAROLINE: Girl. She was a girl.

MARJORY: The coroner's report indicates the baby would have been moving and crying. She cut the cord with nail scissors and found a bag in the hallway and put the baby in it.

CAROLINE: Paul . . .

MARJORY: At this point the baby was suffocated. She cleaned the bathroom, then put the baby next to her and went to bed. She concealed the baby so her boyfriend wouldn't see it.

PAUL: They told me she was out of her mind and that she killed it, but Caroline's story has never changed — she always said it was born dead. There were experts who said it was possible the baby was stillborn, but no one wanted to take the risk of standing trial.

MARJORY: Caroline Hughes pleaded guilty to Manslaughter, Second Degree. She spent eight months on remand in Rikers Island Penitentiary, and a further eight months on bail in Queens. She was then released directly to the Maudsley Hospital in south London for psychological treatment.

CAROLINE: I had to confess if I wanted to go home.

PAUL: I sometimes feel as though I never knew who Caroline was. I'm not sure I'd know where to start if she walked in now. My mum wrote her and told her not to write me again and to stop trying to call me. I'm done speaking to the press about this. I've told you everything there is.

(PAUL starts to exit. He stops when CAROLINE starts speaking. From the start of her speech we begin to hear children on a playground, becoming louder throughout the scene.)

CAROLINE *(brokenly.)*: I imagine Olivia Ann, in the court they call her Baby Jane Doe, but I see her, I have these pictures of her in my head and her name is Olivia Ann. *(Taking comfort in her reverie.)*. And when I miss her I imagine a playground, this most wonderful playground with all of these amazing things. Slides that go on and on and never end and everything is soft, so no one gets hurt. And there's other children playing all around, all the ones who died, that's where they go. They play for so long, they never have to come back home. The older ones help Olivia Ann onto the swing and she's laughing. But I don't know who looks after those dead children. I don't know who's there to take care of them. Do they look after each other? I want to go to that place and take care of them.

(Playground sounds become louder and more distorted until the cacophony is intense — then all noise suddenly stops.).

PAUL: She's just an ordinary girl.

(Blackout.)

END OF PLAY

BOUNDLESS AS THE SEA

Susan W. Thompson

BOUNDLESS AS THE SEA was originally produced by Pilgrim Theatre Research and Performance Collaborative and had its world premiere at the Boston Theater Marathon, May 17, 2009.
Directed by Kim Mancuso
Man .... Kermit Dunkelberg
Woman............................. Susan Thompson

Two aging actors, no longer playing lead roles, meet in their cramped dressing room after a performance of *Romeo and Juliet.* There they hash out their lives and loves using Shakespeare as fodder.

Susan Thompson is a Lecoq-trained artist who performs, directs and teaches in the Boston area. She is a core member of Pilgrim Theatre. Original works include: *The Wild Place,* (co-authored with Jon Lipsky), *Anam Cara,* (co-authored with Judi Wilson and Anne Gottlieb), *Panic* and *Missing Persons.*

CHARACTERS

MAN, late forties to late fifties, a Shakespearean actor with faded elegance, still a bit of a rake but no longer trim. He is dressed in period tights, pantaloons, and slippers, with a period hat. By the end of the play, he will be dressed in street clothes and a winter coat.

WOMAN, late forties to late fifties, a Shakespearean actress, once a star. She is passionate and dramatic. She is dressed in period costume and heavily made up. By the end of the play she will be in street clothes and without makeup.

SETTING

A dressing room backstage in a theater after a performance of *Romeo and Juliet*. It is not a grand affair. Two tables with mirrors, makeup, cold cream, tissue, a basin of water, towel, personal belongings, and a wig stand. There is a clothing rack filled with period costumes.

TIME

Around 11 PM on an autumn night. Now.

NOTE

The conversation should go from conversational and general to combative and personal. The text from *Romeo and Juliet* should be delivered as a wild and desperate fight, dripping with sarcasm, until the actors reconcile and sit together to deliver the final lines.

. . .

The two actors, a MAN and a WOMAN in their late 40s or 50s, are dressed in Elizabethan costume and makeup, both of which are a bit garish and highly theatrical. She is holding flowers. They move together in the space with familiarity. They have known each other for a long time. They have a past together on stage and off. The dressing room is a kind of home for them. Lights up. They are waving and speaking to a young man off-stage who has just performed the role of Romeo in the play.

WOMAN: Good night! Great show! *(Waving and looking offstage.)*
MAN: Yeah! You really nailed the death scene. *(Gesturing and speaking in the same direction off-stage.)*
WOMAN: *(Sotto voce to the MAN, checking to see that the other actor has gone.)* He did not. He dropped about ten lines.

MAN: It was better that way. *(Smiling.)*

WOMAN: You're bad. *(Amused and hitting him gently.)*

MAN: You have to encourage him.

WOMAN: *(Playfully.)* Don't encourage him too much.

MAN: I remember being young enough to play Romeo. I remember being young and in love . . . *(Taking off a his hat and setting it on a wig stand)*

WOMAN: Bullshit!

(She sets her flowers on the table and turns to be unzipped. The man unzips her dress as she speaks and she steps out of her clothes. She is in a bra and slip.)

MAN: I do!

WOMAN: Because I remember being young and it was never like *that. (Gesturing towards the stage.)* That was the promise but the reality was he never looked at me. He never knew I existed or he told me to get lost or, better yet, he confided in me that he loved someone else and I was left holding his coat and smelling him there in the leather while he was rolling in the grass with some long legged, lissome beauty!

MAN: Yeah. Weren't we all promised Romeos and Juliets at one time?

(He takes off his jacket and undershirt through the next few lines.)

WOMAN: Because if love wasn't like that, then something has failed us. Life hasn't given us what we were told we would get. You know? The whole thing! *(She sits and begins removing her makeup. She assesses herself in the mirror through his text.)*

MAN: Yes, the car and the job and health, oh yeah all that, all that "of course" kind of stuff. You know, good hair and teeth and nails, but also *that* . . . the big tamale!

(He begins removing his makeup. They share tissue boxes and cold cream.)

WOMAN: The real thing!

BOTH: LOVE!

WOMAN: Romantic and huge and . . .

MAN: reciprocated!

WOMAN: Hell yes, reciprocated!

MAN: *That* is the miracle. I mean, tragedies about unrequited love happen all the time. Just ask your friends and they will spill out a story like milk on a table.

WOMAN: And tragedies about abuse happen every day in the newspaper. You know, she tries to leave and he shoots up everything in the house! Even her . . .

MAN: even the dog!

WOMAN: and the kids!

MAN: Yes, the kids too. That kind of tragedy is everyday. It is the stuff of the ambulance chasers.

WOMAN: It is in the family.

MAN: But Romeo and Juliet . . . He felt it! *(Exuberantly.)*

WOMAN: And she felt it too! Right away and no problems! *(He gives her a sharp look. She explains.)* I mean, between them.

MAN: Yeah. She didn't play hard to get . . . *(It is obvious that he is speaking about her.)*

WOMAN: and he didn't think about the other girl, what's her name, anymore. *(She is offhand and bitter.)*

MAN: and there weren't any problems . . . *(Silence. They exchange a sharp look again. He gives her a rueful smile.)* with them I mean.

WOMAN: None, no problems. *(Silence.)*

MAN: With them I mean. *(Gently.)*

WOMAN: *(With impatience.)* Yeah, yeah, yeah! I know. *(Silence, but she can't resist making a point.)* And they made promises and they kept them . . .

MAN: *(Pointedly to her.)* and they didn't break them. *(The woman goes to the clothes rack for her street clothes.)*

WOMAN: You'll tell me that Romeo and Juliet didn't have time to break promises. That if they had had time, they would be like all the others, they would break their promises.

MAN: Juliet would have gotten fat.

(He laughs. She takes this personally. He washes his face in a basin of water and dries it through the next few lines.)

WOMAN: *(She speaks as she dresses and directs this at him.)* And Romeo would have begun to go out after work and come home late smelling of cheap perfume.

MAN: Isn't that what they always say? *(Complaining.)* Only there is no such thing as cheap perfume, it's all expensive now. Women and men, real ones, don't come cheap.

(She is dressed and holds a pair of shoes. She sits down and puts her shoes on through the next few lines.)

WOMAN: No, it is loneliness that will haunt *them, (indicating audience),* and drive them into each other's arms, not the promises of Romeo and Juliet. *(He looks out over the audience too.)* They will be alone and that is the worse fricking problem in the entire universe! It's what we are told should never happen and yet, it will happen won't it? Because we come in and go out alone.

MAN: *(To the audience too.)* Yes, we love to say that Romeo and Juliet had to die because, had they lived, they would have had a no fault divorce . . . *(He goes to the clothes rack and begins to change his shirt and pants.)* . . . or she would have thrown it all in his face; how he promised her and now he didn't love her anymore. *(A tired list.)* She would become shrill and . . .

WOMAN: . . . and I will become shrill and accuse you and you will become brutal! *(With emotion.)* And I should leave a shit like you, all my friends will tell me, *(She confronts him.)* but I can't because of this and that and because of those promises, when we were young and we believed them! *(She adjusts his shirt brusquely and without thinking.)* When we were young and promises could be made because we had no sense of history or the repercussions or the crazy compromises that life twists us into. You will tell me that Romeo and Juliet are fantasies! *(They begin to hang up their costumes during the next lines while they argue.)*

MAN: Because they never sat down at the breakfast table, sullen and hung over and each expecting the other to make the coffee . . .

WOMAN: And they never had to struggle over whether they should make love when they didn't feel like it, and breaking it to the other gently that, *(he is in the way and she moves around him to hang her costume),* "Not now, honey. I don't feel like it." *(Silence.)* Do you really think love is bullshit? *(With passion.)* That we can't and won't and shouldn't make that ultimate declaration because, oh no! that only happens in corny movies or daytime television and leads to complications. Or it happens in bodice rippers, those $5.99 books that you buy in the 24/7 drugstore with the lurid covers, you know, stormy skies and satin skirts billowing and all that crap! *(He watches her as she speaks to the audience.)* Or love, did it really only happen when you were little and cherished and cuddled and cooed over, tucked in at night and they lived happily ever after? Is that what love has become? A story told to a child signifying nothing? No! I think true love is responsibility. It is putting in your time. *(Sensual and dangerous.)* It's like vacuuming and doing the dishes; you have to do it everyday, ad nauseam. It isn't always fresh and bitter and wild like that! No! That can't last. Love *is* a wild and delicate plant that needs tending if you want it to grow in *your* garden. *(They are both dressed now. He gets her coat and comes towards her gently. He begins to take on the role of Romeo.)*

MAN: And I am inconstant because I loved Rosaline one day and Juliet the next? But Rosaline had never entered my life really, much less my bedroom. *(He diverges.)* Although, technically, it was Juliet's bedroom that I entered. No. I never saw her, that Rosaline of poetry, I never saw her on my pillow, like Juliet, meaty and fragrant as steak and potatoes. *(He takes her about the waist. Intimately, trying to calm her.)* Juliet nourishes me. Rosaline never did. *(He goes to give her a tender kiss. She pulls away.)* Lady, by yonder blessed moon I swear —

WOMAN: *(She takes on Juliet's lines but is impatient and dismissive.)* Swear not by the moon, the inconstant moon!

MAN: What shall I swear by?

WOMAN: *(With sarcasm.)* Do not swear at all; although I joy in thee, I have no joy of this contract tonight.

MAN: O, wilt thou leave me so unsatisfied?

WOMAN: What satisfaction canst thou have tonight?

(She laughs bitterly as he helps her into a coat.)

MAN: The exchange of thy love's faithful vow for mine.

WOMAN: I gave thee mine before thou didst request it: *(An accusation.)* And yet I would it were to give again.

MAN: Wouldst thou withdraw it? for what purpose, love?

WOMAN: But to be frank, and give it thee again. And yet I wish but for the thing I have: *(Wildly. She has nothing left to give.)* My bounty is as boundless as the sea, My love as deep; the more I give to thee, The more I have, for both are infinite.

(He has his coat on. He gives up and goes to leave.)

WOMAN: Romeo! *(Sharp and desperate.)*

MAN: My dear? *(They are in a stalemate.)*

WOMAN: I have forgot why I did call thee back.

MAN: Let me stand here till thou remember it.

WOMAN: I shall forget, to have thee still stand there, Remembering how I love thy company. *(With sarcasm.)*

MAN: *(He sits down and watches her. She, finally, capitulates and moves to join him.)*
And I'll still stay, to have thee still forget,
Forgetting any other home but this.

(She sits next to him. They sit in silence. Gently they join hands and remember the text together as if a familiar pact.)

WOMAN: Come, night; come, Romeo . . .

MAN: Come, thou day in night . . .

WOMAN: For thou wilt lie upon the wings of night

MAN: Whiter than new snow on a raven's back.

WOMAN: Come, gentle night, come, loving, black-brow'd night,
Give me my . . .

(They speak the text simultaneously.)

WOMAN: Romeo;   MAN: Juliet;
    And, when he shall die,   And, when she shall die,
    Take him and cut him out in little   Take her and cut her out in little
    stars,   stars,
    And he will make the face of   And she will make the face of
    heaven so fine   heaven so fine
    That all the world will be in love   That all the world will be in love
    with night   with night
    And pay no worship   And pay no worship
    to the garish sun.   to the garish sun.
    (They smile.)

WOMAN: *(Intimately to the audience.)* So don't be bitter that we will tell you their tale again . . .

MAN: and again . . . and again.

WOMAN: And you long to be them.

MAN: And you don't dare to because they die.

WOMAN: And if they didn't they would just be here,

MAN: the old couple at the end of the street,

WOMAN: who still smile at each other as they rake their lawn . . .

MAN: and whisper together between the darkness and the dawn.

    (She rests her head upon his shoulder. They begin to reminisce in murmuring tones. Perhaps they are talking about their performance tonight. Perhaps they are speaking about events long past. It is a private matter.)
    (FADE TO BLACK)

END OF PLAY

THE SENTRY

Michael Tooher

Sponsored by Boston Children's Theatre
Directed by Toby Schine
Sentry . . . . Michael Towers
Jill . . . . Penny Hansen
Camera Man . . . . Mike Bash

In *The Sentry* a TV crew on assignment in a war zone interviews a sniper who seems a little too fond of his work.

Michael Tooher's full length works include *The Waiting Room, Iceland, pudding, The Perfect Sameness of Our Days* and the recently completed *The Tree of the Methodists*. His short works have been performed in New York City, San Francisco, Boston, Albuquerque NM, and Portland ME.

CHARACTERS

The Sentry, Male, mid twenties to mid thirties.

Jill, Female, mid twenties to mid thirties. An attractive assignment reporter.

Cameraman, Male, twenties.

Anchorman, A recorded male voice.

SETTING

A rooftop in forward firebase Toro

TIME

Night. Now.

.   .   .

Darkness.

anchorman (v.o): In news from the war, four US Marines were killed when their Humvee ran over an improvised explosive device or IDE. That brings total US deaths from enemy action to three thousand, one hundred and fourteen killed in the last four years since the President declared an end to formal action. *(Beat)* Now we go live to Jill Bellows, embedded with the Golf Company Two/Six, 2nd Division at forward firebase Toro. *(Beat)* Jill, what's the situation there?
(A blue light come up on a SENTRY, slowly scanning the audience through the scope of his rifle. Next to him, slightly crouched down, is JILL, a reporter. JILL is holding a microphone. A CAMERAMAN is crouched down in front of them filming. A harsh white practical light comes from the camera as he signals JILL to start.)

jill: Thank you, Jim. *(Pause)* I'm standing on the top of the north spotting tower here at forward fire base Toro with . . . *(JILL quickly check her notes.)* Corporal Bradley Wilson of the 2nd Division, Golf Company Two/Six. Corporal, how are you tonight?
(The SENTRY lowers his weapon but his eyes are still scanning the middle distance.)

sentry: Fine ma'am, thank you. *(Pause)* Can I say hi to my mom?

jill: Sure

sentry: *(looks quickly into the camera lens)* Hi Mom. Love you.

jill: Corporal Wilson is a rare breed, a young patriot who is on his third tour of duty here. What keeps bringing you back, Corporal?

SENTRY: Well ma'am, the mission isn't done. I feel that the mission needs to be accomplished. And I'd sure rather be fighting them here than at home.

JILL: But three tours? That's a lot . . .

SENTRY: Our enemy hates freedom, ma'am. Someone's got to stand up and fight for freedom. That's what our President says. And I just decided that someone is me. You gotta stand up for what you believe is right. And what we're doing here is right.

JILL: And what's your mission here tonight?

SENTRY: Keeping myself and my buddies alive, ma'am. *(Waves arm in a semi circle)* This is my quadrant. I keep watch on this quarter of the perimeter to guard against infiltrators or insurgents trying to get into the base. *(Pause)* This is my mission. *(Beat)* Every night.

JILL: So tell me and the people watching at home exactly what a typical night for you is . . .

(The camera's light blacks out.)

CAMERAMAN: Cut.

JILL: What?

CAMERAMAN: We're off . . . we lost the uplink.

JILL: Damn.

CAMERAMAN: I got audio. I got New York. They're saying they want to come back here next segment if they can link picture . . .

(Pause.)

SENTRY: We're not on TV no more?

JILL: No.

SENTRY: Ok.

(The SENTRY starts a slow methodical sweep with his rifle. JILL watches. Long pause.)

JILL: How long you been up here, uh . . . Bradley . . . Brad right?

SENTRY: Brad, yes ma'am. Brad's fine.

JILL: So how long you been on duty here, Brad?

SENTRY: *(Pause)* Tonight? *(Pause)* Sun down til sun up.

JILL: Ah, I see. I guess I meant how long have you been here on this tour?

SENTRY: Tour?

JILL: Yes . . .

(The SENTRY lowers his weapon slightly but his eyes never stop scanning the perimeter.)

SENTRY: What month is it?

JILL: October.

SENTRY: It's been . . . *(Pause)* Been awhile.

JILL: You don't know?

SENTRY: I can't think of it. *(Beat)* I try not to do figuring when I'm up here. *(Beat)* It distracts me. *(Pause)* It's not good to be distracted up here. Bad for your health.
(Pause. The SENTRY scans.)
JILL: Oh. So . . . what's it like up here?
SENTRY: Like?*(Pause)* Pretty much the same thing, night after night. *(Pause)* I try to kill Paco and Paco tries to kill me. Doesn't change much.
JILL: Paco?
(The CAMERAMAN looks at the SENTRY curiously.)
SENTRY: Yes ma'am. *(Beat)* Paco . . . *(Pause)* I meet Paco last year during my second tour. I was stationed here, right here. This was before they blew up and bulldozed the buildings that used to surround us. Before they made the kill zone you see here. And I was up here. Right where we are standing. The buildings around the base were really close then. I got sent up here that first night cause I was a disciplinary problem for fighting with my squad mates and I got up here and from the first minute, the first second those damn buildings just poured fire on me, shot at me all night long. It was so . . . exciting. Paco was running around shooting from the houses just 50 yards away and I would shoot back and we'd open up whole fucking ammo clips at each other like it was nothing. And we'd yell at each other. Saying nasty things I can't repeat to a lady like you. *(Pause)* Anyway . . . I loved it. *(Pause)* I volunteered for this post. The squad was saying, oh boy oh boy he it, he wants it, he should get it. They called me Mad Brad. They didn't know what they were missing. And it became my post. Just mine. All mine. And every night me and Paco would be together alone, doing our mission. And I love it. Someone trying to kill you, it starts out being really frightening, you know? But after you get over that, it makes you feel sort of high and really really sharp. Like your senses are completely awake. Like you can see and hear and taste and smell everything in the world . . . *(Beat)* It's great. *(Pause)* Then . . . one day . . . they sent me home. Just up and shipped me stateside.
(Pause. The SENTRY scans.)
JILL: But . . . you came back . . .
SENTRY: Yeah.
JILL: Why?
SENTRY: Cause Paco and me, we had unfinished business.
JILL: But you were home. You were safe.
SENTRY: Yeah, didn't feel like home though. Felt like some weird place, like some amusement park, not really real. Not sharp real. Kind of fuzzy real. And I couldn't sleep cause Paco would talk to me at night . . .

JILL: Talk to you?

SENTRY: Yeah, Paco would call me out every night. Call me a sissy and a coward. Said I was a runner. Said I was a bitch. So I reupped. Had to come back here and straighten Paco out. Told them I wanted to come right back to here and they were fine with it. Said I was a hero. They were happy to have me cause they been having trouble with people not wanting to serve.

JILL: Yes I know.

SENTRY: But I almost didn't make it, cause of some stuff I said. Stuff they said I said. They had me take a whole bunch of tests then talk to a couple of docs. Finally they let me in but they said I had to take these pills everyday.

JILL: What kind of pills, Brad?

SENTRY: I dunno, ma'am. I've only taken them once. I call them stupid pills cause they make you feel stupid. Slow. Can't be slow up here. Gotta bring your A game to play here. You want them?

JILL: No . . . *(Pause)* No.

(Pause.)

CAMERAMAN: Hey Corporal . . .

SENTRY: Sir?

CAMERAMAN: *(Quietly)* Do you ever kill Paco?

SENTRY: Kill Paco? I kill Paco all the damn time. Every chance I get. My second tour I'd come up here and blow Paco's fucking head off 10, 12, 18 times a night. Big mustache Paco, round bottom Paco, those little bitty crying Pacos . . . I see them, I kill them fuckers dead, that's my job. But since we got this 200 yard kill zone now, can't kill Paco so much cause Paco is shifty and fast. Real fast. But I try my best, that's for sure. But so does Paco. Paco's a player. *(Pause)* But we still yell at each other all the time. *(Pause. Then intensely)* You see, Paco is everywhere . . .

(JILL and the CAMERAMAN lock eyes. Then the CAMERAMAN opens his cellphone and starts to talk quietly.)

JILL: I see . . .

CAMERAMAN: Jill, the bird is up. We have New York.

JILL: Oh . . . Ok. Brad, here we go.

SENTRY: We going back on TV?

(JILL quickly fusses with her hair.)

CAMERAMAN: No, we're not going live. We're going to tape. We're . . . we're going to feed them a tag for the stuff we just shot. Then we have to go because we have another assignment.

JILL: What? Wait, we have . . .

CAMERAMAN: Then we have to go because we have another *assignment*, Jill. *(Pause.)*

JILL: Right . . . *(Pause)* Brad, we're going to film a little ending for the story. So why don't you stand the way you normally do, like you're scanning the perimeter, looking though the scope and I'll be next to you, talking and that's how we'll end your story, Ok?

SENTRY: Yes ma'am. *(Pause)* Thanks for coming up here, I don't see lots of people.

JILL: You're welcome. *(Pause)* Ok, get into position and we'll do this..
(The SENTRY scans through his weapons sight. JILL stands next to him holding the microphone.)

CAMERAMAN: We're up. Jill . . . in 3, 2, 1 . . .
(The camera's light comes on. The CAMERAMAN signals JILL to start.)

JILL: Here he is, Corporal Bradley Wilson. A brave young soldier, a patriot. A man who feels his duty so intensely that this is his third tour in this grim war zone. A lone warrior high above his base, scanning for any sign of the enemy, doing his best to keep himself, his comrades and his country protected. An American, another everyday hero . . . *(Pause)* This is Jill Bellows with the Golf Company Two/Six, 2nd Division at forward firebase Toro . . . *(Pause)* Los Angeles, California.
(Long pause. The camera's light blacks out. The CAMERAMAN signals a cut.)

CAMERAMAN: Clear. We're done here *(To JILL)* Let's go.

JILL: Brad, thank you . . .
(The SENTRY lowers his weapon but does not turn to face her, he continues scanning the middle distance.)

SENTRY: *(distantly)* Sure . . .
(The SENTRY shoulders his weapon and scans. JILL hesitates, as if she would speak to the SENTRY again but the CAMERAMAN grabs her arm and leads her off right as the lights start to fade. Pause.)

SENTRY: Ah, there you are . . . .hey buddy . . . .where you been?
(Blackout. A rifle shot rings out.)

END OF PLAY

WHITE PEOPLE
A Ten-Minute Play about Boston

Ken Urban

Sponsored by Huntington Theatre Company.
Directed by M. Bevin O'Gara
Pam. . . . . Kate deLima
Billy . . . . .Scott Sweatt
Passengers . . . . .Cheo Bourne, Michael Cognata

Billy and Pam share a moment of unexpected New England intimacy on the Boston T, leaving these two strangers to ask: is happiness possible when you're a Masshole?

Ken Urban's plays have been produced and developed at SPF @ The Public, The Flea, Wlliamstown Theatre Festival, Playwrights Horizons, New York Theatre Workshop, The Huntington, Theatre of NOTE, and Soho Rep. Winner of the 2008 Weissberger Playwriting Award, the 2007 Huntington Playwriting Fellowship, the 2009 Writers Room of Boston Emerging Writers Fellowship and two MacDowell Colony Fellowships.

CHARACTERS

PAM, white, born and bred in Southie (South Boston), slightly heavy but not obese, her gruff exterior hides the pain that comes with lots of disappointment, late 20s.

BILLY, white, grew up in a Boston suburb, boyish and sporty, his personality combined with the after-effects of his drug use make him chatty in a TMI kind of way, early 30s.

TWO FELLOW PASSENGERS, both African-American, both young, early 20s, the second should be younger than the first.

SETTING

A sparsely populated car on the Red Line going Inbound in Boston, MA. Early Saturday morning.

NOTES

Punctuation gives a sense of the line's delivery.

Lines ending with an (–) are immediately followed by the next line and should overlap slightly.

For non-Boston folk: Dorchester, lovingly referred to as Dot, is a working-class neighborhood of Boston with a large gay population mixed in with a larger African-American population, a rarity in this still-segregated city. Mah = Mom. Sox = Red Sox.

Thanks to Mill 6 Collaborative (John Edward O'Brien, Artistic Director) for giving an early version of the play a home.

. . .

Early Saturday morning. A nearly empty T car on the Red Line, headed inbound. Three passengers are seated near each other: Pam, a white woman in her late 20s, wearing a pantsuit that's a bit tight on her; a Black man in his early 20s; and Billy, a white guys in his 30s, holding jumbo Dunkin Donuts [iced?] coffees in each hand. The white passengers look slightly nervously at the Black passenger: shift in seat, a clutch of the purse. Their eyes meet. They look away. A slightly awkward quiet between the three strangers. A voice announces the station as the T makes a stop. The Black passenger exits. Billy and Pam watch him exit and their eyes meet again. They are forced to share a nervous "hello" smile. The T begins moving again. Billy looks at Pam. He smiles. She glares.

BILLY: Hi. Oh. *(Referring to coffee)* Want one?

PAM: Yeah right I'm gonna drink something from some guy on the T.

BILLY: I can't drink both. Go on. Please.

PAM: Why'd you buy two?

BILLY: Need the caffeine. But I had enough.

PAM: Where you from?

BILLY: Weymouth, live in Dot now.

PAM: You a fag?

BILLY: Yup.

PAM: Fine, alright. Hand it over.

(She takes the coffee and chugs. In the middle of a sip:)

BILLY: I'm a crystal meth addict.

(Pam spits out the coffee.)

PAM: Fuckin hell, you put some weird drug shit in this?

BILLY: I'm in recovery. When I was on meth, all I'd do is read Wikipedia and jack off. Could never seal the deal though. Could beat the meat, couldn't spew the seed. Could get the wood, couldn't launch the load—

PAM: Yeah, yeah, got it, thanks. Erm, why you fuckin tellin me this?

BILLY: I'll never see you again.

PAM: You wanna be friends or somethin?

BILLY: No. Yes. I don't know. Where you going?

PAM: Job interview.

BILLY: On Saturday morning?

PAM: Trial run. Make sure I know how to get there, if this the right outfit—

BILLY: Nope. It's not. Go with vertical stripes, they're slimming.

PAM: And where you goin, you crazy crackhead? AA meeting in a church basement?

BILLY: An orgy. A brunch-time orgy. The host, he makes pancakes, sausages. In the back room, there's lots of anonymous oral action. What's the job?

PAM: Um. Assistant to some assistant.

BILLY: You don't sound jazzed about it.

PAM: Jazzed? No, I'm not fuckin jazzed. I need the money. Badly. I gotta get it. To help Mah—

BILLY: She sick?—

PAM: You think my sister will help out Mah? No, no, she won't. She's frickin useless. Mah and Dad send her to some school with the word "academy" in it. Did I get to go to some academy? No. And what the hell she do with that education? I came home one day from public school and found her getting double-stuffed in the living room. Two boys from the academy double-stuffing her. You don't need to go to the academy to learn how to get double-stuffed. You can learn that in public school. I told my parents, knocked that snooty bitch down a few pegs. She never forgave me though. Nearly killed Dad. His princess double-stuffed just like some public school girl from the magazines he'd hide under the mattress.

BILLY: Is your dad–?

PAM: Dead? Yeah. Remember the Fenway Knife Fights? At least Pops died doing what he loved.

BILLY: Knifing people?

PAM: No, you asshole, watching the Sox.

BILLY: Oh. Well, good luck with your interview. I wish I had a job. Can't work. Cause it makes me wanna use. Who wants to hire me anyways? My family, they used to look up to me, what I made of my life, and now? They look at me like I'm diseased. Won't even let me see my niece. And my love life? Can't date anyone, I mean, who'd want to date me?

PAM: I had a gay boyfriend in middle school. He was very polite. Mah loved him. He was real fruity though. I punched him once. All he did was cry. Wouldn't hit me back. Broke his nose, then his heart, I guess.

BILLY: You got a boyfriend now?

PAM: You're a nosey bastard.

BILLY: Sorry.

PAM: I did. But it had to end. Ten years, we were together. Me and Kevin.

BILLY: Long time.

PAM: Kevin. He wanted to get married.

BILLY: And you–?

PAM: Wouldn't have worked. My mah–

BILLY: She didn't approve–?

PAM: Kevin's Black.

BILLY: Oh.

PAM: Wait, no. That didn't come out right. I know what you're thinking. It's not–

BILLY: No.

PAM: No, just wouldn't work, that's all.

BILLY: Sure.

PAM: She's not a racist. She's a Democrat.

BILLY: I'm, I'm scared of Black people, sometimes. Don't want to be. But the halfway home where I'm getting clean, not a great neighborhood, and I, well, I get nervous. Makes me feel guilty. Because I get nervous.

PAM: Growing up, Pops always told us, you don't, you don't go where the Blacks live, you just don't.

BILLY: My folks said the same.

PAM: But with Kevin, I thought, I mean, ten frickin years–

BILLY: You think you get away from that, you're your own person and then–

PAM: Family's family though, right?

BILLY: Is it?

PAM: Well, yeah.

BILLY: Maybe, I guess.

(Silence. The pair retreat into themselves. The following lines are said mostly to themselves; their inside voices have snuck out.)

PAM: I'm gonna die alone, fat and alone, just like Mah–

BILLY: Never see my niece, never stop judging me–

PAM: I love him, I do, and I let him go–

BILLY: This is not how I thought it'd turn out

BILLY AND PAM: I want it back.

(They face each other.)

PAM: What's your name?

BILLY: Billy.

PAM: Billy, what'd you do before? Your job?

BILLY: Radio and TV stuff in DC.

PAM: Could never do that. Move away from Mah.

BILLY: Sure you could.

PAM: Bet you were good. You're a good talker and all.

BILLY: What about you? What's your name? What do you wanna do?

PAM: Pam. You're gonna laugh.

BILLY: No I won't.

PAM: Be a dancer. You think that's stupid?

BILLY: No not at all, Pam.

PAM: Kevin thought I was really good. And he's *[Black]* — *(Awkward moment.)* Anyways. Pops thought it was stupid.

BILLY: Fuck him. Let me see.

PAM: What? We're on the frickin T.

BILLY: No one's here 'cept us.

PAM: Nah, I couldn't.

BILLY: C'mon, Pam! Here. *(Taking out his iPod.)* Put the headphones in and go for it. I wanna see.

PAM: This is crazy. Crazy.

BILLY: What you got to lose? Show me. You know you want to. C'mon!

(Pam takes the iPod and puts in the headphones. Billy presses "Play." We can hear the music. Perhaps "Single Ladies" by Beyoncé. Pam is tentative at first, but then lets loose. She is pretty good. Billy encourages her. This is a big theatrical moment. The train makes a sudden stop — the screech

of breaks — and Pam tumbles to the ground, landing on her butt. Billy helps her up.)

BILLY: Hey, Pam, you OK?

PAM: Yeah, yeah, I'm fine, I'm fine.

(They sit down. The train resumes. Silence.)

PAM: You tell anyone what I just did, Billy, I'll break your fuckin kneecaps.

(The T enters a station. A voice announces the stop.)

BILLY: This is my stop. I gotta go.

PAM: Maybe I'll see you on TV or somethin. Have fun, Billy, K? Maybe you'll meet a nice guy at the orgy.

BILLY: Pam, you're a good dancer and–

(A young Black guy enters the train. Billy exits just as the doors shut. Pam watches Billy from the window.)

BILLY: *(Not fully audible)* Listen hey it's not too late, to fix things with . . .

(The train departs. Billy is gone. Pam looks as though she might cry. She tries to force the tears back into the locked box where all the pain lives. But she makes eye contact with the other passenger and it all comes out.)

PASSENGER: Hey, lady, you alright?

PAM: Sorry. Yeah. *(Smiles.)* Thanks. *(She decides. She takes out her cell. She has a signal. She makes a call. Into phone:)* Hi. Kevin. Kevin, it's, ah, um, it's, it's me, Pammy.

(Blackout.)

END OF PLAY.

IMPORTEES

Dana Yeaton

Importees was developed at Teatro del Peublo, Minneapolis,.Minnesota, February 2007. It premiered at Boston Theater Marathon 11, produced by Riverside Theatre Works.
Directed by Tara Brooke Watkins.

Rich . . . . Matt Anderson,
Kirsten . . . . .Erin, Pedersen,
Hernando . . . . .Bocar Zilla-Ba.

Kirsten is watching her husband assemble their new changing table and attacking the immorality of his box store purchase when a tiny asylum seeker emerges from the cardboard box.

Dana Yeaton is the recipient of the Heideman Award from the Actor's Theatre of Louisville and the "New Voice in American Theatre" award from the William Inge Theatre Festival. His plays include *Redshirts, Midwives, The Big Random* and *Mad River Rising*. His two-character musical *My Ohio* premiered at Vermont Stage in April, 2010.

CHARACTERS
RICH, An expectant husband.
KIRSTEN, His expectant wife.
HERNANDO, A 29-year old man from Mexico, played by a boy.

SETTING
The nursery of Rich and Kirsten's suburban home. Rich is assembling a changing table. Next to him is the large cardboard box it came in.

TIME & PLACE
Now. Suburban America.

.   .   .

Rich is holding two table parts, preparing to screw them together with a cordless drill. Unsure, he stops, consults the directions and reverses one of the pieces. He puts a screw on the tip of the drill and carefully maneuvers it closer to the hole . . . Easy. Easy . . . Oops, the screw drops and rolls a short distance. He reaches, but it's too far away. He steadies the pieces, and reaches again, this time using the drill. No luck. Stretching a little further, he accidentally pulls the trigger, shrieks, and drops the drill. The table parts crash to the floor.

KIRSTEN: (*Off.*) Rich?
RICH: Nothing.
KIRSTEN: What?
RICH: Don't come in.
    (*KIRSTEN enters. She's eight months pregnant.*)
KIRSTEN: What are you — Are you okay?
RICH: Surprise!
KIRSTEN: What is it?
RICH: It's a change table. I got an excellent deal.
KIRSTEN: I thought we were going to talk to Tim and Barbara about theirs.
RICH: Forty percent off.
KIRSTEN: You have to assemble it?
RICH: No biggie.
KIRSTEN: But do you know how?
RICH: Kirsten, it's a changing table. How difficult can it be?
KIRSTEN: I didn't know we had a screw gun.
RICH: Also on sale.

KIRSTEN: Where did you get all this? And don't tell me WalMart.

RICH: It wasn't WalMart.

KIRSTEN: But it was a box store.

RICH: It was forty percent off.

KIRSTEN: Rich, we agreed! We do not shop at box stores. We support the local economy.

RICH: Who do you think works in those box stores?

KIRSTEN: I don't want something that puts Americans out of work and increases the trade deficit and was probably constructed with child labor in some third world sweat shop.

RICH: You don't want it.

KIRSTEN: I don't want to raise our little girl on something that is morally reprehensible.

RICH: We're not raising her on the table, we're wiping her ass on it.

KIRSTEN: It's wrong, Rich. I'm sorry . . . (*She exits.*)

RICH: So that's it? That's how we're going to make our parenting decisions?

KIRSTEN: (*Off. In tears.*) Look, I said I'm sorry. Isn't that enough?

RICH: All right, I'm taking it back. . . . (*To himself.*) Already I'm outnumbered. (*He picks up a piece of the table and slides it back into the box. It won't fit. He slams it in. We hear a screech from inside the box. Beat. RICH peeks in.*) Jesus!

KIRSTEN: (*Off.*) Rich . . . ? (*She enters and sees him cowering.*) Honey, are you having second thoughts about being a daddy? (*RICH points to the box.*) I guess we'll have something to talk about at our next appointment with — (*Peering into the box.*) Oh for God's sake. (*She tips the box over.*) Come on. Out of there. . . . I said out.

RICH: He could be unconscious.

KIRSTEN: What?

RICH: I hit him pretty hard.

KIRSTEN: First the computer virus, now this, Rich you have got to be more careful what you bring into this house.

RICH: I –

KIRSTEN: Just bring me a dish of tuna. We'll lure him out.

RICH: Maybe if we just return it?

KIRSTEN: What?

RICH: Pack everything up just like it was. (*Producing a sales slip from his shirt pocket.*) I kept the receipt . . .

KIRSTEN: You just said he may be unconscious. You're going to send an unconscious refugee child back to some sweat shop in . . . (*She reads from the side of the box.*) the Czech Republic?

RICH: I knew those directions were confusing.

(While they argue, HERNANDO crawls out of the box. He is played by a 10-year old boy.)

KIRSTEN: Get the tuna, Rich.

RICH: How do you know he likes tuna?

KIRSTEN: He's been trapped in a cardboard box since he left Eastern Europe, I think it stands to —

RICH: Not everyone likes tuna as much as you, Kirsten. People have allergies. Other people —

KIRSTEN: I'll get it myself, thank you.

RICH: I'm just say — Uh oh.

(RICH stares ahead. KIRSTEN turns to see HERNANDO sneaking away.)

KIRSTEN: Hello. *(HERNANDO stop and turns to face them.)*

RICH: *Hola.*

KIRSTEN: Honey, I don't think your high school Spanish is going to help you with a boy from the Czech Republic.

HERNANDO: *(Rapidly.) Hola, me llamo Hernando Salomon. Yo no puedo volver a mi pais porque soy el objetivo de una persecución social, religiosa, o politica. (KIRSTEN looks at RICH, who gestures that it all went over his head. KIRSTEN turns to HERNANDO.)*

KIRSTEN: Slo-o-o-wly.

HERNANDO: Hello. My name is Hernando Salomon. I am unable to return to my country because I am the target of social, religious, or political persecution. *(He holds out a small box.)* Please accept this gift as a token of my willingness to work for scraps of food.

KIRSTEN: Well thank you.

HERNANDO: Except tuna.

RICH: Don't open it.

KIRSTEN: *(Opening it.)* Will you look at that? Russian nesting dolls.

HERNANDO: Also called "matryoshka."

KIRSTEN: My goodness, you little Czech Republicans certainly know a lot of languages.

HERNANDO: I am not Czech, I am from Tijuana, but Americans do not like products from Mexico, so we label them . . . creatively. And I am not a boy. I have 29 years. *(He produces a picture from his wallet.)* My wife, Dominga.

KIRSTEN: She's beautiful. Rich, look.

HERNANDO: Yes. And our four children: Jorge, Angelina, Rosita and little Pepe.

RICH: They're so tiny.

HERNANDO: The photograph is not actual size.

RICH: No, I mean compared to Ameri –

KIRSTEN: Honey, why don't we invite Senor Salomon to –

HERNANDO: Please. Hernando.

KIRSTEN: Why don't we invite Hernando out onto the verandah and do we have any of the Pinot left?

RICH: The *good* Pinot?

HERNANDO: No. Please. First, we must assemble the changing table.

RICH: Actually, we're just gonna take it . . . (*Looks to KIRSTEN, who is staring daggers.*) Easy. Maybe do that later.

HERNANDO: I insist. (*He picks up the drill and begins assembling.*) In the factory, I was able to assemble one of these in 92 seconds.

RICH: Actually, we'd just like to think about it first.

HERNANDO: Of course, that was with the help of my children.

RICH: Before we commit.

HERNANDO: Jorge would hold one piece of the change table, Angelina another. Rosita would dance around me, a handful of screws caught up in her dress. "*Nina de los tornillos,*" I would call to her. "*Un tornillo, por favor.*" (*To RICH.*) If only you had chosen the matching armoire as well, we would still be together.

(*Beat. KIRSTEN picks up a screw and hands it to HERNANDO.*)

RICH: Honey.

KIRSTEN: It will be a marvelous changing table.

RICH: Honey, I think that before —

KIRSTEN: And if there's anything we can do to help you reunite with your family.

HERNANDO: We would have to find them first, at the store . . .

RICH: The box store.

KIRSTEN: They might still be there?

HERNANDO: If not, they are lost to me forever.

RICH: At the *box* store.

KIRSTEN: Rich, we're not going to let some moral code keep us from reuniting a family of refugees facing persecution.

RICH: Kirsten, I don't think someone in our condition should be running around, trying to save the world.

KIRSTEN: What store was it? . . . Rich!

HERNANDO: It may already be too late.

KIRSTEN: What store was it?

RICH: I don't think this —

KIRSTEN: I am going to the store.

RICH: And it doesn't matter what I think? I don't get a vote?

KIRSTEN: Fine. All those in favor of rescuing Hernando's wife and children from certain death or deportation or both . . .
(KIRSTEN raises her hand. She looks at HERNANDO, who raises his.)

RICH: How come he gets a vote?

KIRSTEN: Opposed?

RICH: He's not legal. He's part of a family of illegal aliens.

KIRSTEN: It appears the "ayes" have it. *(She snatches the sales receipt from RICH's shirt pocket. Reads.)* Oh, really, Rich. Target?!

HERNANDO: They're in a Mahogany Baby Armoire. I think it may be from Taiwan.

KIRSTEN: *(To HERNANDO.)* You're not coming?

HERNANDO: I will stay and help Rich.

KIRSTEN: You see how courteous they are? *(KIRSTEN exits.)*

HERNANDO: Hold or screw?

RICH: . . . Screw.

(HERNANDO hands RICH the cordless drill and picks up the two pieces RICH was attempting to join at the beginning.)

HERNANDO: Soon, my friend, you will have a changing table and a beautiful matching armoire, and in each drawer, one of my tiny children. Cute as puppies. Big brown eyes. You will see. Trained to eat nothing, less than a squirrel. And you and your woman will be out watching the sunset on your verandah, sipping Pinot, while Dominga and I take care of your precious little girl.

RICH: . . . Ready?

HERNANDO: Oh yes. . . . I wonder, Senor, who loves this country more . . . you or me? *(RICH pulls the trigger on the drill. Blackout.)*

END OF PLAY

ST. CLOUD

Vladimir Zelevinsky

St. Cloud was produced at the Boston Theater Marathon XI, Boston, MA, on May 11, 2008. Sponsored by Another Country Productions.
Directed by Jeannie-Marie Brown.
Maud . . . . Magalie Neff
Mary . . . . Rachael Hunt
Jess . . . . Kortney Adams.

Small town in Minnesota, roadside diner, early morning. A young woman about to take the first step of a long journey.

Vladimir Zelevinsky spent four years as the playwright-in-residence at the Theatre Cooperative (Somerville, MA), where his full-length plays included *A Brief History of the Soviet Union* (2002), *What Time Is It?* (2004), and *Manifest Destiny* (2006). He is a two-time finalist for the Heideman Award (*Theme and Variations* and *Silence*).

CHARACTERS

MARY, 19, a waitress at her mother's diner.

MAUD, 50, Mary's mother, owns and runs the diner.

JESS, 29, waitress.

SETTING

Back entrance to a diner in Fergus, MN, population 1284.

TIME

September. 5:55AM: five minutes to opening.

. . .

Maud is sitting on a milk crate, massaging her foot. Mary, her daughter, is watching.

MARY: Mom?

MAUD: Mmm?

MARY: How did you feel when you had an abortion?

MAUD: *(She makes a small laugh — half surprised at the question, half pleased her daughter wants to know her better.)* Which one?

MARY: When I was four.

MAUD: You were five.

MARY: I was four. I remember I was four because I remember you took me with you and I sat on the blue couch, I remember the blue couch, and the nurse gave me this floppy doll and I stuck my finger into the doll and pulled out some stuffing and I was thinking — you know what, this is neat, I am four. It's like, you know, those cameras that add the date in little square letters in the low right corner?
(Beat.)

MAUD: I felt good. The first one, before you, that was not good. I didn't know anything, and. . . . But the one when you were — *four* — it's like I'd had, I don't know, cancer, or a virus, or some bug eating at me — and then it was all gone. *(Beat.)* Why? Somebody you know . . . ?

MARY: White Queen.

MAUD: What Queen?

MARY: *(Simply.)* In her white castle in the clouds. *(Beat. Mary shakes her hand in front of her face, getting rid of the image.)* I mean — no. No. Not . . . *(Waves her hand in the air, indicating clouds.)* From "Through the Looking Glass."

MAUD: *(She never read it, but she is willing to go along with this, still happy to be talking about personal stuff with her daughter.)* Oh-kay?

MARY: Like she screams for a while and then pricks herself with a pin and then she doesn't need to scream anymore because she'd done the screaming ahead of time, you know? So — White Queen.

(Mary looks down at her hands, clutched in her lap. Maud rests both feet on the ground and puts her hands on her knees and leans toward Mary. During this motion she ages ten years.)

MAUD: Who's he?

MARY: You don't know him.

MAUD: In this town!?

MARY: I don't *want* you to know him. *(Beat.)* I haven't told him. *(Beat.)* I'll never tell him. *(Beat.)* Why did you get rid of the one before me? *(Beat.)*

MAUD: I was all alone and — *(Notices Mary's unasked question.)* — no, you *don't* know him — and I was at the soda shop, talking to Marcy Jeffreys — she was all long fingers and a pointy nose even back then — and Marcy was all excited how this girl we both knew, this single girl, was — you know — showing — and Marcy kept smiling with all her teeth. Well, you've met Marcy Jeffreys. So I listened to her and then I went to the pay phone in the corner, Yellow Pages chained to the counter, and I found the number and I called 'em and I went there straight out of the soda shop. Same place. They already had the blue couch. *(A long beat as Maud is putting together the most important thing she will ever say in her entire life, and when she is ready, she says it.)* Only, you know, *you* are not alone. I will stay up and I'll change it and I'll do laundry and I'll — *(Mary is looking Maud straight in the face, and Maud can't continue.)*

MARY: What about Marcy Jeffreys?

MAUD: What about her?

MARY: She's still here. I don't know how many teeth she had back then, but now she's got, like, eighty: you can see them all when she smiles. And forty bony fingers. And a nose six inches long. And her friends, the thin lady in purple and the fat lady in green. They sit on her porch and drink warm diet soda and whisper and point with their fingers, the purple finger and the green. I cannot. Mom, I — so — cannot, Mom, I — *(Jess enters, flinty and brittle.)*

JESS: Morning-morning. There's already a rig out front.

MAUD: What rig?

JESS: *(She's too busy putting on her apron to notice things aren't well.)* Yellow.

MAUD: That's Barney. On his way to St. Cloud. Four eggs over easy, ham, coffee. Half coffee, half half-n-half. No toast, he's on a diet.

JESS: Wwwoh-kay.

(Maud looks at Mary. Mary is looking away. Maud suddenly has to get out of here.)

MAUD: I'll open up, Jess.

JESS: If you give me the keys —

MAUD: It's my place, I get to open it.

(Maud goes inside.)

JESS: Wwwoh-kay. *(Rummages in her pockets. To Mary.)* You got a light?

MARY: Did you ever want to have kids?

JESS: Oh for fuck's sake, sweetie, are you for real? D'you read the news!? Here ya go, baby, welcome to the world! It's a great fucking place, baby! It's got gas, soon to be twelve dollars a gallon! It's got mean people who want to kill us, real! fucking!! mean!!!, only you are safe, baby, 'cause we just killed a coupla countries full'a them, for your personal sake, baby, just so you'd be safe, lucky baby you are! So grow up, baby, be good and healthy, real fucking healthy, baby, 'cause if you ever get a toothache, you'll need to fork over forty grand or DIE, and you best learn how to change oil or rotate tires, 'cause here, in Fergus, Minnesota, exit fifty off ninety-fucking-four, that's what you do, unless, of course, my dear fucking baby, you have the luck to be a GIRL, in which case what you do is FRY, you fry and you fry and you FRY, you fry eggs and franks and potatoes and if you want to be real fancy, real fucking fancy, baby, you fry SWEET potatoes, and then you DIE, so welcome, baby, this will be a BLAST! *(Beat.)* No I never wanted to have kids you're welcome.

MARY: Why do you stay here?

JESS: *(Deflates.)* 'Cause it's all the same, sweetie. Trust me — ten years on the open road. All the same. All I remember is rain in Arizona, and dust in Kansas, and snow in Vermont, and pushing the car in Nebraska when we ran out of gas. All those cars whooshing by. Nobody stopped. And that exit fifty was just like this exit fifty, maybe more grease in the fryer. And this sound of tires. Whoosh. All the same, sweetie. All the same, baby. Here's what they don't tell you, baby. It's a big country. This open road — it's all the same.

MARY: Ever been to St. Cloud?

JESS: Why?

MARY: I like the name.

JESS: I'm sure it's also all the same. *(Beat.)* Why do *you* stay here?

MARY: I love it here. The pine trees in Adams Park, they smell like — like

— like pine trees, you know? On Sundays, mom makes tuna casserole, and she spreads mayonnaise on top, and she puts it under the broiler, it's the best food ever. This morning, at five, before the fog was all gone, there was a deer in our garden. Two deer. A mother and a baby. *(She tries not to cry and mostly succeeds.)*

JESS: *(She gets the first hint something isn't right.)* Sweetie — ?

(Maud comes out.)

MAUD: Jess, the fryer is clogged.

JESS: No, it isn't. I cleaned it last night.

MAUD: I want to talk to my daughter.

JESS: So talk — *(Beat. She looks at Mary. Looks at Maud.)* Oh sweet fucking fuck. *(To Mary.)* Sweetie —

MAUD: Jess, go clean the fryer.

JESS: *(Stares at Maud; gives up. To Mary.)* Whooshhhh.

(Jess exits. For a while, Maud and Mary don't look at each other.)

MAUD: The floppy doll you got when you were four. Is that the floppy doll that —

MARY: Yes.

MAUD: I've never seen you run around with any other doll as much as —

MARY: I know.

(Beat.)

MAUD: And now you're telling me you don't want to keep —

MARY: Mom, I want it so much I can't tell you how much, I cannot remember myself not wanting it, only I cannot, because they will all whisper, purple and green, and they will point, and Jake — and *no*, I won't tell you which Jake — he'll just laugh, and all his buddies, they will also laugh, they sound like horses when they laugh — and you called it a bug and a cancer and I still want it more than anything, only there is no way I could keep it, not, not — *(She can't quite say "here." Beat. She is suddenly quiet and thoughtful.)* Did you see the deer in the garden this morning?

MAUD: Was it eating my apple tree?

MARY: Only the apples that fell down. You know, if not for the teeth and the nose and the horsey laughter, this town is — lovely. And I wanted a baby since I was four. Only there is no way I could keep it — and stay — here.

(Beat.)

MAUD: (She runs her hand along the bricks of the diner's wall.) We — can't — you know, we can't leave. The diner is so not paid off and —

MARY: Not we, mom. Not — we.

(Beat. All the cards are on the table.)

MAUD: Where would you go?

MARY: First, to St. Cloud. Then maybe to St. Paul. Then — I don't know. Plenty of saints to go around.

MAUD: How will you —

MARY: I make the best sweet potato fries. Ever.

MAUD: *(She's barely audible.)* Why?

MARY: Because I think — no, I don't think, I don't know, I just guess — I guess there's a world out there, and there's an open road, and I want to feel the snow in Vermont, and hear the rain in Arizona, and taste the dust in Kansas, I want this open road, Mom, only — only — you see — you'll have to tell me to go, because you are strong and I'm not, and I can't decide for myself, so if I am to go, Mom, you have to tell me to go.
(Long beat. Event of the play.)

MAUD: Go.
(Beat.)

MARY: Thank you.
(Beat.)

MAUD: You want to take the day off?

MARY: No. Just five minutes. *(Maud nods, turns, and goes into the diner. Before disappearing inside, she turns, looks at Mary, and semi-smiles. Mary stands all alone, and looks around, and puts her arms around herself, because the morning wind has picked up and it is cold.)* Afoot and light-hearted, I take to the open road — *(Beat.)* Afoot and — *(It's not working: she feels so far from light-hearted she's starting to hyperventilate. Then she looks up, and takes a deep breath, and speaks, as an incantation.)* St. Cloud. *(Beat. A spell.)* St. Cloud. *(Beat. A prayer.)* St. Cloud.

END OF PLAY

BOSTON THEATER MARATHON XI
THEATERS, 2009

Actors' Shakespeare Project, www.actorsshakespeareproject.org
Actors' Studio of Newburyport, www.newburyportacting.org
American Repertory Theatre, www.americanrepertorytheater.org
Another Country Productions, www.anothercountry.org
Apollinaire Theatre Company, www.apollinairetheatre.com
Barefoot Theatre Company, www.barefoottheatrecompany.org
Battleground State, battlegroundstate@gmail.com
Blackburn Performing Arts, www.blackburnperformingarts.com
Boston Actors' Theater, www.bostonactorstheater.com
Boston Center for American Performance, www.bu.edu/cfa/theater
Boston Children's Theatre, www.bostonchildrenstheatre.org
Boston Playwrights' Theatre, www.bostonplaywrights.org
Cape Repertory Theater, www.caperep.org
Centastage, www.centastage.org
Company One, www.companyone.org
Elemental Theatre Collective, www.elementaltheatre.org
Emerson Stage at Emerson College, www.emerson.edu/emersonstage
Foothills Theatre Company, TBD
Fort Point Theatre Channel, www.fortpointtheatrechannel.org
FortyMagnolias Productions, www.wrestlingpatient.com
Gloucester Stage Company, www.gloucesterstage.org
Gold Dust Orphans, www.golddustorphans.com
Holland Productions, www.hollandproductions.org
Huntington Theatre Company, www.HuntingtonTheatre.org
Image Theatre Company, www.imagetheater.com
Lyric Stage Company of Boston, www.lyricstage.com
Metro Stage Company, www.metrostagecompany.com.
Mill 6 Collaborative, www.mill6.org
New Century Theatre, www.newcenturytheatre.org
New Repertory Theatre, www.newrep.org
Nora Theatre Company, www.centralsquaretheater.org
Orfeo Theatre, www.orfeogroup.org
Our Place Theatre Company, www.ourplacetheatreproject.com
Perishable Theatre, www.perishable.org
Phoenix Theatre Artists, www.phoenixtheatre.org
Pilgrim Theatre Research and Performance Collaborative, www.pilgrimtheatre.org/
Playwrights' Platform, www.playwrightsplatform.org
Publick Theatre Boston, www.publicktheatre.com

Riverside Theatre Works www.rtwboston.org

Rough & Tumble Theatre, www.rough-and-tumble.org

Roxbury Crossroads Theatre, 37 Vine Street, Roxbury, MA 02119-3354

Salem Theatre Company, www.salemtheatre.com

Shakespeare & Co., www.shakespeare.org

Speakeasy Stage Company, www.speakeasystage.com

Stoneham Theatre, www.stonehamtheatre.org

Turtle Lane Playhouse, www.turtlelane.org

Underground Railway Theater, www.centralsquaretheater.org

Village Theatre Project, www.vtpboston.org

Wellesley Summer Theatre, www.wellesleysummertheatre.com

Wheelock Family Theatre, www.wheelock.edu/wft

Zeitgeist Stage, www.zeitgeiststage.com

RIGHTS AND PERMISSIONS

310